Sojourners in the Sun

Francis Danby, gouache, "Sunset over the Sea," ca. 1850. Reproduced by permission of the Henry E. Huntington Library and Art Gallery, San Marino, California.

Sojourners in the Sun

Scottish Migrants in Jamaica
and the Chesapeake,
1740–1800

Alan L. Karras

Cornell University Press

Ithaca and London

First published 1992 by Cornell University Press.

International Standard Book Number 0-8014-2691-X
Library of Congress Catalog Card Number 92-52763
Printed in the United States of America
*Librarians: Library of Congress cataloging information
appears on the last page of the book.*

♾ The paper in this book meets the minimum requirements of the American National Standard for Information Sciences—Permanence of Paper for Printed Library Materials, ANSI Z39.48-1984.

FOR AUNT BEA
who taught me
to love learning

Contents

Illustrations

Tables

Maps

Charts

Preface

Alexander Johnston came of age in the mid-eighteenth century along Scotland's blustery northeastern coast. With hopes of making his fortune as a physician, he traveled south, stopping first in Edinburgh and later in Britain's Caribbean colonies. Though Johnston did not much like life in the West Indies, he spent twenty-four years in St. Ann's Parish, Jamaica. As I read through his surviving letters, journals, and accounts, a whole field of unanswered questions sprouted. The most obvious was whether Alexander Johnston's records, now located in Philadelphia, could represent anyone or anything other than himself. Did his behavior and ideas typify a group, or was he an isolated case? To answer these questions, I began to explore one of the broadest characteristics of Johnston's existence—his ethnicity.

Beginning in the winter of 1985–86 and continuing over the course of the next several years, I discovered substantial caches of unmined manuscripts in Jamaica, the United States, and (especially) Britain. These collections consisted principally of letters and accounts that Scots resident in the American colonies sent to their correspondents in Britain. As I read these documents, it became clear to me that for a period, Scottish ethnicity combined with a professional education to produce a group of people with a uniformly strong desire to leave Scotland temporarily. These Scottish migrants chose to voyage to certain colonies because they expected they could earn a fortune quickly. Borrowing a sociological term I dubbed them "sojourners"; the behavioral patterns that the documents revealed among the Scots form this book's principal subject.

Migration history has usually been written in ways that make it easy to exclude transient migrants. Their numbers never seemed to be very great, at least as far as we knew, so their functions within both their host and their home societies have gone relatively unnoticed. Still, as this book has progressed, I have become convinced that the Scots were only one of several groups of sojourners which dotted the American historical landscape. We know so little about sojourning in American history that questions about other groups of transients are nearly impossible to answer without much additional research.

We need, in general, to discover whence sojourners came, where they went, what they did after they arrived, and how they fared. Did some ethnic groups tend to be sojourners more than others? What precise socioeconomic and cultural conditions spawned the transient migrant in each generation? What treatment did sojourners receive from their host communities, and what perceptions did native-born residents of the communities exhibit?

Alexander Johnston's small career, in the 1770s and 1780s, has thus suggested a whole range of questions about other peoples at other times and in other places. Here I have, for the most part, worked only on Johnston's eighteenth-century contemporaries. It is my hope that the texture of sojourners' lives in three British colonies, which this book provides, will provoke others to explore sojourning in other contexts.

A project such as this one is like a tree with many branches. If I were to recognize properly all the help I received along the way, I would most likely present readers with a book shorter than its acknowledgments. Rather than do so, I apologize here to anyone who has been omitted.

I am grateful to the following, both for permission to quote from the rich sources they superintend and for making my days as a researcher pleasant ones: the Trustees of the National Library of Scotland, Scottish Record Office, Strathclyde Regional Archives, Aberdeen University Library, Edinburgh University Library, Glasgow University Archives, Library of Congress, Liverpool Record Office, Lloyd House at the Alexandria Library, the Huntington Library, Historical Society of Pennsylvania, Virginia Historical Society, and the Virginia State Library.

Mr. Oliver Tweedie-Stodart, Lord Moncreiff, Lord Seafield, and Mr. Archibald Stirling have generously provided permission to quote from letters in their care.

Staff at the Public Record Office at Kew and the Jamaica Archives in Spanish Town were of great assistance as I perused masses of documents in their possession. I also used documents belonging to Marion Campbell of Kilberry and Mrs. E. Hanbury-Tenison. While they are not quoted here, they have informed the arguments presented.

Early on, James Munson, Jean Russo, and Adele Hast all pointed me to sources that I might otherwise have overlooked.

My colleagues and students at Georgetown University have generally been tremendously supportive over the last four years. I am particularly grateful to Richard Duncan and Marcus Rediker for reading various parts of the manuscript and offering helpful suggestions. Graduate students Roger Haughey, Eileen Scully, and Stephen Manaker have also contributed to the version of the argument which appears here. Timothy Lane read the manuscript in its semi-final form and provided insightful and detailed criticisms. John McNeill has not only been a terrific reader, friend, and source of inspiration; he has also suffered through many team-taught classes that always seemed to end on the subject of Scots sojourners.

Georgetown University's publication fund and a generous grant from the Huntington Library allowed me the time needed to complete the research and begin final revisions.

Cornell University Press has been supportive of the project since first hearing about it. I am indebted to Roger Haydon for his efforts on my behalf. Lisa Turner, who copy-edited the book, did much to clarify my prose. I am also grateful to Ned Landsman and Richard Sheridan, who provided criticisms that helped to make this a more articulate book.

Friends across the world have helped me in one form or another when I've been "in town" researching and writing. I know they will forgive me for only listing them here: Andy Bell and Angela Frain, Trevor Burnard, Kirsty Wark and Alan Clements, Saul Cornell and Susan Selleck, Allan Little, Steve Pahides, Loren Ratner, Alan Schoen, Ian Sherwood, Gigi Sohn, and Kevin Traynor.

Finally, I owe Richard S. Dunn, Roy F. and Jeanette P. Nichols Professor of American History at the University of Pennsylvania, a tremendous intellectual debt—not only for reading many versions of the manuscript but for always having new insights and suggestions for improvement. I simply could not have studied under anyone better. Along the way, Michael Zuckerman and Richard Beeman also provided much useful assistance and encouragement.

ALAN L. KARRAS

Washington, D.C.

Abbreviations

AUL	Aberdeen University Library
BL	British Library
EHR	*Economic History Review*
EUL	Edinburgh University Library
GUA	Glasgow University Archives
HL	Henry E. Huntington Library
HSP	Historical Society of Pennsylvania
JA	Jamaica Archives
JAH	*Journal of American History*
JEH	*Journal of Economic History*
LC	Library of Congress
LRO	Liverpool Record Office
LT	Loyalist Transcripts
NLS	National Library of Scotland
NRA(S)	National Register of Archives (Scotland)
NYPL	New York Public Library
PRO	Public Record Office
SRA	Strathclyde Regional Archives
SRO	Scottish Record Office
VHS	Virginia Historical Society
VSL	Virginia State Library
WMQ	*William and Mary Quarterly*

Sojourners in the Sun

INTRODUCTION

But what comes here? Methinks I see
A *walking* University.
See how they press to cross the TWEED,
And strain their Limbs with eager speed!
While SCOTLAND from her *fertile* shore,
Cries, On My Sons, return no more.

Hither they haste, with willing mind,
Nor cast one *longing* look behind;
On *ten-toe* carriage to salute,
The K——g, and Q——n, and Earl of B——e.

These two stanzas lampoon Caledonian migration to London.[1] Written by an Englishman who objected to the earl of Bute's regular appointments of Scots to positions in the British government, the verse could also characterize the general exodus of educated people from Scotland to Britain's American colonies in the mid-eighteenth century. But the poem has got it only partly correct. The poet, like more modern historical scholars, did not seem to realize that these people usually left Scotland intending to return to their homeland with increased wealth.

Though the Scots operated in two worlds (separated by the Tweed in the poem), they did not wholly belong to either. It is, then, only natural that a book about such people straddles rigid historiographical boundaries. Mono-

---

[1]Untitled poem, in *The British Antidote to Caledonian Poison: Consisting of the most humourous Satirical Political Prints, for the Year 1762* (London, 1762).

graphs in early American history generally focus on one place or one event in British North America. This book compares two different colonial regions, one of them in the Caribbean. Histories of immigration to the United States tend to begin in the nineteenth century, after about 1820—precisely when this book concludes. Moreover, many immigration histories have been concerned with the immigrant's adjustment and integration into "American" life. This book describes very different processes because its subjects never had any intention of integration, let alone prolonged residency. Because Jamaica was never a part of the United States, matters are further complicated.

Standing at the confluence of several distinct historical traditions, this is clearly a work of migration history. Frank Thistlewaite, in 1960, suggested that students of human migration have been overly concerned with only one phase of the movement of people: immigration to the United States. "As a result," he asserted, "it has been the consequences and not the causes of migration which have received most attention; and, moreover, the consequences in the receiving, not the sending country."[2] He argued that scholars needed to look at the Atlantic system as a whole in order to understand the movements of people. Prescribing a program of comparative research, Thistlewaite, and later John Higham, maintained that comparing one group of migrants in two or more different receiving societies—cross-cultural history—would allow us to recapture the richness of the migratory processes and experiences. More than thirty years on, these observations and pleas for innovation remain valid.[3]

Just as migration historians have not generally undertaken comparative studies, they have not often enough concerned themselves with the variety of conditions in the "old world" which fueled emigration.[4] Scholarship has

[2]Frank Thistlewaite, "Migration from Europe Overseas in the Nineteenth and Twentieth Centuries," reprinted in *Population Movements in Modern European History*, ed. Herbert Moller (New York, 1964), p. 73.

[3]See John Higham, "Immigration," in *The Comparative Approach to American History*, ed. C. Vann Woodward (New York, 1968), pp. 91–105. Higham was still most concerned with the United States, despite his recognition of the advantages of comparative history. For an example of the possibilities cross-cultural history provides, see Samuel L. Baily, "Cross-Cultural Comparison and the Writing of Migration History: Some Thoughts on How to Study Italians in the New World," in *Immigration Reconsidered: History, Sociology, and Politics*, ed. Virginia Yans-McLaughlin (Oxford, 1990), pp. 241–53.

[4]The traditional view has been that immigration resulted because economic and living conditions were better in the United States than they were in Europe. This assumption is beginning to change; there are now scholars working on describing conditions on both sides of the Atlantic and, increasingly, the Pacific oceans. For an example, see John Bodnar, *The Transplanted: A History of Immigrants in Urban America* (Bloomington, Ind., 1985). Virginia Yans-McLaughlin has edited an excellent series of essays that discuss the problem. Her introduction provides the best assessment I have seen of this literature. See *Immigration Reconsidered*.

very little to say about the "quality" of the migrating people; surely they were not all members of an agricultural peasantry in search of a better life. Only in doing such research can we discover the richness of texture that characterized the various movements of people from one place to another.[5] This book pursues the experiences of one group of people—identifying them in the context of their native country, describing the reasons that "pushed" them out of it, identifying new world conditions that "pulled" them to different places, and then discussing their positions and careers within the colonies. But, again following Thistlewaite's cue, it does not stop there.

The book's subjects—educated and professionally trained Scots—did not intend to stay permanently in the colonies. They went to earn a fortune as quickly as possible and return home with it. Thistlewaite claimed that perhaps a third of the immigrants to the United States in the nineteenth and twentieth centuries re-emigrated, "thereby considerably reducing the intensity of the immigrant impact." John Bodnar has recently stated that return migration was very common, from about 25 to 60 percent in the twentieth century. Rowland Berthoff has suggested that the rate of Scottish remigration at the turn of the twentieth century was between 14 and 46 percent.[6] But these estimates derive from a later period, when statistical record-keeping was more regular and documentation more complete.

Though we know about the size and contributions of a reasonably large number of groups who immigrated to the American colonies in the eighteenth century, there has been virtually no recognition that some people moved only temporarily across the Atlantic. Historians of colonial America, like most American historians, have tacitly accepted the model of a one-directional westward flow of people. As far as it has been possible to determine, few have seriously considered the possibility that remigration took place.[7]

---

[5]For a statement of the general problem see Thistlewaite, pp. 80–84. For a discussion of some of the responses to Thistlewaite in this area, see Yans-McLaughlin, *Immigration Reconsidered*, pp. 8–9. For discussions of the different types of colonial migrants see Bernard Bailyn, *Voyagers to the West* (New York, 1986). A. Roger Ekirch in *Bound for America: The Transportation of British Convicts to the Colonies, 1718–1775* (New York, 1987), describes a stream of migration which shows that some migrants did not have a choice about where they would go.

[6]Thistlewaite, p. 75; Bodnar, pp. 52–53. Both authors recognize that the rate of return migration varied between ethnic groups. Both also acknowledge that the available statistics for the twentieth century are woefully inadequate for more precise measurements. There are virtually no statistics available for earlier periods. For Berthoff's discussion of British remigration in the late nineteenth and early twentieth centuries, see Rowland Tappan Berthoff, *British Immigrants in Industrial America, 1790–1950* (Cambridge, Mass., 1953), p. 10 and passim. The large range of his figures derives from the idiosyncrasies of surviving records.

[7]For the eighteenth century, there are no records of return migration. Only Ekirch, in *Bound for America*, argues that convicts frequently returned to England after leaving (either legally or illegally) their service obligations. Among the most recent studies of migration to the colonies

Knowing something about migrants in the nineteenth and twentieth centuries makes it possible to extrapolate backward in time. Temporary migrants over the past two hundred years tended to be single males. We might, therefore, logically expect to see more temporary migration in eighteenth-century societies that drew a high ratio of unmarried men to family units. Bernard Bailyn has shown that families generally went more to the northern colonies and single men more to the southern, a pattern established from the very outset of English migration to the North American mainland in the seventeenth century.[8]

This migration and remigration—sociologists call it sojourning—was important both to the receiving and to the sending societies. All were not created equal, however. Transients, because of their goals, would have found some places much more attractive than others.[9] As Thistlewaite claimed, "It is clear that in South, even more than in North, America and for an important fraction of individuals, migration was temporary and transitory." Though he wrote about the nineteenth century, he could have been describing the eighteenth-century British Atlantic world.[10] The proportion of sojourners to permanent white settlers was greater in the tropical islands than it was in the mainland colonies simply because there were fewer whites in the Caribbean. With large slave populations, few creole institutions, and an unhealthful climate, the island colonies needed imported skilled labor more than did Massachusetts, Pennsylvania, or Virginia. Beyond their skilled labor, however, what did the Scottish transients contribute to the host society?[11] Like later Chinese migrants to the United States, these Scots found themselves

---

are Jon Butler, *The Huguenots in America* (Cambridge, Mass., 1983); David Cressy, *Coming Over: Migration and Communication between England and New England in the Seventeenth Century* (New York, 1987); Ned Landsman, *Scotland and Its First American Colony* (Princeton, N.J., 1985), and Stephanie Wolf, *Urban Village: Population, Community, and Family Structure in Germantown, Pennsylvania 1683–1800* (Princeton, N.J., 1976).

[8]Thistlewaite, pp. 76–77. Bailyn, *Voyagers to the West*, pp. 208, 210–11.

[9]Two sociologists have done a great deal to characterize this "type" of migrant. See Paul C. P. Siu, "The Sojourner," *American Journal of Sociology* 58 (1952–53): 34–44, and Edna Bonacich, "A Theory of Middlemen Minorities," *American Sociological Review* 38 (1973): 583–94. Also see Sucheng Chan, "European and Asian Immigration into the United States in Comparative Perspective, 1820s to 1920s," in Yans-McLaughlin, *Immigration Reconsidered*, esp. pp. 37–38. Chan argues that calling a group "sojourners" has tended to exclude them from discussions of immigration to the United States. While her argument applies to Chinese migrants in the nineteenth century, it is no less instructive for those interested in other groups and periods.

[10]Thistlewaite, p. 76. Also see Rowland Berthoff, *British Immigrants*. Berthoff discusses a high proportion of remigration in the nineteenth century; he is not, however, specific as to place. Geographer D. W. Meinig in *Atlantic America, 1492–1800* (New Haven, Conn., 1987) notes that the Scots in Virginia were "young males, salaried sojourners rather than family settlers" (p. 158). Though Meinig uses the same terminology, he neither elaborates nor identifies his source.

[11]See Yans-McLaughlin, pp. 12–13.

socially segregated. In part, this isolation derived from their own career choices; in part, it resulted from social discrimination. But the sojourner's ultimate goal of returning home lay at the heart of the matter. The process of trying to accrue enough capital to escape the colonies for a more comfortable existence at home ultimately informed decisions and dictated behavior. The only way to understand such a *mentalité* is to explore, qualitatively, the careers of identifiable transients. Such analysis brings the contributions they made to the host societies into sharp focus.

Sojourners' connections to the sending society are also difficult to describe. On the surface, these people left their native countries, just like emigrants. Their significance to their homeland would, it has been assumed, cease as their ships sailed off into the sunset. But this assumption is inaccurate. Because transients intended to return, they worked toward "old world" goals. Some sent wealth acquired abroad back to their native country, quietly adding capital to its supply. Others found employ for their countrymen and thus provided an outlet for their native country's excess labor supply. Still others used their country's social and cultural institutions—schools, for example—to educate themselves and their families. None of these linkages is inconsequential, yet the historical profession's tendency has been to overlook them.

Just as this book's subject clearly belongs to migration history, so its chronological and geographical boundaries make it a work of early American history. Set in the eighteenth-century British Atlantic world, it integrates the histories of three separate societies: Jamaica, the Chesapeake, and Scotland. History based principally, if not entirely, on national boundaries has long been the unit of analysis accepted by the members of the historical "guild."[12] Though scholars recognize that ideas, actions, and reactions travel across mountain ranges, seas, and continents—from one nation to another—it is simply easier to study them in one place. To remain bound to this tradition, however, can only allow only an incomplete recovery and reconstruction of the past.

The Atlantic Ocean both separates and links societies in Africa, the Americas, and Europe. It did so in the eighteenth century; it does so now. By examining these connections from a vantage point somewhere in the middle of the ocean, the historian can see a great deal that might otherwise be obscured.[13] In this book I urgently suggest a real need for further com-

---

[12]See C. Vann Woodward, "The Comparability of American History," in *The Comparative Approach*, pp. 3–17, for a discussion of the pros and cons of history based on national boundaries.

[13]Though Atlantic history has been in existence for several decades, it has remained on the periphery of colonial American history. Among recent examples of Atlantic history are: Alfred Crosby, *The Columbian Exchange* (Westport, Conn., 1972); Ian Steele, *The English Atlantic,*

parisons, both inside and outside the British Empire. I argue that some groups of people might well have been at least as important to the Atlantic world as a whole as they were to any one of its constituent elements.

Just as the sojourner's aims dictated his behavior, so too did the sojourner's origin and destination influence his experiences. Scottish transients carefully chose their destinations; certain colonies held much more appeal to them than others. Jamaica, for example, was the largest and most important of the British sugar islands. These islands were, in turn, the jewels of the country's imperial crown. Of all Britain's far-flung possessions, the Caribbean colonies generated the most revenue for the metropolis.[14] As a result, the British population perceived the islands to be places where fortunes could be rapidly made. Opportunities for those with skills and training abounded. But the Caribbean remained an unhealthy and dangerous place for Europeans to visit for a week, let alone live for a prolonged time. Moreover, at least to many Scots, the islands were corrupt and vice-ridden societies. Though money could easily be made there, it was easy to become addicted to luxury and excess. Absenteeism thus became a goal. Very few people went to the West Indies in the eighteenth century expecting to settle permanently or to start a new life and family in the same way in which those who went to Pennsylvania or New England did.

The Chesapeake offered similar opportunities. Maryland and Virginia, right up until the War of Independence, existed primarily—at least in the British mind—as a place from which tobacco could be exported for the financial benefit of those in the metropolis. Profits could be increased even more by reexporting the crop to the continent. Scots began to dominate this trade after 1740. As a result, they reinforced their ethnic identity with economic power. In the mind of the Virginia resident, Scots and tobacco had become inextricably linked. The financial success of these early Scottish "middle men" entrepreneurs encouraged even more of their countrymen to begin Chesapeake sojourns.[15]

1675–1740 (Oxford, 1986); John McNeill, *Atlantic Empires of France and Spain* (Chapel Hill, N.C., 1986); Marcus Rediker, *Between the Devil and the Deep Blue Sea* (New York, 1987); David Geggus, *Slavery, War and Revolution: The British Occupation of St. Domingue* (Oxford, 1982); and Pierre Chaunu, *Les Ameriques, xvie, xviie, xviiie siècles* (Paris, 1977).

[14]For an excellent discussion of the West Indies' importance to Britain and Jamaica's preeminence among the islands, see Seymour Drescher, *Econocide* (Pittsburgh, 1977).

[15]The links between Scotland and the Chesapeake have been delineated by Jacob Price. See his *Capital and Credit in British Overseas Trade: The View from the Chesapeake, 1700–1776* (Cambridge, Mass., 1980); *France and the Chesapeake* (Ann Arbor, Mich., 1973); "The Rise of Glasgow in the Chesapeake Tobacco Trade, 1707–1775," *WMQ* 11 (1954): 177–99, and "Buchanan and Simson, 1759–1763: A Different Kind of Glasgow Firm Trading to the Chesapeake," *WMQ* 40 (1983): 3–41. Also see T. M. Devine, *The Tobacco Lords* (Edinburgh, 1975).

Both Jamaica and the Chesapeake were societies that rested firmly upon slave labor. This foundation, in turn, dictated that certain kinds of opportunities for whites (e.g., as physicians, bookkeepers, overseers, managers, and attorneys) would exist in them. The Scottish colonial residents therefore had to reconcile their own cultural identities with those prevalent in the "new world" societies. At the same time that they capitalized on opportunities provided by slave societies, however, the Scots worried about being corrupted by the avarice and vice to which they believed many white colonists had succumbed. As a group, they did not especially like either the system of slavery or the slave trade. They viewed it simply as something to be tolerated for as long as they were resident in a society outside Scotland. They only indirectly profited from it. When occasionally some of them thought about gaining profits directly from slavery, they did not want their countrymen to know. Virtuous behavior did not include trafficking in other human beings. Dr. Alexander Johnston wrote his brother from Jamaica with "some thoughts of entering into the slave trade and selling each year in the parish and two-neighboring ones . . . perhaps 250 or 300 slaves." But he wanted his family and neighbors to remain ignorant about this potential source of wealth. He, therefore, instructed his brother to keep "these matters . . . entirely to yourself—not even to Mr. Hay or your sisters—for they will only blab it about."[16]

To compare the sojourners' experiences in Jamaica and in the Chesapeake, I have organized the book along parallel thematic lines. The first chapter identifies the sojourners, their origins in Scotland, and their destinations in the colonies. It then examines the social and economic climates which spawned sojourners. At the same time that it characterizes the (mostly negative) images of Jamaica, Maryland, and Virginia circulating in Scotland, it explains why these ideas were not terribly likely to deter a sojourner from leaving. Chapters 2 and 3 chronicle the experiences of Scottish transients in Jamaica and the Chesapeake respectively. Both chapters use biographical sketches to present a detailed picture of the daily life experienced by sojourners, as well as the career choices open to them. The fourth chapter demonstrates the existence of strong Scottish communities and

[16]Alexander Johnston to James Johnston, 21 August 1784, legal papers, Alexander Johnston Section, Powel papers, Historical Society of Pennsylvania, Philadelphia. In general, the Scots tried to remain virtuous as they pursued their own financial aims. The attitudes of the moderate party in the Church of Scotland seem to me to encapsulate the attitudes the Scots demonstrated as they pursued wealth in corrupt societies. See Richard Sher, *Church and University in the Scottish Enlightenment: The Moderate Literati of Edinburgh* (Princeton, N.J., 1985). Also see Istvan Hont and Michael Ignatieff, eds., *Wealth and Virtue: The Shaping of Political Economy in the Scottish Enlightenment* (Cambridge, 1983), for a useful discussion about the virtuous way to acquire wealth (pp. 1–26).

well-spun ethnic patronage webs in both Jamaica and the Chesapeake and compares the differing ways in which they functioned. Finally, Chapter 5 uses a two-pronged approach to examine the fates Scottish sojourners met in Jamaica and the Chesapeake. It answers, in several ways, the question of whether or not they were successful. As part of that process, the chapter explores Scottish loyalism during the American War for Independence and demonstrates that the meaning of "independence" underwent some sort of transformation.

The book's chronological boundaries, 1740–1800, are designed to make the comparisons as precise as possible. In 1740, the movement of Scottish sojourners to both Jamaica and the Chesapeake really began in earnest. Travelers continued to voyage to Maryland and Virginia right up until the American Revolution. After the peace was signed in 1783, they returned to the former colonies, but they soon discovered that their old places within them had disappeared. By 1800, Scottish sojourns in the Chesapeake had become a thing of the past. No disruption in patterns of migration to Jamaica took place in 1776, and sojourners continued to flock there in the hopes that they would strike it rich. Yet though their involvement in the colony went on well past 1800, their numbers probably diminished. With the British Empire's acquisition of new Caribbean colonies and expansion into the East Indies and, later, Australia, more numerous opportunities for sojourners arose in other parts of the world.

I hope that the questions this book raises will serve as useful points of departure for scholars of migration and colonialists alike. Historical sources located outside the United States can and should be examined to provide a different perspective on the past. Our units of analyses might also profitably be changed. Since we have such a clear idea of how things operated *within* individual societies, we need now to begin exploring the connections *between* these same places. Equally important, statistical data alone do not begin even to hint at the complexity of the movements of people from one place to another. It is therefore vital for us to blend the qualitative with the quantitative as we begin to reconstruct the migrant's milieu.

I

TRANSATLANTIC TRANSIENCY: THE CHARACTER AND CONTEXT OF THE SOJOURNING MOVEMENT

Men and women in various Scottish localities encountered decidedly different opportunities to travel to the New World. Popular awareness of Jamaica and the Chesapeake (or, for that matter, any other colony) varied across Scotland. Glasgow's rise to prominence in the tobacco trade after 1740 is now a famous story. It made sense for Glaswegians to go to Virginia and Maryland because the city's economic well-being for several decades had become tightly tied to commerce in the "sot weed." As a result, the number of opportunities to travel from Glasgow to the Chesapeake exceeded those for any other British colony. The links between Scotland's growing professional classes, residing principally in Edinburgh, and the West Indies are equally demonstrable, though far less well known. Jamaica became home to more of these transient Scots than any of the other islands.

An examination of contemporary sources can reveal much about the significance of this overlooked stream of migration. The sojourners, a group of well-educated, middle-class professionals, were an integral part of the British Atlantic world of the eighteenth century. Records on both sides of the ocean provide information on their identity, motives, and numbers.

METHOD AND SAMPLE

There are generally two ways to measure the size of a movement from one place to another. The first necessitates counting the people who actually traveled. In many cases, however, there are no documents available that list either their names or their numbers. In such instances, the second method—studying the forms of transportation which these individuals and families employed—can be used to provide an approximation of the migration's total size.

Bernard Bailyn found an excellent source through which to measure the movement of people from Britain to the colonies over a three-year period. For *Voyagers to the West*, he gleaned impressive data from emigration registers created between 1773 and 1776.[1] Unfortunately, the registers consciously excluded sojourners. The captain of every ship carrying even one passenger who did not intend to return to Britain was required to register his vessel. An Act of Parliament, passed in response to high emigration levels, also obligated the captain to provide certain information about every person on board who admitted to permanently leaving the United Kingdom. Those who planned on returning, however, were exempted from any interrogation.

Just as Parliament did not mandate a record of travelers embarking before 1773 and after that date registered only those who did not plan to come back, the American colonies did not systematically record the names of any passengers (with the possible exception of indentured servants) who arrived in the colonies.[2] Thus, sojourners also escaped official enumeration on the Atlantic's western side. Any aggregate measure of such people must therefore be compiled from unofficial, and thus irregular, sources.

One way of tracking transients is to count the names of Scots known to be sojourning in the colonies. This is, perhaps, easier said than done. I surveyed and then examined all collections of family papers located in British repositories which had correspondence from Jamaica, Virginia, and Maryland. (The sample was later expanded to include United States and Jamaican archives.) I then compiled a list of all those correspondents in Jamaica or the Chesapeake who expressed plans to return home. I also included others mentioned by name in those letters in connection with a desire to go back to Scotland.

The next step involved checking to make sure that these individuals were really Scottish. Using corroborating evidence, such as baptism and matriculation records, I established, whenever possible, that the migrants in the colonies had spent their earlier days in Scotland. It is quite possible that some of the people identified as Scots were in fact creoles born in the West Indies who were sent to Scotland for their education. By including these

[1]See Bailyn, *Voyagers*, chap. 3, pp. 67–84, for a complete description of the emigration registers, including a candid characterization of their strengths and weaknesses.

[2]Exceptions to this general practice are "Certificates of Importation." Such lists were compiled when a proprietor sought to increase his landholdings. Virginia's George Mason entered a series of these lists into the public record when he sought in 1773 to obtain the land rights of indentured servants who had arrived thirty years earlier from the individuals who had imported them. These lists can be found in the Brock Collection, Box 78 (1), Huntington Library, San Marino, California. Though the bulk of the names are English and Irish, several lists include only Scots. These are BR Box 78 (1[c, f, g, v]).

Table 1.1. Occupations of Jamaican Scots

Occupation	Number	Percent
Apprentices	7	3.6
Artisans	3	1.6
Attorneys	26	13.5
Bureaucrats	5	2.6
Bookkeepers	1	0.5
Estate managers	20	10.4
Lawyers	6	3.1
Merchants	51	26.6
Military officers	3	1.6
Merchant captains	2	1.0
Ministers	1	0.5
Overseers	12	6.2
Physicians	37	19.3
Planters	13	6.8
Surveyors	3	1.6
Tavernkeepers	2	1.0
TOTAL	192	99.9

individuals I am consciously making some assumptions that Scottish identity encompasses more than birthplace.[3]

In several cases, a letter writer clearly indicated that the person with whom or about whom he corresponded was Scottish. For example, Alexander Wilson, who had returned from Virginia to Glasgow, wrote to his friend Alexander Miller: "A Few Days ago I was up at your House drinking Tea, when your Mama told me that you liked the place exceedingly Well."[4] This letter established Miller's ties to Scotland. Such techniques yielded the names of 267 men for Jamaica between 1739 and 1801, and 139 in the Chesapeake for the same period.

Moreover, when the occupations of these 406 individuals are taken into account, profiles of a highly trained, preponderantly middle-class group emerge. They are presented in Tables 1.1 and 1.2 as they referred to themselves. The occupations of eighty-five men are unknown. In Jamaica, an extraordinary tendency toward jobs which required some level of expertise characterized the sample. More than one-quarter of those whose occupations are known began their careers as merchants, or were otherwise involved in trade, and over one-half could be classified as "professionals" or what we would today call "white collar." Not unsurprisingly, the sample is

[3]A Scot is here defined as a person who was born in Scotland or formally educated there. See Forrest Macdonald and Ellen Shapiro Macdonald, "The Ethnic Origins of the American People, 1790," *WMQ* 37 (1980): 179–99. Also see Ned Landsman's "Communication" in *WMQ* 41 (1984): 680–81.

[4]Alexander Wilson to Alexander Miller, 29 July 1771, TD 1/1070, f. 24, SRA.

Table 1.2. Occupations of Chesapeake Scots

Occupation	Number	Percent
Apprentices (merchants)	12	9.3
Attorneys and lawyers	7	5.4
Bureaucrats	3	2.3
Landowners and planters	3	2.3
Merchants and tobacco factors	52	40.3
Ministers	3	2.3
Physicians	15	11.6
Teachers	2	1.6
Tobacco factors	32	24.8
TOTAL	129	99.9

devoid of unskilled laborers, small farmers, and skilled craftsmen. It is, however, a relatively diverse group, with its ranks composed of doctors, lawyers, merchants, and bookkeepers.

Most sojourners in the Chesapeake participated in some aspect of Glasgow's commercial relationship with Maryland and Virginia. Many served as factors to the merchant firms, many more acted as assistants to these factors, and a few, especially during the early years of this period, attempted to set up and operate their own mercantile businesses. A smattering of doctors, several teachers and tutors, and the odd minister and government bureaucrat filled out the Scottish ranks, but they were nowhere near as numerous as their neighbors engaged in trade.[5]

Identifying transient Scots from surviving correspondence has a decided advantage. It provides an important qualitative understanding of not only the character of the sojourners and their movement but also their motivations for leaving Scotland and their behavior abroad. But it is also an uneven technique. Much more is known about people who left records than about others who did not. Those like Alexander Wilson, whose letters have survived, and their friends, like Alexander Miller, who were simply mentioned in them assume a perhaps undeserved importance. Though the descriptive informa-

[5]A small idiosyncrasy in the classification scheme in Table 1.2 should be pointed out. Some people considered themselves merchants, while others who did the same job called themselves tobacco factors. Most people who referred to themselves as merchants dealt primarily with tobacco for one of the Glasgow houses; they probably preferred the term "merchant" because it implied an independent business and carried more prestige. Apprentices were the shop assistants who actually oversaw the shop activities and kept the books. Tobacco factors controlled the local stores in direct consultation with the Glasgow houses which employed them. The Merchants category contains three types of people: those who acted as merchants, those who called themselves merchants even if they clearly acted as factors, and those who did not refer to themselves as members of any particular trading subgroup.

tion yielded by the correspondence allows the sojourners' worlds to be reconstructed and their significance within the developing Atlantic context posited, it does not provide an entirely satisfactory measure of the size of the sojourning movement.

CONDITIONS IN EIGHTEENTH-CENTURY SCOTLAND

Historians of pre-industrial Scotland have long maintained that the country was one of Europe's most backward. For them, the central historical markers have been the Union of [Scottish and English] Parliaments in 1707 and industrialization. They have questioned, for example, whether or not the Union of Parliaments had any effect, positive or negative, upon either their country or its people. So too have they examined the importance of industrialization in changing the country's social and economic structure. Most scholars had concurred, at least until relatively recently, that the average Scot's life changed little or not at all as a result of the Union. It has been argued that most Caledonians, at least through the first seventy-five years of the eighteenth century, remained tied to their land, dependent upon outdated agricultural techniques, undiversified crops, and—if they were lucky—indifferent landlords. T. C. Smout, Scotland's best-known social historian, characterized the period from 1675 to 1750 as one of deep stagnation "in which very little economic growth or benevolent change occurred."[6]

More recent scholarship asserts that this may not have been entirely the case for everyone in "North Britain." Therefore, specifying about whom we are talking becomes essential. Revisionists have persuasively argued that positive social and economic transformations, at several levels of society, took place both in the years at the close of the seventeenth century and in the middle decades of the eighteenth century. Ian Whyte, for example, demonstrated that double-family farms became single-tenant farms years before

---

[6]T. C. Smout, "Where Had the Scottish Economy Got to by the Third Quarter of the Eighteenth Century?" in *Wealth and Virtue*, p. 45. The traditional wisdom long held that the Union of Parliaments, at least in the short run, failed woefully to meet its proponents' expectations and claims. See, for example, Smout, *History of the Scottish People* (London, 1969); R. H. Campbell, *Scotland since 1707* (Oxford, 1965), p. xx; and Bruce Lenman, *An Economic History of Modern Scotland 1660–1976* (London, 1977). Among more recent scholars, John Stuart Shaw argues in *The Management of Scottish Society* (Edinburgh, 1983) that most of Scotland's wealth, before and after the Union, lay at the very top of society, with the landed gentry and those bureaucrats who had moved south to England (p. 41). This position is also expressed in Nicholas Phillipson, "Politics, Politeness, and the Anglicisation of Early Eighteenth-Century Scottish Culture," in *Scotland and England, 1286–1815*, ed. Roger Mason (Edinburgh, 1987). Phillipson asserts that Scotland was an infant in the 1750s compared with its neighbor to the south (p. 227).

the enclosure movement really took off in the later eighteenth century. He has also discovered incidents (albeit not terribly widespread) of experiments with crop rotation.[7] Farmers who participated in such experiments would have seen improvements to the circumstances of their lives. Nonetheless, the fact still remains that both before and after 1707, most of Scotland's population remained agriculturally oriented. They generally earned enough to subsist from one year to the next and in good years even produced more than they could easily consume on their own.[8]

Recent demographic, historical, and geographic scholarship has also demonstrated that during the eighteenth century, several segments of the Scottish population moved to the cities. The percentage of city dwellers (in towns of over 10,000) nearly doubled, from 5 to 9 percent, between 1700 and 1750. Along with England's, Scotland's urban development was the fastest in Europe.[9] This increase in the urban population, combined with some years of agricultural surplus, led to the development of new internal markets and centers for trade and social interaction.[10] Also considering the access to the external markets which the Union of Parliaments provided, one could easily argue that the roots of a commercial society began to take hold in the country.[11]

At the higher elevations of Scotland's socioeconomic hierarchy, these changes contributed to external migration. Historians have generally agreed that post-Union Scotland saw a period of occupational specialization and the emergence of an educated middle class. As Smout has argued, there is reason to suppose that "improvement in personal incomes was occurring, and was being concentrated in the pockets of middle and higher social

[7]See Ian Whyte, "The Emergence of the New Estate Structure," in *The Making of the Scottish Countryside*, ed. M. L. Parry and T. R. Slater (London, 1980), pp. 117–35, and "Early Modern Scotland: Continuity and Change," in *An Historical Geography of Scotland*, ed. G. Whittington and I. D. Whyte (London, 1983), pp. 119–39.

[8]See R. A. Houston and I. D. White, "Introduction: Scottish Society in Perspective," in *Scottish Society, 1500–1800*, ed. Houston and Whyte (Cambridge, 1989), pp. 1–36, and Smout, "The Third Quarter."

[9]Houston and Whyte, "Introduction," p. 5. Also see T. M. Devine, "Urbanisation," in *People and Society in Scotland, I, 1760–1830*, ed. T. M. Devine and Rosalind Mitchison (Edinburgh, 1988), pp. 27–30.

[10]Christopher A. Whatley, "How Tame Were the Scottish Lowlanders during the Eighteenth Century," in *Conflict and Stability in Scottish Society, 1700–1850*, ed. T. M. Devine (Edinburgh, 1990), says that by 1800, 17 percent of the Scottish population lived in urban centers, the third highest rate in all of Europe (p. 4). Also see Houston and Whyte, "Introduction," p. 15, and M. Lynch, "Continuity and Change in Urban Society," in Houston and Whyte, *Scottish Society*, pp. 85–117.

[11]Scotland's east coast had in the seventeenth century developed European trading routes; these also greatly contributed to the country's urbanization. See R. A. Dodgshon, *Land and Society in Early Scotland* (Oxford, 1981).

groups."[12] The reasons are thus. Landowners began to consolidate their holdings at the same time that the general population increased, so that there were fewer estates for more people. The country's aristocracy and the largest landlords consolidated their holdings first, which effectively squeezed out those between them and the lower orders. These "lairds" and "bonnet lairds" then found themselves wanting income and fearing downward mobility. They joined members of the mercantile and professional classes and seized available opportunities to migrate to London, Europe, or the British colonies.[13] In general, such people were lowlanders; they lived along the country's east coast south of Aberdeen and in Ayrshire and the counties bordering Glasgow. As will become clear below, these were exactly the groups of people who became sojourners.

The caricature of the enterprising Scot, long a favorite in the Scottish imagination as well as the national historiography, needs therefore to be revised. J. M. Bumsted has claimed: "Countless numbers of Scots, mainly those skilled at making war or conducting trade, had ventured to England or to the continent of Europe throughout the Middle Ages and the Reformation, seeking employment and prosperity not possible at home."[14] Though Bumsted defined his cohort of Scots by singling out certain groups of people, he did not draw an overt connection between social and economic changes, class, and migration. To make his characterization more precise, one needs to understand that most "enterprising Scots" in the eighteenth century began with at least a small advantage. Their families had always been members of one of Scotland's better-off classes. "Better-off" is a relative term. While they were near the top of Scotland's social hierarchy, when compared to their counterparts in countries like the Netherlands, France, or England, they were disadvantaged. The inadequacies of the Scottish economy generally meant that all but the wealthiest landowners looked for ways to supplement their incomes.

Many of these people chose to learn a trade or profession. But the prevailing economic conditions ensured that this advantage would prove insufficient. If conditions in eighteenth-century Scotland constricted opportunities for socioeconomic advancement, they also limited the amount of income that

---

[12]See Smout, "The Third Quarter," p. 61, and Houston and Whyte, "Introduction," pp. 18–20. Also see R. A. Houston, "The Demographic Regime," in *People and Society*, p. 20.

[13]I have simplified and adapted the model presented by L. Timperley in "The Pattern of Landholding in Eighteenth-Century Scotland," in Parry and Slater, *Making of the Scottish Countryside*.

[14]Bumsted, *The People's Clearance: Highland Emigration to British North America, 1770–1815* (Edinburgh, 1982), p. 1.

"The Caledonian Voyage to Moneyland," Plate 17, *The British Antidote to Caledonian Poison* (1762), shows Scots lining up to travel south to England in search of their fortunes. The cartoonist believed that Scots were unfairly claiming patronage from the head of the Westminster Government, then under the charge of Lord Bute. Reproduced by permission of the Henry E. Huntington Library and Art Gallery, San Marino, California. (Rare Book 343170)

could be accrued from a professional career. In other words, it was simply impossible to increase one's wealth very much by serving as a physician in a country where many—if not most—people could not afford to pay their medical bills. Similarly, only those Scots who owned land had any significant need for legal advice. Their numbers were not enough to support a large community of lawyers. Greater opportunities existed for those involved in trade, but new markets would eventually have to be found if growth was to continue. For all of these professionals, going abroad to practice one's vocation provided an alternative.[15] But they were not the only groups to cross the Atlantic.

[15]See Stana Nenadic, "The Rise of the Urban Middle Class," in *People and Society*, esp. p. 117. For a discussion of the position of Scottish lawyers in Edinburgh society, see John Stuart Shaw, *Management of Scottish Society*, p. 19. T. C. Smout has drawn the connection between

"The Caledonians' Arrival in Moneyland," Plate 18, *The British Antidote to Caledonian Poison* (1762), pictures Scots lining up to receive sacks of cash, presumably from Lord Bute and his minions. Reproduced by permission of the Henry E. Huntington Library and Art Gallery, San Marino, California. (Rare Book 343170)

Permanent emigrants were almost universally drawn from the lower echelons of Scottish agricultural society, either in the highlands or the lowlands.[16] In both areas, they generally had to contend with marginal land. If they had land, it was not likely to be productive enough to guarantee them anything beyond subsistence. Even if the family farm provided more than its tenants needed, a surplus did not promise them much socioeconomic mobility. If they did not have land, then they needed to earn a living in some other way, which was usually even more difficult. Such people were not especially

---

Edinburgh and the professions in his *History of the Scottish People*, pp. 366–79. He also calls attention to the importance of merchants in Glasgow, pp. 379–90.

[16]For an example of the fusion of sojourners and emigrants, see L. M. Cullen, "Scotland and Ireland, 1600–1800: Their Role in the Evolution of British Society," in *Scottish Society*, pp. 228–44. Previously, distinctions have been made between highlanders and lowlanders or between "adventurers" and "servants." The distinction I make ultimately considers plans, occupations, and locations.

well educated, though they had more opportunities for education than most Europeans.[17]

Scots highlanders who left their country during the eighteenth century did so, as Bumsted puts it, in a "protest against alterations in their traditional patterns of life."[18] Highland tacksmen, for example, were second in command of the clans, after the lairds. They were tenants of the chiefs, and had many tenants of their own. Following the unsuccessful Jacobite uprising in 1745, the lairds began to take back for themselves much of the economic power which they had delegated to the tacksmen. Rather than endure further humiliation and a possible decline in their standard of living at home, many tacksmen decided to leave the country. They brought as many of their tenants with them as they possibly could. As a result, they left Scotland to recreate (or preserve), in the colonies, a hierarchical system that had come under attack not only from Westminster's punishment for 1745 but also from the gradually metamorphosing Scottish economy. The tacksmen expected to be at the top of the social order in the "new world."[19]

Many tenant farmers (and indeed other poor highlanders and lowlanders) who willingly left home also had misgivings about staying in Britain. Most must have feared that their rents would rise (as Scottish economic development began to affect land values) without corresponding increases in yield, or changes in methods of cultivation.[20] Some were certainly afraid that they would lose their small farms, which had little margin for unforeseeable fiscal problems, to circumstances beyond their control, such as eviction or drought. If so, they would be caught in an unhappy economic position without support from the familiar quasi-feudal system or, in the lowland case, from landlords who also lived off the land.

Many lowland landholders moved to England after the Union; they had

[17]I will address questions of the Scottish educational system more fully in the next chapter. See Donald J. Withrington, "Schooling, Literacy and Society," in *People and Society*, pp. 163–87.

[18]Bumsted, *The People's Clearance*, p. 2.

[19]According to Henry Graham, (*Colonists from Scotland* [Ithaca, N.Y., 1956] pp. 68–69), "the tacksman would farm part of his tack and let the rest to undertenants. The tacksman was responsible to his superior for the payment of rent on the whole of his tack. So the more he got from the crofters the less he had to pay out of his own pocket." A brief discussion of changing social relationships in the Scottish Highlands can be found in Houston and Whyte, "Introduction," pp. 24–29. For a summation of the punishments which the Crown inflicted on the clans, see Smout, *History*, p. 343.

[20]L. Timperley, in "Pattern of Landholding," p. 141, demonstrates that real rents increased three times over between c. 1660 and c. 1770, and between c. 1660 and c. 1793, they increased 7.6 times. Smout, in his *History*, maintains that rents which were "stationary from 1700 to 1750, began to lift markedly from 1763, doubled from 1783 to 1793, and doubled again from 1794 to 1815" (p. 310). Graham, in *Colonists from Scotland*, p. 64, is more specific: in the Highlands, rents rose between 33 and 300 percent after 1763 and between 200 and 400 percent in the Lowlands, indicating the general level of "improvements" made.

arranged to have their rents sent to them there.[21] Residing away from their property and in a place where it was extremely easy to spend money made them forget important truths. If they persisted in collecting rents during a bad year, the tenants would not have enough to support themselves. The growing gulf between landlord and tenant worried many lowlanders. "Improvement" of a property often meant a worse life for those who actually lived on it once the owner had gone south or otherwise moved off the land. Emigration, therefore, became an increasingly attractive option for the tenants.

Another group of emigrants, mostly from the lowlands, left Scotland for purely personal motivations. They were perhaps a bit less disaffected. In their estimations, the colonies simply allowed them more than they could reasonably have hoped to achieve at home. As William Brock has suggested:

> The prospect of acquiring large tracts [of land] at what must have seemed to be very low prices, or paying the normal rents demanded by some land speculators, must have attracted ambitious young men whose families had struggled along for generations on small holdings or poor soil, and to younger sons who had little to hope from their patrimony.[22]

Such people did not believe that changes in the Scottish economy would ever benefit them or satisfy their desire for property. Scholars have not missed the irony in this situation: "Emigration from Scotland in the eighteenth century grew from a trickle to a stream in the very years when the country experienced an unprecedented acquisition of wealth."[23] The unknown of the new world seemed better to them than the familiar of the old. They did not intend to return to their native country; it had failed to provide adequately for them.

These are precisely the people whom Bernard Bailyn has recently studied. His findings tend to confirm the proposition that Scottish historians have put forth. In his three-year sample (1773–76), Bailyn demonstrates that nearly twice as many people left Scotland for negative reasons (i.e., unemployment, poverty, high rents, or economic conditions) as for positive ones (i.e., to

[21]The tendency of the Scottish landlord to become Anglicized and the increasing gulf between landlord and tenant is discussed in G. Whittington, "Agriculture and Society in Lowland Scotland, 1750–1870," in *An Historical Geography of Scotland*, pp. 148–50.

[22]Brock, *Scotus Americanus* (Edinburgh, 1982), p. 17.

[23]Graham, *Colonists from Scotland*, p. 8. Graham paints too simplistic a picture of changes in Scottish society. The migrants which he describes were largely rural laborers and farmers; wealth began to increase slowly for these people only during the second half of the eighteenth century. But those farther up the social hierarchy experienced changes much earlier. Also see T. M. Devine, "The Failure of Radical Reform in Scotland in the late Eighteenth Century," in *Conflict and Stability*, pp. 57–60.

better themselves, to settle, to follow an occupation). Fully one-third of those who left for negative reasons came from the highlands (330 of 992). Of the other six Scottish regions used in Bailyn's analysis, only the west lowlands came close to matching this figure (264 of 992). There was little, if anything, to pull such people back to their native country from the colonies.[24]

The other group of people, sojourners who went to the colonies in search of fortunes, were obviously not so alienated. They intended to return home as soon as they could with as much as they could. Though they faced some of the same economic conditions which drove out many emigrants, two characteristics distinguished transients from emigrants. First, those who were sojourners generally came from higher social and economic positions than did the American immigrants. Their families began with more and therefore benefited earlier from the Scottish economy's increasing attention to commerce. Land pressure was of a different kind. Rents were still an issue, but these people collected them rather than paid them. According to William Brock, the typical transient might have "come from a family in comfortable circumstances, but if so he was probably a younger son with poor expectations at home. Though he might eventually hope to own land in the colonies, his first objective was normally to succeed in business or medicine."[25]

Furthermore, owning land in the colonies served as a temporary substitute for possessing Scottish property. As T. C. Smout has said of the growing Scottish middle class, "There is also no doubt . . . that more people were ambitious for estates after the middle of the eighteenth century in Scotland than ever before."[26] Because small Scottish estates had begun to be enclosed by larger ones during the eighteenth century, less land was available to satisfy increasing demand. And though the urban and commercially oriented population increased, the demand for landed estates did not abate. Properties that yielded an annual rental income continued to indicate status. As R. H. Campbell has noted, "the possession of property was the way to social prestige and political power, but its economic potential was necessary if that

[24]See Bailyn, *Voyagers*, pp. 190–98. The negative and positive reasons for emigration differed significantly between Scotland and England. South of the border, travelers were more evenly divided about their reasons for leaving the United Kingdom.

[25]Brock, *Scotus Americanus*, p. 15. Smout in *History*, pp. 258–67, has noted that the poor Scottish land had to support a growing number of people. Younger sons of the well-off would have had nearly as much trouble getting land as those in less fortunate circumstances, because their relatives would have required more upon which to live themselves, given the rising standard of living.

[26]Smout, *History*, p. 283.

social prestige was to be perpetuated."[27] Working in the colonies, therefore, could generate an income which could be used to purchase property abroad at a lower price than at home. More important, that colonial estate would produce enough revenue, it was believed, for the owner to procure Scottish property when it became available at the right price. (The Scots did not plan for property inflation to increase faster than wage inflation.)

The second trait that distinguished the two groups of migrants was simply that sojourners had one or several reasons to return to Scotland. The colonies, they believed, were to be exploited, not settled.[28] They discerned no reason to stay permanently in a place in which they had no formal or historical ties, and which they perceived to be unhealthy and unpleasant. Any property acquired in the colonies, they thought, could easily be directed from abroad. And it could certainly provide its owners with power and status in Scotland, which they had all along sought and which generally unfavorable economic conditions had denied them.

At first glance, it might seem odd, even puzzling, that a group of people who felt compelled to leave one place, tacitly acknowledging a lack of sufficient opportunity for mobility, should also feel so compelled to return to it. Yet, among eighteenth-century middle-class Scots such behavior was completely to be expected. The reasons are fairly straightforward. In the first place, ambitious Scots of this class did have a long tradition of moving in search of increased opportunities and returning home better off than when they left. They did not perceive the move from one side of the ocean to the other as a barrier against increased status at home. Rather, migration became an aid to, if not a necessity for, upward mobility. In effect, going to the American colonies was nothing more than a geographic expansion of old migration patterns.[29] In addition, an extremely strong sense of family, community, and nation, along with all the corresponding cultural characteristics, permeated the society from which these people came. The Scots simply did not want to be *corrupted* by an alien and vice-ridden culture. As the eighteenth-century Scots saw it, they required only enough to live comfortably.

[27]R. H. Campbell, "The Landed Classes," in *People and Society*, p. 96.

[28]This is precisely the attitude that many Scots demonstrated during the heyday of the British Empire in the nineteenth and early twentieth centuries. Several essays that make similar observations about Scots in Canada, Australia, New Zealand, and India can be found in R. A. Cage, ed., *Scots Abroad: Labour, Capital, Enterprise, 1750–1914* (London, 1985).

[29]Such migratory behavior would later expand to include the East Indies. Yet Scots who had status at home did not care for the *nouveaux riches* nabobs, finding them ill-mannered and grotesque caricatures of themselves. See Dwyer, *Virtuous Discourse: Sensibility and Community in Late Eighteenth Century Scotland* (Edinburgh, 1987), p. 44. This experience generated the literati's fear of some of the effects of commercial society. See also L. M. Cullen, "Scotland and Ireland," pp. 238–40.

Residents of the colonies, they believed, generally had riches and possessions merely for the sake of having them. Scottish character, no doubt the
product of both ingrained Calvinist logic and Enlightenment thought about
commercial society, deplored (indeed, still deplores) ostentatious display.
This attitude distinguished them from many of their neighbors, who were
considered fortune-hunting pleasure seekers.[30]

As if to demonstrate their intentions, those Scots who emigrated permanently had a strong tendency to leave the country in company with their
families or other relatives.[31] Those who went over as sojourners did so on
their own. It was much easier for an ambitious young man to leave Scotland
if he believed that he would return to his relatives (who acted as a sort of
human collateral) as a success. The inevitability of the sojourner's home-
coming was never seriously questioned until he had passed many years in the
colonies.[32] Finally, most, if not all, of the Scottish transients were drawn
back to Scotland by the promise of what they could have there if they were
successful abroad. The Scottish sojourner saw his social rank (the middle
class) becoming wealthier, a clear result of the rising commercial economy.
Many could not think of a better way to take advantage of it than by increasing their fortunes abroad in order to live comfortably in their old age at
home. They did not realize that they would face different problems.

With this basic knowledge of the migrating population and the changes
taking place in eighteenth-century Scotland, we can now look more closely
at how sojourners became informed about events in the places to which they
contemplated traveling. What did they know about colonial America?

[30]See Smout, *History*, pp. 71–87, for a discussion of the rigid attitudes of the Church of
Scotland which could have contributed to this fear of corruption. Smout's argument seems too
monolithic. For Scots of the middle classes, the relationship between economic thought and
virtuous behavior could very probably have been tied to the Scottish enlighteners who were
members of the Church of Scotland's "Moderate" group. These people "sought a rational basis
for religious belief in view of Enlightenment thinking . . . which despised 'enthusiasm' and
excess in religion" (Callum G. Brown, *The Social History of Religion in Scotland since 1730*
[London, 1987], p. 30). See also Dwyer, *Virtuous Discourse*, pp. 1–7; Hont and Igantieff, "Needs
and Justice in the Wealth of Nations: An introductory essay," in *Wealth and Virtue*, pp. 2–6;
Adam Smith, *The Theory of Moral Sentiments*, ed. D. D. Raphael and A. L. Mactie (Oxford,
1976); and Richard Sher, *Church and University*. All provide excellent analyses of the connections between socioeconomic mobility and virtuous behavior.

[31]According to Bailyn, nearly half of the highlanders emigrated in groups. See *Voyagers*, p.
140. According to Ned Landsman, 40 percent of early Scottish immigrants to New Jersey
arrived in family units and a majority of them came with at least some relatives. See Landsman,
Scotland and Its First American Colony, pp. 114–15.

[32]See Siu, *The Chinese Laundryman* (New York, 1987), pp. 294–99, and Bonacich, "Middleman Minorities," pp. 592–93, for other examples of this phenomenon in the twentieth
century.

PUBLIC PERCEPTIONS: JAMAICA, THE CHESAPEAKE AND THE PRESS

Analyzing Scottish newspapers allows a glimpse of the information that potential migrants—emigrants as well as sojourners—had available to them as they decided whether to strike out for British America. The papers clearly served as a forum on a range of issues. Their pages contributed to public opinion and awareness; indeed, more than one historian has argued that the press molded and reinforced the social and economic views of their readers.[33] It is, therefore, slightly unnerving to discover that much reporting about Jamaica and the Chesapeake (as well as about other colonies) was negative.

Table 1.3 presents the results of an analysis of the content of stories about Jamaica or the Chesapeake in the Glasgow and Edinburgh papers between 1750 and 1775 and also between 1778 and 1790.[34] Stories about wars, battles, conquests, and the like have all been omitted from the survey.[35] The remaining reports have then been divided into four categories. Stories about Jamaica that were essentially negative in character described slave rebellions, sickness and disease, murder plots, and poor weather. Negative reports about the Chesapeake included extravagant living, storms and flooding, runaway slaves, and problems between the governor and House of Burgesses. Positive articles about both colonies described improvements to commercial relationships with Britain, the success of a particular crop, or political decisions that favorably affected the economic and social climate in both societies. Neutral reports simply reprinted the Legislative Journals, which merely demonstrated that the colonial legislatures sometimes deliberated.

---

[33]On the question of audience, see Mary Elizabeth Craig, *The Scottish Periodical Press, 1750–1789* (Edinburgh, 1931). Craig correctly argued that newspaper readers were more numerous than purchasers. Together subscribers and readers constituted the upper echelons of Scottish society. John Dwyer in *Virtuous Discourse*, p. 12, argues that both the landed gentry and the literati viewed the *Caledonian Mercury* as an impartial organ. Though modern readers may not find it impartial, they will certainly discover compelling reading—on a host of subjects—in its pages.

[34]Because of the difference in the number of years covered in the two components of Table 1.3, 26 and 13 years, I have calculated a per annum (p.a.) figure, the total number of stories divided by the number of years covered in each part. This will allow more direct comparison between the two samples.

[35]Battle reports, despite their large number, are omitted because they resembled more the journalistic reporting we associate with twentieth-century newspapers than the extended editorial commentary so prevalent in the eighteenth century. Since we can safely assume that the British public supported the British side during the French and Indian War and the American Revolution, we can surmise that these reports would not have led to new or reformulated opinions.

Table 1.3. Analysis of story content

City		1750–1775			1778–1790		
		N	%	P.A.	N	%	P.A.
Edinburgh	Total Chesapeake stories	29	100	1.1	30	100	2.3
	Negative	25	86	0.96	17	56	1.3
	Positive	2	7	0.07	3	10	0.23
	Neutral	1	3.5	0.035	10	33.3	0.77
	Personal	1	3.5	0.035	0	0	0.00
	Total Jamaica stories	33	100	1.27	9	100	0.69
	Negative	21	64	0.78	7	77.8	0.54
	Positive	5	15	0.175	0	0	0.00
	Neutral	4	12	0.14	0	0	0.00
	Personal	3	9	0.105	2	22.2	0.15
Glasgow	Total Chesapeake stories	44	100	1.69	27	100	2.08
	Negative	27	61	1.04	10	14.81	0.77
	Positive	7	16	0.27	4	37.03	0.31
	Neutral	7	16	0.27	8	29.62	0.62
	Personal	3	7	0.11	5	18.51	0.38
	Total Jamaica stories	26	100	1.00	14	100	1.08
	Negative	13	50	0.50	5	35.71	0.38
	Positive	3	11.5	0.11	4	28.57	0.31
	Neutral	3	11.5	0.11	0	0.00	0.00
	Personal	7	27	0.27	5	35.71	0.39

Personal stories generally provided notices about the lives of Scottish individuals already residing in the colonies. Marriage, death, and increased prosperity were the events most frequently mentioned.

In Edinburgh between 1750 and 1775, 64 percent of the stories about Jamaica and 86 percent of those about the Chesapeake were negative in character. In Glasgow, the figures were similar: 50 percent of the stories about Jamaica were negative as were 61 percent of those concerning the Chesapeake. The newspapers' regular readers before the American War, in both cities, almost certainly (perhaps subliminally) received the message that trouble and misfortune were not particularly unusual in these colonies. The same arguments apply to the years between 1778 and 1790. In all categories negative reporting accounted for the greatest percentage of the total number of stories. Nevertheless, the manner in which the press presented the stories invariably indicated that any problems could be controlled.

Quite often, negative stories expressed little more than whites' fear of those whom they had subjugated—blacks and Indians. In 1742, the *Caledonian Mercury* printed a description of an Indian insurrection planned against European residents of Maryland:

A Design is lately discovered of the Indians in Somerset and Dorchester Counties [on Maryland's Eastern Shore] intending to massacre all the white People; after which they were to proceed to Philadelphia, and be joined by their swarthy Brethren the French and Northern Indians.[36]

Though it might seem illogical, such reports probably did not dissuade many of those considering an Atlantic move. One factor found in many of the stories served to ameliorate a potentially damaging situation: virtually all such tales of rebellion ended in a way that allowed the Europeans to claim victory. In the case described above, the plot was discovered with just enough time to prevent anyone (who was white, and thus innocent) from being hurt. In other instances, discovery came too late to save everyone involved. But in the final analysis, justice—in the form of retribution—always prevailed. As the *Glasgow Journal* of 5–12 February 1761 reported about Jamaica:

By our latest accounts from the country, there are not above 30 of the rebellious negroes now left; and yet that small body came down last week on an estate . . . and burnt the whole sugar works. . . . They made an attempt upon Mr. Wallace's [the nextdoor neighbor] at the same time, but were beat off . . . on . . . killing some of them the rest retired to the woods. The governor has raised three companies of free negroes to suppress them, and allows a reward of 20 l. for every one they shall kill or take prisoner.[37]

While the slaves had indeed managed to damage British planters' property, they were ultimately made to pay, almost certainly with their lives, for their insubordinate and homicidal actions. By portraying such incidents in this fashion, the Scottish newspapers conveyed to their regular readers both a sense of the unusual and the comforting knowledge that their rights, lives, and property would, and could, be safely protected in the colonies. Any risks were ultimately worth taking. Two more examples point out both the negative character of the reporting and the vindication property owners almost always received. On 2 March 1770, the *Edinburgh Advertiser* published a magnificent murder story from Jamaica:

There has been a dreadful murder committed . . . upon the body of one Watts, a Planter, by his wife and the overseer of his plantation. They went into his bed chamber in the night whilst he was asleep, armed with clubs . . . and

[36]*Caledonian Mercury*, 9 November 1742.
[37]The single best account of the original rebellion, which took place during April 1760 in St. Mary's parish, can be found in the *Caledonian Mercury's* one and one-half column story of 9 July 1760.

attended by three negroes; the wife and negroes struck him first, but, he crying out, the overseer finished at two blows. . . . About a fortnight after[,] the overseer came to Kingston, and lost his pocket-book, having made a memorandum of the said murder in it.[38]

The overseer, of course, confessed to the crime (and probably to his own stupidity for jotting down a murder he had committed!) after the magistrates arrested and imprisoned him. He and the widow allegedly planned the death so that they could later be married. Both were hanged. The slave accomplices were acquitted, because the homicidal actions were not their own choice. It is not a little ironic that obedience to ill-intentioned and petty masters was thus rewarded. Surely if the plot had been of the slaves' own design, as an act of resistance against oppression, they would have faced immediate execution. The *Glasgow Journal* three years later, and in much the same vein, reported that,

> There has been an insurrection of a plantation on . . . [Jamaica] belonging to Mr. M'Donald, by his slaves who rose upon the family to destroy it, but happily he had got some intelligence of their design: and had got a body of men whom he placed in ambush & as they were making for the dwelling house, the people suddenly rushed out upon them and secured them all. Three of the ring leaders were immediately hung up.[39]

Once again, justice prevailed. White lives were spared from certain suffering at the hands of blacks. Europeans had little to fear in Jamaica, provided they were willing to trust in and abide by the law (which, after all, they had created for their own benefit).

Regular readers of Scottish newspapers also learned quite a lot about natural disasters (such as hurricanes and severe flooding) which were either unknown or uncommon in Britain. Such misfortunes usually had deleterious results for resident planters and merchants alike. But in the press, these crises could not be seen to impede the long-term accumulation of wealth. As an example, a two-column account of the havoc a devastating hurricane wreaked in Virginia (including damage to the Scottish tobacco warehouses there) at the end of 1769 was quickly followed by the more positive story which reassured readers that life in Virginia remained safe.[40] "Authentick advices from Virginia say, that the greatest harmony subsists among the

---

[38]Extract of a letter from Kingston, dated 18 November 1769, *Edinburgh Advertiser*, 2 March 1770.

[39]*Glasgow Journal*, week ending 7 January 1773.

[40]Stories about the storm can be found in the *Glasgow Mercury* issue of 9–16 November 1769 as well as the *Caledonian Mercury* of 18 November 1769.

inhabitants of that place, and that commerce seems to be in the most flourishing situation."[41]

Such reports amounted to effective damage control. As a general rule, negative reporting could only have hurt the Scots' determination to relocate. But the reporting of unfavorable incidents with favorable outcomes surely compensated for any lost ground.

Scottish newspapers regularly contained references to individual sojourners who had gone to live in the colonies. Stories that described, for example, the marriage of a Scot in the Chesapeake or the death of one in Jamaica often found their way into print, indicating that the part of Scottish society which had some connections to the newspapers did not write off those who had left temporarily for the colonies. Though the total number of such stories was small, we can surmise that those whose experiences appeared in the newspaper were among the group's most prominent members. The *Caledonian Mercury* of 23 August 1766 recorded: "A few days ago [14 June] died at Montego Bay, William Gordon, Esq; Copartner of George Richards, Esq.; and late one of the members of the Hon. Assembly."[42]

Gordon's obituary indicated that his labors had been rewarded; he had served as a member of the Jamaica Assembly. Notices like this one provided readers with two important ideas. First, life (and death) in the colonies went on just as normally as it did in Scotland. Thus, places in the new world were not frightening or intolerably strange. Second, some Scots who went there encountered recognition and success.

In addition, some of the stories that concerned other (usually negative) subjects contained references to Scottish people living in the colonies. For example, it is likely that Wallace, who beat back the band of marauding slaves, and M'Donald, who ambushed the slave insurrection on his plantation, were both Scottish. Certainly an account of the uprising at one Wedderburn's Westmoreland parish plantation in 1766 was published in the Scottish press because Wedderburn was an important landowner in Jamaica who happened to be Scottish.[43] Publishing reports with references to Scottish subjects insured that more readers could relate to the story because they knew the subjects or their families personally. And, because these subjects were usually vindicated (or otherwise pictured as successful), the Scots saw that they were capable of enduring any hardships that they might encounter. I could find no newspaper reports of Scots who had completely failed to achieve anything at all in the colonies. Such a noticeable omission, especially when people sometimes did not accomplish what they had set out to achieve,

[41]*Edinburgh Advertiser*, 5 January 1770.
[42]This and similar stories are included in the "personal" categories of Table 1.3. For a few other brief examples, see the *Caledonian Mercury*, 15 April 1756 and 18 June 1764.
[43]See the *Caledonian Mercury*, 4 February 1767.

strongly confirms the notion that the press did what it could to prevent a negative backlash against traveling to the colonies.

Three general points emerge. First, the Scottish newspapers would have had little interest in reporting the experiences of *emigrant* Scots. In almost all cases, once a person permanently left Scotland, his or her ties with it were weakened, if not completely severed—particularly if other family members left at the same time. Therefore we can safely assume that reports about expatriates in the Scottish press concerned transients. Second, stories about Scots already in the colonies demonstrated to those who contemplated a trip that they would not be alone. Some of their countrymen already lived there, and the ones who had been depicted in the newspapers encountered success in one form or another.

Third, many well-read, middle-class Scots worried about too vigorously pursuing wealth that could not be obtained at home. They belonged to a culture that, more than almost anything else, feared avarice, greed, and luxury. Their newspapers constantly reminded them what their aims in the colonies should be; they were warned away from the opulent lifestyles that lurked beyond the River Tweed. By 1760, Jamaica's reputation as a place for slothful derelicts was already well established. The *Caledonian Mercury* noted: "Fortunes are made at Jamaica almost instantly, while the people appear to live in such a state of luxury and profusion; as in all other places, are the sure tokens of approaching beggary."[44]

The Chesapeake was not far behind. In 1767, the *Caledonian Mercury* published part of a letter from Virginia that described the typical Chesapeake planter's tendency to borrow in order to cover the costs of high living: "The people in general are naturally very extravagant; and this inclination of theirs (for very good reasons) has been but too much encouraged by the merchants on your side of the water."[45]

These sorts of warnings coincide with the Scot's ambivalence toward the changes wrought by commercial society. While the assumption in Scotland was that fortunes could be made in both Jamaica and the Chesapeake, Scots also knew that their gains would be devalued, at least in the eyes of their native society, if prosperity led to increased opulence and extravagance. This belief, which was almost a fear of faring too well financially, often contributed to a sojourner's perpetual desire to return to Scotland; at least it was not corrupt.[46]

---

[44]*Caledonian Mercury*, 25 October 1760.

[45]Letter dated 20 June 1767 published in *Caledonian Mercury*, 19 September 1767.

[46]A fine, though incomplete, discussion of the embracing of commerce with a simultaneous antipathy toward luxury can be found in David Spadafora, *The Idea of Progress in Eighteenth-Century Britain* (New Haven, Conn., 1990), pp. 275–84. John Dwyer in *Virtuous Discourse*, pp. 1–5 and 39–46, illuminates the problems the Scottish enlighteners had with commercial

The press portrayed the colonies in an ambivalent manner at best, yet we know that Scots went to America in considerable numbers. Scottish newspapers published other information, which provides the basis for estimating those numbers. They help us to gauge the size of the movement of people from one side of the Atlantic to the other.

THE SCALE OF THE SOJOURNING MOVEMENT

Because transient's letters indicate that most of them traveled on board the merchant ships which regularly plied the north Atlantic, examining extant shipping records is a logical step. Unfortunately, where official or public documents have survived, only the inanimate cargoes which these vessels transported have been recorded. Neither Scottish nor colonial authorities kept track of the number of voyagers on these ships. This means that unofficial sources must next be considered.[47]

The best available method for estimating the movement's size derives from analyzing Scottish newspapers. Ships that traded across the Atlantic generally advertised in one or more of the Scottish papers in Glasgow, Edinburgh, and, to a lesser extent, Aberdeen. And they did so with increasing frequency as the century progressed. By the mid 1760s, most ships, as far as it has been possible to determine, advertised.[48] Simply counting the

---

activity and the avarice and love of luxury that could result. He uses the examples of the returned nabobs from India, whose desire for wealth and opulence was considered a moral cancer within Scottish society. Also see Hont and Ignatieff, "Needs and Justice in the Wealth of Nations: An Introductory Essay," in *Wealth and Virtue*, p. 2; and Adam Smith, *The Theory of Moral Sentiments*, esp. pp. 223, 226, 256–57. Smith sees the distinction between Scotland and England diminishing as Scotland's commercial activity increases. In general, the Scots put the English and "excess" on one side of the line and themselves and "moderation" on the other side.

[47]The official eighteenth-century Virginia Shipping Returns, both inward and outward, can be found (when they have survived) in CO 5/1445–1450 at the PRO. Similar records for Jamaica are located in CO 142/16–20. The Scottish customs records for the mid and late eighteenth century, which noted ships' cargoes entering and leaving Greenock and Port Glasgow, are located in E 504/28 (Port Glasgow) and E 504/15 (Greenock), both at the SRO. Some colonial papers also listed the local arrival of British ships, identifying their home ports (and sometimes their cargoes) and whether or not they were carrying any passengers. I have not carried out a systematic analysis of these papers, because spot-checked years have shown that lists of arrivals and departures appeared quite irregularly. Sometimes no port of origin was given; usually no list of passengers was printed; sometimes just departures or just arrivals were published.

[48]The newspapers consulted are as follows: for Edinburgh, *Caledonian Mercury*, 1740–99, except 1748 and 1757 (*Edinburgh Evening Courant*), and 1770 (*Edinburgh Advertiser*); for Glasgow, *Glasgow Journal*, 1741–47, 1758–59, 1761–74, *Glasgow Courant*, 1747–58, 1759–60, *Glasgow Chronicle*, 1775, *Glasgow Mercury*, 1778–95, and the *Glasgow Courier*, 1796–99; for Aberdeen, *The Journal*, 1748–99.

Quarter Deck of the Lime

"Drawing of the Quarter Deck of the *Lime*," made by Robert Johnston probably while traveling between Jamaica and Scotland, ca. 1813. Powel Collection, R. Johnston, Drawings, The Historical Society of Pennsylvania.

ads and recording the destinations reveals a clear image of trading patterns between Scotland and the colonies. To validate this method of analysis, one can compare the same newspapers' published lists of arrivals and departures in Port Glasgow and Greenock with the names of ships that advertised. Such a technique provides an estimate of the number of advertised ships as a percentage of the number of ships that actually crossed the Atlantic.[49]

It is therefore useful to consider commercial intercourse between Scotland and Jamaica and Scotland and the Chesapeake in a manner that accounts for the number of ships per year between North Britain and the colonies. Each sailing provided an opportunity for Scottish transients to transport themselves across the Atlantic. Using the same sources, one can also identify the ships' ports of origin and destination. Analyzing these should then indicate the places where Scottish sojourners resided in both the old and new worlds. An imperfect method, it does allow us to distinguish among Edinburgh, Glasgow, and Aberdeen, and helps to provide a focused picture of the movement's changing character.

OPPORTUNITIES TO TRAVEL

Advertising analysis demonstrates that at least two distinct markets existed within Scotland. It also indicates that commercial interests in particular Scottish regions favored one group of colonies over the other. Tables 1.4 and 1.5 depict the total number of ships that advertised passages from the Clyde ports, that is, Port Glasgow and Greenock, and Leith, which is just north of Edinburgh, to Jamaica and the Chesapeake between 1740 and 1799.[50] The combined total of ships advertising in Scotland's two principal metropolises and departing for either the Chesapeake or Jamaica is presented in Table 1.6, along with the component totals for each of the two cities.

As should be apparent from these tables, Glasgow's ports always overshadowed Leith, the capital's port, in terms of shipping to both Jamaica and Virginia. Because more ships crossed the Atlantic from Glasgow than from

[49] I have not carried this analysis out because spot checks in Edinburgh and Glasgow papers revealed the figure to be well over 90 percent. By contrast, checks of advertisements in Aberdeen with the published lists of arrivals and departures reveal many more ships coming and going to this port than used the press to advertise. Even so, the number of vessels is less than four or five per year to either the Chesapeake or Jamaica.

[50] The only gaps come in the Glasgow papers before 1746 and between 1775 and 1778. With the exception of an odd issue or two, no papers from the first years of the American Revolution are known to have survived. As a result, the historian has no way of knowing just how quickly and completely the Chesapeake trade fell off and was replaced by West Indian commerce. Table 1.6 certainly shows that the drop was quite precipitous. Papers from the 1740s reveal little. Few ships advertised in them and, in Glasgow's case, very few of them have survived. The city's tobacco trade was still in its infancy, however, making the gaps less important than they otherwise might have been. The big commercial increases came in the later years of the 1750s.

Table 1.4. Glasgow ships, as advertised, to Jamaica and the Chesapeake

Year	Chesa-peake	Jamaica	Total	Year	Chesa-peake	Jamaica	Total
1750	6	2	8	1778	0	16	16
1751	6	4	10	1779	0	23	23
1752	14	3	17	1780	0	16	16
1753	13	5	18	1781	0	14	14
1754	16	3	19	1782	0	17	17
AVERAGE	11	3.4	14.4	AVERAGE	0	17.2	17.2
1755	18	7	25	1783	9	20	29
1756	22	4	26	1784	17	11	28
1757	21	6	27	1785	23	20	43
1758	15	6	21	1786	30	18	48
1759	16	6	22	1787	27	20	47
AVERAGE	18.4	5.8	24.2	AVERAGE	21.2	17.8	39.0
1760	18	6	24	1788	26	19	45
1761	25	5	30	1789	21	25	46
1762	28	9	37	1790	14	21	35
1763	27	10	37	1791	25	16	41
1764	20	9	29	1792	4	12	16
AVERAGE	25.6	7.8	31.4	AVERAGE	18	18.6	36.6
1765	22	9	31	1793	0	7	7
1766	25	8	33	1794	0	8	8
1767	26	10	37	1795	0	4	4
1768	26	12	38	1796	2	20	22
1769	34	13	47	1797	3	27	30
AVERAGE	26.6	10.4	37.0	AVERAGE	1.0	13.2	14.2
1770	33	8	41	1798	2	21	23
1771	41	15	56	1799	3	18	21
1772	37	11	48	AVERAGE	2.5	19.5	22
1773	32	13	45				
1774	35	12	47				
AVERAGE	35.6	11.8	47.4				

Edinburgh, a difference that can be explained principally by Scottish geography in the days before the Clyde and Forth canal, more passengers could be carried in them. Furthermore, for those in Glasgow, there were fewer opportunities to go to Jamaica than there were to go to the Chesapeake. In Edinburgh, the reverse was true. Not only did two different markets exist, but they differed in the places they served.

Tables 1.7 and 1.8 further define Glasgow's and Edinburgh's shipping by including all advertisements, not just those of ships bound for either Jamaica or the Chesapeake. For Glasgow, during the pre-war period, Chesapeake

Table 1.5. Advertised Edinburgh ships to Jamaica and the Chesapeake

Year	Chesa-peake	Jamaica	Total	Year	Chesa-peake	Jamaica	Total
1746	1	1	2	1775	0	9	9
1747	3	1	4	1776	0	6	6
1748	0	3	3	1777	0	11	11
1749	0	4	4	1778	0	12	12
AVERAGE	1	2.25	3.25	1779	0	17	17
				1780	0	10	10
1750	1	3	4	1781	0	4	4
1751	1	2	3	1782	0	0	0
1752	2	3	5	AVERAGE	0	8.6	8.6
1753	2	3	5				
1754	1	4	5	1783	4	7	11
AVERAGE	1.4	3	4.4	1784	5	10	15
				1785	2	13	15
1755	0	2	2	1786	5	7	12
1756	4	2	6	1787	4	9	13
1757	3	7	10	AVERAGE	4	9.2	13.2
1758	2	6	8				
1759	1	2	3	1788	0	14	14
AVERAGE	2	3.8	5.8	1789	3	11	14
				1790	1	16	17
1760	1	3	4	1791	0	9	9
1761	0	6	6	1792	1	10	11
1762	0	5	5	AVERAGE	1	12	13
1763	0	9	9				
1764	1	5	6	1793	2	7	9
AVERAGE	0.4	5.6	6	1794	1	8	9
				1795	0	5	5
1765	4	7	11	1796	1	9	10
1766	2	4	6	1797	0	4	4
1767	2	5	7	AVERAGE	0.8	6.6	7.4
1768	0	9	9				
1769	1	6	7	1798	1	8	9
AVERAGE	1.8	6.2	8	1799	0	8	8
				AVERAGE	3.3	6.7	10
1770	0	3	3				
1771	2	5	7				
1772	1	5	6				
1773	1	4	5				
1774	1	6	7				
AVERAGE	1	4.6	5.6				

and Jamaican destinations (combined) claimed more than 50 percent of all advertisements. After a precipitous decline accompanying the loss of Glasgow's tobacco trade during and after the American Revolution, advertised opportunities to go to the West Indies increased. Edinburgh, on the other hand, was always much more of a European port; the Chesapeake and

Table 1.6. Ships from city to colony: Combined totals for Chesapeake and Jamaica

YEAR	GL/JA	GL/CH	ED/JA	ED/CH	TOT/JA	TOT/CH
1750	2	6	3	1	5	7
1751	4	6	2	1	6	7
1752	3	14	3	2	6	16
1753	5	13	3	2	5	15
1754	3	16	4	1	7	17
1755	7	18	2	0	9	18
1756	4	22	2	4	6	26
1757	6	21	7	3	13	24
1758	6	15	6	2	12	17
1759	6	16	2	1	8	17
1760	6	18	3	1	9	19
1761	5	25	6	0	11	25
1762	9	28	5	0	14	28
1763	10	27	9	0	19	27
1764	9	20	5	1	14	21
1765	9	22	7	4	16	26
1766	8	25	4	2	12	27
1767	10	26	5	2	15	31
1768	12	26	9	1	21	26
1769	13	34	6	1	19	35
1770	8	33	3	0	11	33
1771	15	41	5	2	20	43
1772	11	37	5	1	16	38
1773	13	32	4	1	17	33
1774	12	35	6	1	18	36
1778	16	0	12	0	28	0
1779	23	0	17	0	40	0
1780	16	0	10	0	26	0
1781	14	0	4	0	18	0
1782	17	0	0	0	17	0
1783	20	9	7	4	27	13
1784	11	17	10	5	21	22
1785	20	23	13	2	33	25
1786	18	30	7	5	25	35
1787	20	27	9	4	29	31
1788	19	26	14	0	33	26
1789	25	21	11	3	26	24
1790	21	14	16	1	37	15
1791	16	25	9	0	25	25
1792	12	4	10	1	22	5
1793	7	0	7	2	14	2
1794	8	0	8	1	16	1
1795	4	0	5	0	9	0
1796	20	2	9	1	29	3
1797	27	3	4	0	31	3
1798	21	2	8	1	29	3
1799	18	3	8	0	26	3

Abbreviations: GL = Glasgow
ED = Edinburgh
JA = Jamaica
CH = Chesapeake
TOT = Total to each place

Table 1.7. Glasgow ships to all destinations, as advertised

YEAR	CH/JA	BR/E	NE	MC	SC	WI	CA	TOTAL
1751	10	3	2	0	0	0	0	15
1756	26	5	5	0	1	4	0	41
1761	30	4	3	5	4	7	0	53
1766	33	9	6	3	5	8	4	68
1771	56	17	8	6	7	5	0	99
1778	16	5	0	6	0	12	4	43
1781	14	17	0	11	5	7	3	57
1786	48	7	0	4	12	23	10	114
1791	41	16	2	6	6	19	11	101
1796	22	9	5	12	5	27	7	87

Table 1.8. Edinburgh ships to all destinations, as advertised

YEAR	CH/JA	BR/E	NE	MC	SC	WI	CA	TOTAL
1746	2	12	0	0	0	0	0	14
1751	3	17	0	1	3	0	0	24
1756	6	21	0	0	3	3	0	33
1761	6	15	0	0	4	3	1	29
1766	6	49	1	1	5	4	2	68
1771	7	53	3	3	6	11	0	83
1778	12	50	0	1	0	6	0	69
1781	4	37	0	1	1	1	0	44
1786	12	83	1	4	3	15	7	125
1791	9	87	0	1	1	14	7	119
1796	10	63	2	8	1	9	4	97

Abbreviations: CH/JA = Chesapeake and Jamaica combined (see Tables 1.4–1.5)
BR/E = Britain and European ports
NE = New England colonies
MC = New York, New Jersey, Pennsylvania (Middle Colonies)
SC = Southern Colonies (Carolinas, Georgia)
WI = West India islands other than Jamaica
CA = Canada (Quebec and Nova Scotia)

Jamaica accounted for small components of its total trade. Ships regularly plied the waters between Leith and London, Spain, Portugal, and France. They occasionally roamed as far east as St. Petersburg, Riga, and Danzig. While Jamaica and the Chesapeake were far less significant routes for Leith than others, shippers there showed a preference for the West Indies over the mainland colonies. This strongly suggests that Glasgow and the Chesapeake had very strong ties to each other. *Scotland* and the Chesapeake did not.[51]

The number of ships that advertised trips to Jamaica and the Chesapeake in Edinburgh remained fairly constant, averaging between seven and eight per year. Those that advertised similar trips in Glasgow increased from an average of twenty-one per year before 1760 to thirty-eight per year from 1760 to 1775. Immediately after the 1783 peace, and until the end of the decade, Glasgow sent an average of forty-two ships per year to these two American areas. The number of ships trading to Jamaica and the Chesapeake settled down to an average of only thirteen per year in the last decade of the century, despite increases in the number of ships going to other West Indian islands, particularly Grenada, St. Vincent's, and To-bago.[52] The Edinburgh figure, however, is misleading, because Clyde shippers began to advertise their ships in the capital, probably because they encountered trouble filling them. When this double listing is corrected, less than four ships per year, on average, sailed from Leith to Jamaica and the Chesapeake combined, throughout the period.[53]

For shippers, advertising in the capital city's thrice-weekly newspaper, with its larger circulation, was not as important as publishing an ad in the weekly Glasgow press.[54] Cross advertising between the cities, as indicated above, did take place. Such multiple listings accounted for about 65 percent of Edinburgh's total advertisements for the two largest American destinations alone, the Chesapeake and Jamaica, between 1750 and 1799.[55]

[51]Such regional variations are precisely the sort of questions which Frank Thistlewaite suggested in 1960. See Thistlewaite, p. 80. Also see Chan, p. 44.

[52]The exact figure for Edinburgh between 1750 and 1799 is 7.78 ships per year on average. The wartime figure for Glasgow between 1778 and 1782 was 17.2, exclusively to Jamaica. This figure is well below even those from before the tobacco trade boom.

[53]The exact figures are 3.16 from 1750 to 1775 and 3.4 from 1750 to 1799.

[54]This was true despite a substantially larger population in Edinburgh. Between 1751 and 1755, Edinburgh and Leith together had around 57,000 people while Glasgow had around 31,700, and Aberdeen around 15,600. In terms of the total population of Scotland at this time, Edinburgh had only a little over 4 percent, Glasgow, just over 2 percent and Aberdeen just under 2 percent. See J. G. Kyd, ed., *Scottish Population Statistics* (Edinburgh, 1952). Only one census was carried out, in 1755, before the nineteenth century. For a good discussion of the census and its findings, see Lenman, p. 72.

[55]To be exact, 233 of 363 advertisements in the years when comparison is possible. This means, however, that Edinburgh still maintained a transatlantic trade of its own, despite an unfavorable geographic position for it. Those coming to Edinburgh to leave for the colonies

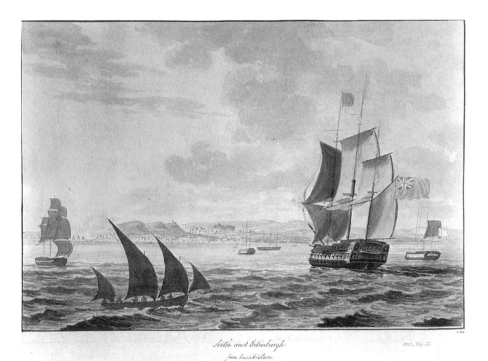

C. Hamilton Smith, "View of Leith and Edinburgh, from Inchkillan," portrays a variety of ships cruising the Firth of Forth. Reproduced by permission of the Henry E. Huntington Library and Art Gallery, San Marino, California.

The development of cross advertising paralleled Glasgow's growing trade. The *Caledonian Mercury* increasingly carried Glasgow ships' advertisements for Jamaica and the Chesapeake. There was no reciprocity. Of ships leaving from Leith, none used the Glasgow press.[56] Between 1743 (the year the first meaningful comparisons could be made) and 1757, only 36.4 percent of ships advertising in Edinburgh had also advertised in Glasgow. At this point there were two completely separate markets. From 1758 to 1760, the figure increased to 53.3 percent. Between 1761 and 1769, 68.2 percent of ships advertising in Edinburgh also advertised in Glasgow. This change indicates a

would have had to wait longer for an opportunity to go to the colony of their choice, if they were intent on leaving from Edinburgh. Alternately, they could have taken a coach to Glasgow or caught one of the weekly ships to London and made arrangements for the transatlantic passage there.

[56]However, a number of ships going from Leith to London placed advertisements in the Glasgow press with increasing frequency after 1771. This certainly helped to compensate for Glasgow's lack of trade to the English capital.

fairly rapid decline in Leith's importance as a market for American destinations in its own right as well as the terrific expansion of Port Glasgow and Greenock. The same drop can be substantiated by examining Table 1.8. In 1761, American trade represented 48.2 percent of Leith's advertisements. In 1766, it had fallen to 27.9 percent and in 1771, it had recovered to 36.1 percent.

Between 1770 and the outbreak of war in 1775, only 23 percent of ships advertised in both cities, which illustrated more Glasgow's superior ability to fill its own ships than it did Edinburgh's continued decline. From 1778 to 1787, as a direct consequence of the loss of Glasgow's Chesapeake trade, nearly 90 percent of ships crossing the Atlantic advertised in both papers. As a straightforward result of the American Revolution, Glasgow experienced difficulty finding enough cargo (people and goods) to fill all its available ships; the "tobacco lords" needed assistance from their countrymen in the capital or their ships would have to go empty or, worse, not go at all. Unfilled ships meant lost revenue. Between 1788 and 1791, as Glasgow began to redirect its trade away from the Chesapeake and explore new (especially West Indian) markets, the number of ships that advertised in both cities topped 70 percent. Scottish merchants banded together at these crucial junctures to maintain and recover as much trade as they could. Their regional differences blurred as the threat of losing money loomed so large on the horizon. After 1792, comparison becomes difficult because of Glasgow's rapidly changing newspaper situation.[57]

To include Aberdeen in this comparison of Scottish markets simplifies matters as much as it complicates them. Put simply, there was little direct trade between Scotland's far northeast and the American colonies. The *Aberdeen Journal*, for its entire run in the eighteenth century, consisted of little more than reprints from the London, Glasgow, and Edinburgh papers. By virtue of its easy sea connections, London was by far the most important of the three. As a result, there are very few advertisements for opportunities to the new world and very many to London, from whence further travel would have taken place. Examination of the *Journal's* published arrivals and departures lists does reveal that several more ships went to and from the Chesapeake and Jamaica each year than actually advertised. Even so, no more than four per year plied the waters between Scotland's northeast metropolis and these particular American colonies. Only a few more went to some of the other colonies, mostly in the West Indies.[58]

[57]The city saw the decline of one newspaper, the *Glasgow Mercury* and its replacement by the *Glasgow Courier*. Comparisons during the transition years, 1793–94, are somewhat unreliable as a result.
[58]We know from the correspondence that many Scots from Aberdeen and the northeast went to Jamaica. It is very likely that these people moved first to London; trading ships frequently

DESTINATIONS

Newspaper advertisements have made it remarkably easy to determine where passengers on ships from Scottish ports intended to disembark in the colonies. Graphs 1, 2, and 3 illustrate the information from the Glasgow papers. In the twenty-two years from 1747 to 1769, most Scottish merchant ships went to the James River in Virginia, with the next highest concentration going to docks on the Rappahannock River, closely followed by those on both the Virginia and Maryland sides of the Potomac. Looking at the second period, from 1769 to 1774, we see the James's continued popularity. By then the Potomac had surpassed the Rappahannock as the second most popular destination. When trade resumed in 1783 after the war, the same pattern emerged, though the total number of voyages continued to decline.[59]

Aside from revealing where Chesapeake ships planned to go, these figures identify where "Glasgow" Scots who had decided to leave Scotland for the Chesapeake had chances to travel. Of course, it is impossible to rule out movement around the colony after arrival on a particular river, and there is some indication that such moving took place. But because so many ships left Glasgow each year for the Chesapeake, it is not unreasonable to argue that most travelers waited for a ship going to the place in which they intended to reside. In addition, most people going to the Chesapeake went over with specific jobs arranged with particular firms, further increasing the likelihood that they waited for a ship which could take them as near to their final destination as possible. Some, who usually had not arranged for their employ in advance, did change locales upon their arrival; even so they went from one area where Scots were concentrated to another. Consulting the ship's advertised destinations, one can confirm the existence of sizable Scottish enclaves and networks along the James and Potomac rivers.[60]

---

sailed the North Sea between the two ports. From the *Aberdeen Journal*, it has been possible to determine that 56 of 73 advertised ships listed ports of call in the West Indies between 1748 and 1787. The others went principally to the Chesapeake, the Carolinas, or New York, the last two being areas with significant populations of Scottish emigrants.

[59]Note how consistently small the direct trade from Glasgow to Maryland remained throughout the period. Apart from ships which called on the north side of the Potomac, very few ships indeed went to Annapolis, Baltimore, or any of the eastern shore points. The Loyalist Claim Series of documents created during and after the Revolution confirm that the transient Scots population was considerably smaller north of the Potomac than south of it. Jacob Price's "New Time Series for Scotland's and Britain's Trade with the Thirteen Colonies and States, 1740–1791," *WMQ* 32 (1975): 307–25, shows again that the Maryland trade was far less important to Scotland than Virginia's, though it did outstrip that of other mainland colonies.

[60]For example, Alexander Wilson landed in Port Tobacco, Maryland, crossed the Potomac to Colchester, Virginia, and made his way up the river to Alexandria. He had a specific employ arranged before he went across. See A. Wilson to his father, 30 October 1768, Letterbook, Smiths of Jordanhill, TD1/1070, SRA. On the opposite side of the coin, schoolmaster David

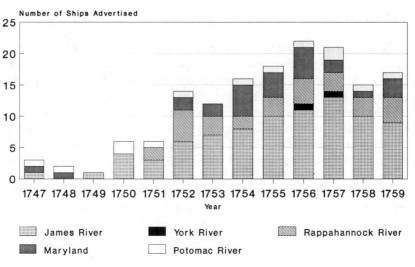

Graph 1. Destinations of Glasgow ships to the Chesapeake, 1747–1759

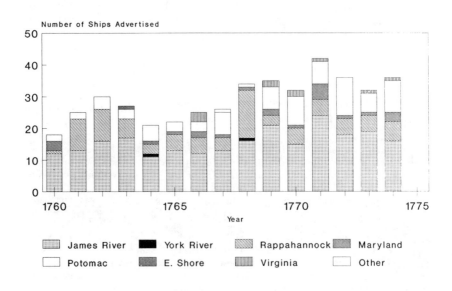

Note: Data incomplete for 1775.

Graph 2. Destinations of Glasgow ships to the Chesapeake, 1760–1775

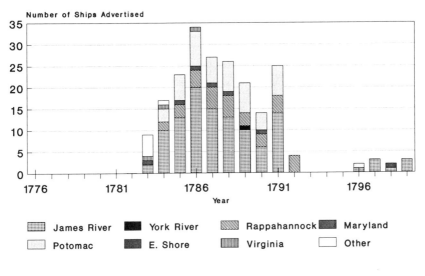

Graph 3. Destinations of Glasgow ships to the Chesapeake, 1776–1799

Jamaica-bound ships also listed destinations other than Kingston with growing regularity, especially after 1778. Even then, nearly all advertisements named Kingston as a port of call; most listed one or several other island ports, usually situated near each other. As should become clear from Graphs 4, 5, and 6, Kingston's share of the total Scottish trade became less significant while the ports in the northern and western parts of the island continued to grow in importance as a destination for Scottish mercantile voyages. Unlike Virginia, the island had no resident Scottish factors. Therefore the Scots needed trading partners within the colony. It is obvious that they began to go where they had contracts and allies and where there would have been a demand for their goods. This increasingly came to be the island's northern and western corners, and to a lesser extent, its eastern tip. Who would trade with a Scot? The answer should be perfectly clear—other Scots.

Duff (almost certainly from Aberdeen) went first to Glasgow, but missed by four hours the packet he intended to take from Glasgow to Maryland (Potomac). Instead, he had to take passage to Norfolk and make his way to Port Tobacco by another ship. He had no specific offer of employment. See David Duff to James Grant, n.d. [docketed 1772], Seafield Muniments, GD 248/349/3/5, SRO.

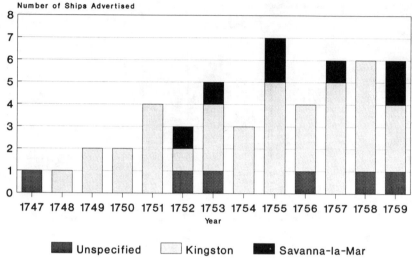

Graph 4. Destinations of Glasgow ships to Jamaica, 1747–1759

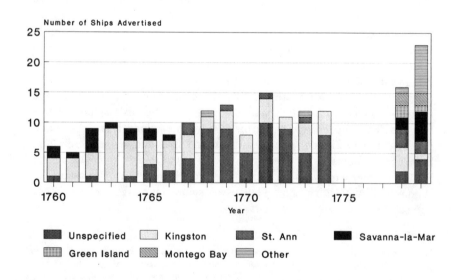

Note: Data incomplete for
1775, 1776, 1777.

Graph 5. Destinations of Glasgow ships to Jamaica, 1760–1779

Number of Ships Advertised

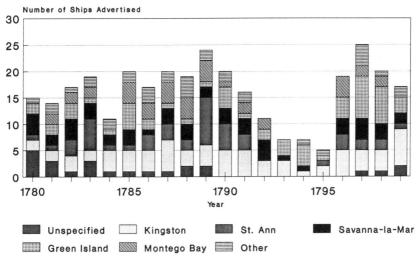

Graph 6. Destinations of Glasgow ships to Jamaica, 1780–1799

SCALE: A PRELIMINARY ESTIMATE

The number of Scottish ships traversing the Atlantic can also be used to arrive at a preliminary estimate of the total size of the sojourner movement. Transients have told us that they went to the colonies on merchant ships, as opposed to crowded immigrant vessels.[61] The rationale for the Act of Parliament that generated the emigration registers used by Bailyn also suggests that those planning to return to Britain traveled separately from immigrants. With this is mind, therefore, we can usefully multiple the total number of ships traveling between Scotland and Jamaica and Scotland and the Chesapeake by an estimate of the number of passengers that each ship might have carried. This method also has some significant weaknesses. Though many of the trading ships advertised accommodation for passengers, and provided some information about the quality and amount available, we have no way of knowing whether the cabins and state rooms went full or empty. Nor do we know that every ship carried passengers.

Between 1750 and 1799, 782 ships advertised trading voyages between Glasgow and the Chesapeake (Table 1.6). Two hundred thirty-one ships

[61]See, for example, Alexander Wilson to his father, 30 October 1768. I do not wish to imply that all sojourners went on advertised merchant ships. In all probability, some traveled on board emigrant ships. Some sojourners may also have traveled to other colonies first and arrived in their final destinations on board intercolonial trading vessels.

advertised trips to the Chesapeake in Edinburgh. Multiplying the total of 1,013 ships by five results in an approximation of 5,065 passengers traveling between the two principal Scottish ports and the Chesapeake.[62] Voyages advertised to Jamaica during the same period totaled 569 from Glasgow and 314 from Edinburgh. Thus 883 ships could have carried 4,415 passengers. Glasgow and Edinburgh together, according to this estimate, saw 9,480 people travel to Jamaica and the Chesapeake. But, 233 of 363 ships that advertised in Edinburgh also advertised in Glasgow. Therefore, it becomes essential to subtract the 1,165 passengers who are double counted in the above estimate. A figure of 8,215 results. When Aberdeen ships are added, (30 were advertised) another 150 people traveled to the two colonies, raising the total to 8,365 over a sixty-year period. A sizable number of Scots sojourners could also have left through English ports—London, Bristol, or Liverpool—further increasing the total.[63] If we use Bailyn's figure of 5.6 percent of the total Scottish migration leaving from English ports (for want of anything more precise), then the revised estimate of the total number of transients increases to 8,861. There is also no doubt that a few sojourners traveled on board emigrant ships. It is, therefore, my estimate that the maximum number of Scottish sojourners traveling to the Chesapeake and Jamaica between 1750 and 1800 amounted to nine or ten thousand.

If the Scottish population in 1755 was a million and a quarter, then we are only talking about one percent of the entire population sojourning in one of these two places. But women did not sojourn as far as I have been able to tell, and many males were too old or too young to travel. The proportion of men of working age who sojourned abroad might then have been as high as 3 percent.

[62]A multiplier of five derives from several sources. Bailyn has found that five was the median number of passengers on ships carrying immigrants who left from England between 1773 and 1776. See *Voyagers*, p. 94. The brig and the snow, the two principal transatlantic merchant ships after 1720, had carrying capacities of 80 to 100 tons. During the eighteenth century, it was common practice to have one crew member for each ten to twelve tons. That meant that these ships would have had crews of seven or eight. The number of passengers would therefore have been less than the size of the crew. See Ralph Davis, *The Rise of English Shipping* (London, 1962), pp. 59, 77–79; William Falconer, *Falconer's Marine Dictionary* (1769; reprinted, 1970); Alan McGowan, *The Ship: The Century before Steam* (London, 1980), pp. 24, 34.

Contemporary descriptions are all too rare. Janet Schaw voyaged from Burntisland, near Edinburgh, to the West Indies with four adults and two children. She remarked that "a state room" was no more than thirty square feet, making for cramped accommodations. [Janet Schaw], *Journal of a Lady of Quality*, Evangeline Andrews, ed., (New Haven, Conn., 1921), pp. 20, 22. I am indebted to Marcus Rediker and John McNeill for pointing me to the right sources on this subject.

[63]Bailyn's three-year sample shows that 5.6 percent of all Scots emigrating from Britain used English ports, principally London (p. 122). Those more likely to have done so would either have come down the east coast or have already been resident in England.

From the perspective of the other side, the number of Scottish transients was not large. Virginia and Maryland's combined white population in 1750 was around 300,000. The Scottish sojourner population seems small in comparison. The white population of Jamaica, however, was only about 20,000, so the number of Scottish sojourners becomes more important. Approximately 65 percent of the sojourners I have identified individually went to Jamaica.

Given the total size of European and African migration to the American colonies, nine thousand people seems a rather small movement; indeed, on the basis of numbers alone one could argue that it is trifling and insignificant. But the numbers do not dictate the group's importance. Rather, as will be seen, these people occupied particularly significant places within the developing British Atlantic economy.

2

The Caribbean Connection: Scots in Jamaica

Mr. Gillespie expressed the intentions held by many Scots in Jamaica throughout the period between 1740 and 1800 when he remarked that "we all come here to improve and not spend fortunes, and of consequence, devote our whole thoughts and attention to the former."[1] Though increasing one's wealth in the colony was a principal aim, leaving Jamaica with it as soon as possible was no less important. The Scots generally found much in their new environment to dislike. Unavoidable elements of tropical life—climate, for example—often justified plans for a hasty departure. Lewis Grant expressed this opinion in 1742, just as Scottish transients began to come to the colony in significant numbers:

> I look upon us Europeans in this part of the World to be in the Same Condition with West Indian Planters when carry'd to Britain, if they are carefully kept in Green houses the heat of the Sun doubl'd upon them in Summer & kept warm with fires in winter, they will doe tollerably weall, but when expos'd to the inclemency of our air in the open fields they quickly decay and dye, it is just soe with us hear, if we can afford the Conveanancy's of Life & use them temporaly we may doe prittie weall but if wee are oblidged to march or Labor in the heat of the day, and Lye out in the night it is certain Death.[2]

Attitudes such as Grant's have not gone unnoticed by scholars who have studied the eighteenth-century British West Indian colonies in any detail. As

---

[1]Mr. [James] Gillespie to Archibald Grant, 7 October 1767, Grant of Monymusk Papers, GD 345/1171/1/128-129x, SRO.

[2]Lewis Grant to Ludovick Grant, 8 February 1742, Grant of Grant papers, GD 248/99/5/24, SRO. The Scots were not especially fond of slavery, though there is little overt evidence of severe condemnation.

early as 1928, historian Lowell Ragatz concluded: "No considerable body of persons inspired by motives higher than the desire to extract the greatest possible amount of wealth from them in the shortest possible time ever reached the smiling shores of the Caribbean colonies."[3]

Like many island residents, the Scots simply did not want to be there. Until early in the nineteenth century, the number of social institutions in the island was small, given its population. The residents were unwilling to invest in collective institutions like schools or churches. At the same time, however, most recognized that the colony provided a growing number of economic opportunities of a kind that did not exist for most of them at home. In some sense, then, they needed to be in Jamaica if they wanted to satisfy their own ambitions.[4]

The colony, by the middle of the eighteenth century, had entered a prolonged period of economic growth. According to Richard Sheridan, the century between 1673 and 1774 witnessed a doubling of the island's white population and a twenty-fold increase in the number of slaves. Livestock increased nineteen-fold and the number of sugar plantations rose to fourteen times original levels. Most of this expansion took place after 1739. For example, though the value of exports from the island to Britain doubled from £325,000 in 1701–4 to £652,000 in 1736–40, that rate was easily surpassed in the next three decades. Exports increased to £1,025,000 in 1751–55 and £2,400,000, nearly four times greater than 1740 levels, by 1771–75. The island, which from its earliest days had tied so much of its economic well-being to sugar, benefited from rising demand for its chief agricultural product.[5]

British mercantile policy combined with European political events to accelerate further Jamaica's economic development. The Seven Years' War (1756–63) was perhaps the single most important contribution to that growth.

---

[3]Lowell Ragatz, *The Fall of the Planter Class in the British Caribbean* (New York, 1963), p. 3. Indeed, several other scholars have written on the theme of absenteeism. Orlando Patterson in *The Sociology of Slavery* (London, 1967) views the colonials' quest for riches and the resulting absenteeism as inherently evil, especially as it concerned the slaves' living conditions (p. 33). Richard Pares, in *A West India Fortune* (London, 1950), notices the impermanent nature of West Indian life, especially in Nevis (pp. 20, 23–31). Michael Craton and James Walvin in *A Jamaican Plantation* (New York, 1970) have commented that absenteeism was the "most notorious of all the burdens laid upon the West Indian estates" (p. 120).

[4]Here I must disagree with Jack P. Greene, *Pursuits of Happiness* (Chapel Hill, N.C., 1989), p. 182. I do not believe that what could be called a creole society had developed in the eighteenth century. See also Edward Brathwaite, *The Development of Creole Society in Jamaica* (Oxford, 1971), pp. 269–74.

[5]Richard Sheridan, *Sugar and Slavery* (Baltimore, 1974), pp. 216–17, 220–22. Sheridan also points out that the slower growth of the first half of the century can be explained by the low state of the world sugar market. Also see Sidney Mintz, *Sweetness and Power* (New York, 1985), pp. 61–73.

The British captured the important French sugar islands of Martinique and Guadeloupe, effectively gaining control of exports and imports to these islands. Britain made trade between the captured islands and France so difficult that the neutral Dutch had to carry it out when it was permitted at all. French sugar therefore became more expensive and British sugar, which came predominantly from Jamaica, much cheaper and thus more attractive on world markets. When the Peace of Paris ended the war in 1763, the British kept Canada (to concentrate on their North American markets) and returned the Caribbean sugar islands to France. While the settlement allowed the French to resume sugar trading, it effectively removed any competition to Jamaica as the most important sugar producer within the British imperial system. The Jamaican sugar economy continued to prosper.[6]

The average sugar plantation increased in size, and more of the island's land was given over to cultivation. People who had gone to the island (some with very little indeed) before the boom created by the war earned substantial amounts of money. Many of them returned to consume conspicuously in London.[7] Jamaica thus became more attractive to prospective fortune-hunters; Britain made clear in 1763 that it would protect the island colony's economy. Protection and growth continued well into the nineteenth century.[8]

The island's economic development could never have been sustained without a greatly increased slave labor force. Such an importation necessitated an increased white presence. In the earlier days of expansion, few Europeans were willing to forsake limited opportunities at home for the, as yet, unproven chances on offer in Jamaica. As a result, the black to white ratio became so unbalanced that "deficiency laws" had to be enacted. These measures required that all plantations employ a minimum number of whites for every slave (usually one white for every ten slaves) or pay a fine for each default. The laws did not have the desired effect of increasing settlement, because many planters found it cheaper to pay the penalty than provide a

---

[6]Craton and Walvin, *A Jamaican Plantation*, p. 75. Sheridan, *Sugar and Slavery*, pp. 448–59, also discusses the importance of the Seven Years' War to Jamaica. While the French sugar colonies, especially St. Domingue, outproduced the British islands, the British protected their metropolitan and colonial markets. After the war, French sugars were no longer attractive to traders in these places.

[7]See Sheridan, *Sugar and Slavery*, pp. 12–13.

[8]There is some debate about when the period of economic growth actually ended. I accept Seymour Drescher's view in *Econocide* that it lasted until well after 1800. Others, including Ragatz, in *The Fall of the Planter Class*, Craton and Walvin in *A Jamaican Plantation*, and Patterson, *Sociology of Slavery*, have all put the decline around the time of the American Revolution. British trade statistics that support Drescher's argument can be found in B. R. Mitchell, *British Historical Statistics* (Cambridge, 1988), esp. pp. 492–97. Much of the evidence presented in this chapter comes from the period where the earlier authors have argued for decline, providing some additional support for Drescher's argument.

salary for a white servant whose utility was limited.[9] In the end, it took obvious displays of opulence at home to draw sizable numbers of whites to the colony.

Most people who left Britain for Jamaica hoped to emulate those who had already returned home from the island with handsome fortunes. These whites generally occupied the vocational niches that black slaves could not fill, working as overseers and bookkeepers. As those who made fortunes departed, absenteeism increased. As a result, demand for attorneys and estate managers expanded. The island's growing population, both slave and free, required health care. This magnified the need for qualified physicians. To provide shelter for newcomers and build new boiling and curing houses, island residents recruited skilled artisans. Many of these people came from Scotland.

Personal correspondence in Britain's record offices, libraries, and private homes has provided invaluable information about the careers and aspirations of many Scots who went to Jamaica. From these documents, characteristics common among Scottish residents in the colony can be established. The vast majority of people identified through systematic examination of these records came from middling and educated backgrounds. Most had absolutely no intention of staying permanently in the tropics. Because they shared the belief that they were living only temporarily in Jamaica, they took certain decisions and behaved accordingly. Whether they actually returned to Scotland is not at issue here, because the sojourner's original motivation for traveling abroad limits the cohort. Those who changed their minds after residing for several years in the island also do not need to be separated at this point. All began their careers as sojourners.

Scotland's very wealthy would have had little reason to exchange a relatively easy country existence on the family estates for the Caribbean's more peripatetic lifestyle.[10] If wealthier families had any Jamaican involvement at all, the patriarch might own an absentee estate or two, purchased as an investment or, with noticeable regularity, acquired by marriage to Jamaican heiresses. Such properties frequently provided employ for their less fortunate relations. Nor were the very poorest and least educated inhabitants of Scotland likely to embark temporarily for places unknown. If they emigrated,

---

[9]See Ragatz, *Fall of the Planter Class*, p. 8, and Sheridan, *Sugar and Slavery*, p. 221.

[10]A few of Scotland's very rich during this period procured places for their sons in the East Indies. As the century drew to a close, however, and Jamaica began to become old-hat as a place to earn money quickly with small efforts, especially in comparison with new opportunities in the East Indies, more and more middle class families chose the latter. See James G. Parker, "Scottish Enterprise in India, 1750–1914," in *The Scots Abroad*, ed. R. A. Cage, pp. 191–219. The pattern in India appears to follow the pattern in Jamaica.

and many did, they chose the colonies that had the most available land and greatest opportunities for permanent settlers without special skills, the American mainland.

The second and third sons, nephews, and cousins of Scottish landowners did turn up regularly in Jamaica. As Archibald Sinclair, a Scottish merchant and attorney resident in Jamaica, observed in 1760, Jamaica's "Inhabitants are Chiefly Younger Brothers and Sons of Fortune." They had been to Edinburgh, Glasgow, or Aberdeen for their general or professional educations. A few had even gone to London to learn commercial skills. In many cases, their guardians or mentors had decided that their training could generate income more quickly in the Caribbean than in the British isles. Sinclair continued:

> In this Island . . . it is Just as Consistant for a Barister at Law or a Doctor of Phisuk to Lease or Purchase a Plantation or Estate as it is for an Overseer or any other man, nay, in my opinion, the former on Account of their Profession's being (in General) more Lucrative are most Likelie to get a Preference.[11]

The surest way to wealth in Jamaica, at least according to Scottish belief, was to enter the island with a profession. By practicing it, and earning and saving capital along the way, the upwardly mobile would have little difficulty acquiring an estate, returning to Scotland, and living comfortably off of the property's proceeds. In some cases, however, a family's financial (or other) obligations prevented extensive secondary education before migration. Those who found themselves in this position often assumed that traveling to Jamaica and learning the planting business once there was the best available option. For these people, the established route went from bookkeeper to overseer and then to manager or to owner. This path appears to have been much more common among the island's English adventurers.[12]

The Scottish practice of sending trained individuals abroad was almost certainly connected to the country's educational system and an economy that could not support everyone with professional training. Throughout the second half of the eighteenth century, Scotland, especially the non-highland

---

[11]Archibald Sinclair to Sir Robert Gordon, 25 June 1760, MS La. II. 498, EUL. Sinclair's remark indicates the widely held belief that professionals, who earned quite a bit of money, and had more acquaintances (and thus easier access to credit), would have an easier time purchasing a property. This, in fact, was probably true, though the professionals' income was also dependent upon plantation success. They would not be paid if the island's crops had a bad year.

[12]For details of one such adventurer, see the Diaries of Thomas Thistlewood, microfilm at American Philosophical Society and Colonial Williamsburg's Library (originals at Lincolnshire Archives Office, Lincoln). Also see Douglas Hall, *In Miserable Slavery: Thomas Thistlewood in Jamaica, 1750–1786* (London, 1989).

regions, provided some of the best opportunities for education in the Anglophone world.[13] The law required every parish in Scotland to have a school. Students who could not afford to pay school fees were often supported by local authorities. Those who came from wealthier backgrounds, of course, had access to more classical education and private lessons. All Scots, however, were subjected to a fairly authoritarian form of teaching, though less so as Calvinism adapted to the changes in eighteenth-century Scottish secular society.

Both at home and abroad, middling Scots attached tremendous value to the utilitarian functions of an education. "Education is a noble Portion," wrote Dr. Robert Glasgow from St. Vincent's in the Caribbean, "it is a fortune sufficient of itself to carry a person genteelly thro' life with a small share of industry."[14] To Scots in all but the highest ranks, learning took the place of inherited money, property, and status. It became a catalyst for the acquisition of fortune.

Of course, an influx of credit from home provided the other great catalyst, both to Jamaica's expanding plantation economy and to individual guests for wealth. The ways in which West Indian economies became dependent upon credit are superbly set forth in Richard Sheridan's *Sugar and Slavery*. British agents granted estate owners credit against revenue gained from the sale of sugar and other staple crops. The planters then loaned each other money by trading the balances with their agents and merchants among themselves. Everyone was both debtor and creditor.

Sugar plantations had been built up over many years and financed by reinvested profits. Because trade credit from Britain was only granted for one year, against one crop, it became difficult to expand production very rapidly and boost profits in order to pay off debts. Thus, to conserve capital, planters frequently postponed debts or made them difficult for their cred-

[13]The traditional view holds that Scotland's educational system was among the best in Europe. See Charles Camic, *Experience and Enlightenment: Socialization for Cultural Change in Eighteenth Century Scotland* (Edinburgh, 1983), chap. 5, "Early Educational Experiences," pp. 141–63. Also see T. C. Smout, *History*, pp. 449–66. These arguments have recently been questioned by R. A. Houston in *Scottish Literacy and the Scottish Identity* (Cambridge, 1985), who argues that literacy rates in Scotland and (northern) England were not noticeably different. He suggests the Scottish schools were both inadequately funded and poorly attended. He further argues that Scottish nationalism has colored its past so much that education was romanticized into existence. While there can be no doubt that Scottish schools were inadequately funded, it seems to me that he should not deny the impact that the availability of education and mandatory schooling had on much of the population. Moreover, his evidence has been challenged by Donald J. Withrington in "Schooling, Literacy and Society," in *People and Society*, pp. 163–88. Withrington finds a very high rate of school attendance among various groups of Scots, some of which Houston claimed had no access to education.

[14]Robert Glasgow to William Glasgow, 4 June 1774, Hunter of Hunterston Papers (Cochran-Patrick of Ladyland), Bundle 169. Privately owned, accessible through NRA(S).

itors to collect, leading to a new cycle of indebtedness.[15] Credit became the fuel for the island's economic development.

As a result, colonial residents frequently found themselves entangled in endless webs of debt. Though they intended to return home, and though they accrued capital in their books, fear of losing that cash in the transition from Jamaica to Britain prevented them from leaving the island permanently. The reality of daily life in the Caribbean guaranteed that even the most carefully earned fortune would not easily cross the Atlantic, unless it had been collected all along and immediately remitted to Britain. In the words of Dr. Walter Grant,

> If I could send to Britain the little Fortune I have acquired I should certainly leave this part of the world & never think of Returning! But you find from Experience how difficult it is to get Money from this place & I assure you I am not luckier in that Respect, tho I am on the Spot.[16]

Island residents effectively loaned their services to customers, clients, and patients by debiting their accounts with a cash value.[17] Surviving account books regularly reveal that the credit side of the ledger was greater than the debit side. But this is creative accounting. Monies owed proved extremely difficult to collect, especially given the cycle just described. While it was sometimes possible to find a bill of exchange, such notes could only be purchased at roughly a 25 percent discount from face value. After deducting the seller's commission, a substantial part of the remittance had already been eliminated. All of this work and cost, simply to remove the balance from a Jamaican account book and place it on the credit side of a British ledger, might not have seemed worth the effort. Such conditions encouraged people in the island to deal with each other, and not extract their money from the island's economy. They could thus avoid substantial financial losses. Further complicating the problem, wealth in the island was measured primarily in land and slaves. Neither of these traveled well to Britain.

If removing money from the colony caused trepidation and uncertainty, keeping money in Jamaica had very clear benefits. Planters could maintain the styles of living to which they had become accustomed. And, they could increase profitability of their estates. Any white man in the island, therefore, who had even one interaction with one planter, became hostage to the credit-dominated society. Dr. Walter Grant, writing from Jamaica in 1763, was certainly aware of the difficulties.

---

[15]See Sheridan, *Sugar and Slavery*, pp. 262–305, esp. 271–74, 294, and 305.

[16]Dr. Walter Grant to Captain Archibald Grant, 2 September 1763, GD 345/1180, SRO.

[17]See John Mack Faragher, *Sugar Creek* (New Haven, Conn., 1986) for a discussion of similar behavior, the "borrowing system" on the Illinois prairie during the nineteenth century (pp. 133–36).

This is such a Fluctuating Country of Adventurers that neither Man their Families or Estates are so permanent as in Great Britain and after a few years They & their Estates (if they had any) disappear & their is scarce any tracing them, even the most Prudent and Active make debts here.

It is apparent that little had changed in the twenty years since merchant Robert Hamilton wrote home, "I am now resolv'd in all Events . . . to leave this Island, in two or three years at most, by which tyme I am in great hopes, I shall have my matters brought to an issue, without which . . . there can be no retiring with true satisfaction." Nor would things change in the next twenty years. Andrew MacFarlane wrote his sister in 1782: "a few years more will fully satisfy my ambition here and enable me to return amongst you to enjoy the fruits of a few years Most painfull Labour; but I never wish to be too sanguine in my expectations for fear of disapointments, experience has taught me this."[18]

In short, earning money in the booming Jamaican economy did not pose a problem. Extracting it, however, frequently proved more difficult than most sojourners reckoned. Jamaica had a growth economy, fuelled by credit infusions from home and reinvested profits, which prevented the participants from achieving their aims at the very same time that it assisted them. If the Scots sojourners, who were well-educated and had clearly defined aims, had problems, then others must have experienced even greater difficulty.

THE CALEDONIAN PRESENCE

Contemporaries observed the overwhelming preponderance of Scottish men in certain occupations. As late as 1801, Lady Maria Nugent reckoned that "almost all the agents, attorneys, merchants, and shopkeepers are of that country [Scotland], and really do deserve to thrive in this, they are so industrious."[19] She might have exaggerated the numbers of Scots in these businesses. She was, however, correct to notice that certain occupations had more Scottish practitioners than others. But a sample of correspondence cannot provide an estimate of the total number of Scots residing either temporarily or permanently in the island. Many more lived in Jamaica throughout the period 1740–1800 than the 267 sojourners I have identified.

Public records provide information that can be used to arrive at an approximation of the Scottish population in a particular year. Scottish sur-

---

[18]Dr. Walter Grant to Captain Archibald Grant, 2 September 1763. Robert Hamilton to Thomas Garvine, 31 August 1740, Hamilton of Rozelle Papers, volume 3, p. 15, GUA. Andrew MacFarlane to his sister, 9 November 1782, T-MJ 369, SRA.

[19]*Lady Nugent's Journal of her Residence in Jamaica from 1801 to 1805*, ed. P. Wright (Kingston, 1966), p. 29.

names not otherwise identified as belonging to a free mulatto or black man or woman can usually be picked out of available lists.[20] Comparing their number to the total number of recorded names provides a very rough estimate of the Caledonian presence in the white population. Based upon such sampling for the entire island, a minimum of ten percent of island landowners in 1754 were Scottish.[21] Given the increase in shipping connections between Scotland and Jamaica after 1760, we would expect the number of resident Caledonians to be ascending. Qualitative data that support this extrapolation are not difficult to find.

Edward Long, the island historian, reckoned in 1774 that

> Jamaica, indeed, is greatly indebted to North-Britain, as very near one third of the inhabitants are either natives of that country, or descendants from those who were. Many have come . . . every year, less in quest of fame than of fortunes; and such is their industry and address, that few of them have been disappointed.[22]

Long's claim that Scots represented a third of the white population is not unrealistic. His observation that they were a successful group suggests that the Scottish presence was conspicuously recognizable. Even assuming that Long erred on the generous side, his remarks nonetheless indicate that Jamaica's Scottish population noticeably increased in the two decades between 1754 and 1774. By the century's close, 40 percent of the residents in some parishes may well have been Scottish.

THE CAREERS

Dr. Colin Maclarty described himself and his compatriots approvingly:

> For what more commendable character than a professional man of extensive information, unassuming manner, void of pedantry, unremitting application to

[20]There is some precedent for this practice. See Forrest Macdonald and Ellen Shapiro Macdonald, "The Ethnic Origins of the American People, 1790." For a synopsis of the very interesting debate which arose from their thesis, and which culminated in Ned Landsman's astute criticism, see "Communications," *WMQ* 41 (1984): 680–81. Landsman is correct in asserting that ethnicity has more to do with cultural identification than simply coming from a particular country. In Jamaica, such self-identification was sharpened both by outsiders classifying the Scots as Scots and by the people themselves, searching for something in common in an alien environment.

[21]I have not counted anyone whose surname could have been either Scottish or English, nor have I considered any of those whose ethnicity was otherwise questionable. The figure, from the 1754 landowner's list, is 140 Scots out of 1564 total names. The actual number of Scots is very probably greater. See CO 142/31, PRO, Kew. Sheridan, in *Sugar and Slavery,* pp. 369–70, has used the same source, and estimates the proportion of Scots to be nearer 25 percent.

[22]Edward Long, *A History of Jamaica* (London, 1774), v. 2, p. 287.

business, and to crown all, for without it the rest is a mere nothing, inflexible integrity.[23]

His remarks lend credence to the epithet "industrious" that other observers, such as Edward Long and Lady Nugent, applied to the Scots. Many sojourning Scots came to Jamaica with the idea that they would achieve their goals simply by adhering to principles similar to those espoused by the young physician. Whether they were doctors, attorneys, merchants, or clerks, all shared a common sense of professional integrity and, at least superficially, demonstrated diligence to their affairs. Perhaps as important, little changed in the way Scots perceived and practiced their professions from 1740 onward.

MEDICINE

Colin Maclarty's story provides a glimpse into the workings of Jamaica's medical community, and the Scottish presence in it. When Maclarty entered the colony in mid 1787, his first task was to meet "the right people." He sought out those who would be most able to help him achieve his ambitions. Writing his cousin Peggy, he indicated that he found island society "exceeding genteel" with a number of "well bred people . . . most of whom I have already got acquainted with."[24]

His enthusiasm quickly evaporated; Dr. Maclarty faced substantial problems. His father, a Glasgow merchant ship's captain, had only been able to provide his son with a few connections in the island.[25] They proved inadequate; young Maclarty encountered considerable difficulty setting himself up in a practice. The overabundance of physicians which he discovered upon his arrival made good employment near impossible, even for men who might have been better connected.

"I am convinced their protestations were sincere," he wrote his cousin Betty, referring to his patrons,

> but such . . . is the unfavourable state of this country at present, for Men of my Profession that it is as bad as can be. . . . [T]his country owing to the vast number of Medical people who were either *refugees*, or deprived of em-

[23]Dr. Colin Maclarty to his father, 23 July 1792, John Cunningham Letters, Acc. 7285, NLS.
[24]Colin Maclarty to Peggy Maclarty, 23 July 1787, Cunningham Letters, Acc. 7285, NLS.
[25]Maclarty's father served as captain of several ships. According to newspaper advertisements, he traveled to the Chesapeake until 1774 and to Jamaica in 1778–79. After that time, he no longer appears in the advertisements, perhaps because the houses which employed him could no longer afford to run trading ventures. It appears that Captain Maclarty's career suffered when Glasgow lost the Chesapeake markets.

ployment by the place, is so perfectly overrun with them that almost every small plantation has got its Doctor.[26]

Maclarty believed that he could not have arrived at a worse time. Though loyalist refugees of all professions flocked to the island in the years after the American Revolution, they could not be blamed for Maclarty's difficulties. Jamaica frequently had too many physicians. Scots practitioners continued to flow in, because Jamaica had a reputation for being a place to earn a quick fortune. And chances for socioeconomic mobility at home were limited by a sizable population which generally could not afford much medical care. According to Richard Sheridan, Scots may well have accounted for up to two-thirds of all the island's doctors.[27] Opportunities in Jamaica were not imaginary; the overabundance of physicians resulted from the colony's real need.

The problem came because doctors, like Maclarty, believed that being a plantation doctor was simply too slow a path to wealth. David Grant wrote Sir Archibald Grant in 1766, "I am much perplexed about myself," he complained, "in what sphere of life to act—the attending of plantations is much trouble and fatigue, with small profits besides . . . they are already stocked & more."[28] Fourteen years earlier, Dr. Robert Ewart wrote his brother with a similar complaint: "This place does not at all answer the notion we have of it in Scotland, for it is as much overstocked with people of my profession as any part in Great Britain, and what is worse there is neither money nor trade in The Island."[29]

The white population needed medical practitioners for its slaves. But physicians did not like to devote very much time to their care. Dr. John Williamson explained the reasons.

The medical profession in Jamaica, particularly for plantations . . . is not placed on that system of respectability and independence which is due it.

[26]Colin Maclarty to Betty Maclarty, 23 July 1787, Cunningham Letters, NLS.

[27]Sheridan, in *Doctors and Slaves* (Cambridge, 1985), notes that doctors were in short supply during war-time but there was an overabundance of them in times of peace (p. 44). Maclarty arrived during a year of peace in the West Indies. See also Sheridan's *Sugar and Slavery*, p. 372. *The Medical Register for the Year 1780* (London, 1780) lists seventy-two Jamaican doctors.

[28]David Grant to Sir Archibald Grant, 12 November 1764, GD 345/1170, SRO.

[29]Dr. Robert Ewart to Adam Ewart, 6 July 1750, Bundle 47, Tweedie-Stoddart of Oliver papers, privately owned, accessible through NRA(S). Charles Leslie had maintained that there were too many doctors in 1740 (*A New History of Jamaica* [London, 1740], p. 49). Archibald Sinclair, in 1760, saw physick as a profession from which enough money could be made to purchase property (to Sir Robert Gordon, 25 June 1760, MS La. II. 498, EUL). He said nothing about the supply of physicians. Dr. Alexander Johnston noted an overabundance of practitioners in 1784. See Alexander Johnston to James Johnston, 20 January 1784, A. Johnston papers, letters, HSP.

> There are few things . . . which appear . . . to be more in want of radical
> reform, [than] . . . our profession being better rewarded for their labours. . . .
> it is believed that plantation doctors, in many parts of the interior, do not make
> good horse-hire for the number of miles they ride, on average, daily.[30]

Prospective physicians always tried to avoid serving on a plantation because they would only be paid a flat rate, perhaps five shillings, for the care
of each slave per year. The only way to make a profit was not to visit or treat
the slaves. Since they could charge the white inhabitants for every individual
treatment and visit, the financial disadvantages of plantation medicine were
obvious to them all. Nevertheless, some plantation doctors who also had
private practices did manage to acquire capital.[31]

Few opportunities existed for Maclarty to join a white practice immediately, so he spent his first year in Jamaica moving from place to place, trying to
find a job. Like a number of Scots, he began in St. Thomas in the East
parish, around Port Morant, and then moved to Kingston. After an unsuccessful attempt to join a medical firm there, he returned to St. Thomas in
the East to lament his failures.

> What renders it peculiarly distressing to me is a change which took place about
> six months ago amongst the medical people here and had I then been on the
> spot, with the interest I had procured, I would beyond all doubt have suc-
> ceeded to an immediate practice of, from five to seven hundred a year but my
> evil genius presided.

Frustration reigned supreme. "Matters being thus situated," he continued, "there are two things which I regret without being able to redress.
The first is, that I did not come here some years ago; and the last, that I came
here when I did."[32]

The way in which medical positions were acquired had not changed
dramatically between 1760 and 1787. Having the right connections remained of paramount importance. Recommendations from suitable people
followed by a short apprenticeship became the norm for "buying" a share of
the practice. As early as 1760, Dr. Robert Ewart wrote that he had to advance

[30]John Williamson, *Medical and Miscellaneous Observations Relative to the West India Islands*
(Edinburgh, 1817), v. 2, pp. 8–9.
[31]I have published a biography of one of these physicians, "The World of Alexander
Johnston: The Creolization of Ambition, 1762–1787," *Historical Journal* 30 (1987): 53–76.
Johnston tried to visit his slave patients as infrequently as possible.
[32]Colin Maclarty to Betty Maclarty, 23 July 1787, Cunningham Letters, NLS. I have been
unable to determine what a physician might have expected to earn in Scotland, in order to
estimate whether Maclarty would have been better off staying at home. It is not likely that he
would have been.

a thousand pounds before "I ever recovered one hundred pounds from the profits of my business." In 1776, Dr. William Bryant paid two thousand pounds in return for a 50 percent share of a Kingston business with an annual income of six thousand pounds. He remarked that someone who paid that much six years before had "now a fortune of upwards of Twenty thousand pounds, which he has acquired by close application to Bussiness in that short time."[33] Alexander Johnston, in 1763, paid half of the business expenses in return for one-third of the business revenues for two years and fifty percent after that.

Maclarty, for his part, when he was trying to join the "first medical house in Kingston" would have had to post £1500 security in return for a third of a £7000 per annum practice. However, he would not have been subject to apprenticeship before he purchased his practice. By 1787, all it took to acquire a stake in a practice was cash or credit in hand. Investing British security in a practice was little more than a means of injecting capital into the internal Jamaican economy.

In early 1788, Maclarty again moved from St. Thomas in the East parish to Kingston "to get into the House of Drysdale & McGlashan," a medical firm in town. He wrote his cousin excitedly, "if I can accomplish it I think my chance of acquiring something hansome will undoubtedly be greater as their business is perhaps the most extensive of any medical people in the West Indies."[34] It could not have come at a better time. Maclarty had already expressed his intentions. "I am determined to do all in my power to succeed & if I do not, I shall positively return to Greenock however disagreeable such a step may be to me."[35]

By 1790, Maclarty had become a partner. He had found the security to do so through borrowing; thus, he had to worry about earning enough to repay the loan and still become independent. "Our income last year," he penned his father, "fell rather short . . . tho not near so much as most of the medical Houses in Town, as we were uncommonly healthy, however my proportion, after allotting the contingent charges which were particularly high, say £1000 . . . amounted to £840 and of that there may, perhaps be 50 or sixty pounds doubtful debts."[36] Even in a bad year Maclarty earned a reasonable salary (£840 currency was the equivalent of £600 sterling), which was at least as much as he had hoped for when he came to the island three years earlier. But the form in which the £840 was paid him became the issue. What he

[33]Robert Ewart to Adam Ewart [ca. 1760], Bundle 44, Tweedie-Stoddart of Oliver; privately owned, accessible through NRA(S). William Bryant to the Earl of Fife, 29 March 1776, Tayler Manuscripts, 2226/19/17, AUL.

[34]Colin Maclarty to Peggy Maclarty, 14 March 1788, Cunningham Letters, NLS.

[35]Colin Maclarty to Betty Maclarty, 23 July 1787, Cunningham Letters, NLS.

[36]Colin Maclarty to his father, 8 May 1790, Cunningham Letters, NLS.

collected in currency negotiable outside the island, he feared, would only be a small fraction of that to which he was entitled. Thus, assuming that he obtained all but the "doubtful debts" (a big assumption), he would be able to do quite a lot in Jamaica but nothing in Britain until he could get bills which would be paid there at face value.

This central problem placed the sojourners in awkward positions. Like so many other Scots in the island, Maclarty despised greed, and saw it in the tendency of Jamaican residents to look at every thing in terms of the profit generated. Yet, most Caledonians knew that they had to look after their own interests. If that meant trying to make sure that they were paid in British notes, or constantly keeping after their debtors, they showed no aversion to doing so. Maclarty condemned avarice at the same time that he was obsessed with earning his independence.

> Madness, Consumption &ca are not more certainly transmitted than that most detestable of all principles, Avarice. I do not say but liberal education and generous example may possibly correct it in the infant & growing mind; but when the soil is favourable and it is early implanted, melancholy is the possessor indeed.[37]

Here Maclarty reveals that, like many of his countrymen, he adheres to the idea that education could illuminate the distinction between greed and the pursuit of independence. Clearly, very little had changed in the island as the century wore down. Lieutenant Governor Archibald Campbell had remarked the same thing just ten years earlier.

> There is another motive for my returning home, which even surpasses those already mentioned. That is a Passionate desire to get out of exceeding bad company. Avarice seems to pervade every department in the Island. Extortionate jobs, and every Species of abuse go on with impunity.

"And," he continued, "I have neither temper . . . nor inclination to remain a spectator of such infamy."[38] Scots deplored heavy-handed displays of wealth. These people were not trying to become flashy members of any island aristocracy. Robert Hamilton had expressed similar intentions forty years earlier.

> And as my ambition never aim'd higher, than that of being Independent, and haveing it in my power to be usefull & serviceable to my friends, I am hopefull

---

[37]Ibid.
[38]Archibald Campbell to Allan Ramsay, 24 June 1780, Campbell of Inverneil Papers, M. 1430 (Microfilm), EUL.

I shall be able to find my Self in these circumstances when my scatter'd affairs are brought together.[39]

The Scots believed that Jamaica was a place to practice one's trade to earn enough to purchase property and become an absentee landowner, or even better, to sell out at a profit. But a shortage of capital and an excess of easily obtained credit prevented such success from occurring more regularly. In other words, good British money invested in Jamaica, particularly in property, became virtually impossible to extract without going to court. As Dr. Robert Ewart remarked: "A man in business here, altho he is worth ten thousand pounds, may goe to Jail for five hundred pounds, money is so hard to be called in, unless you are quitting Bussiness altogether."[40]

It is unclear how successful Colin Maclarty was; only a handful of his letters exist today. No record of him has been found in the island's estate inventories, so it seems unlikely that he left property in the island when he died.[41] In 1791, he urged his brother Alexander to be trained as a physician and, in 1797, Colin welcomed Alexander to Jamaica.[42] He obviously had done well enough, in island terms, to assist those coming up in the business. Ambitious in an avaricious environment, the Scottish medical practitioner tried to reconcile his values with his aspirations. "Independence" was the reward.

THE LAW

Scottish and English law remained separate after the Union of Parliaments in 1707; those who learned to practice law in Edinburgh could practice it only in Scotland. The colonies, because they were English in origin,

[39]Robert Hamilton to Thomas Garvin, 31 August 1740, Hamilton of Rozelle Papers, v.3, p. 15, GUA.

[40]Robert Ewart to Adam Ewart [n.d., 1755?], Bundle 44, Tweedie-Stoddart of Oliver; privately owned, NRA(S).

[41]When the Jamaica Deeds Series is transferred from the Island Record Office to the Jamaica Archives, it will be possible to verify Maclarty's island interactions.

[42]Alexander Maclarty was the youngest son of Captain Alex. Maclarty. An Alex. Maclarty matriculated at Glasgow University's medical school in 1791. The matriculation album suggests that this might have been Alexr. Johnston Maclarty who died on 23 June 1794, eight days after arriving in Jamaica. Because Colin Maclarty wrote to his brother on 11 December 1796, his brother may well have been the Glasgow matriculant but not Alexander Johnston Maclarty. See *The Matriculation Albums of the University of Glasgow from 1728 to 1858*, ed. W. Innes Addison (Glasgow, 1913). Colin Maclarty was the apprentice of a Dr. Fullarton in Glasgow when he trained as a physician. Both Edward Brathwaite in *Creole Society*, pp. 282–83, and Richard Sheridan in *Doctors and Slaves*, p. 260–61, refer to a Dr. Alexander Maclarty in the early nineteenth century. He was the director of the island's vaccine establishment and probably Colin Maclarty's brother.

utilized England's legal system. One of the most marked and obvious distinctions between being English and being Scottish arose here.

After surmounting the obstacles that Jamaica's legal system placed in their way, some Scots used their training to advantage. The colony's litigious nature provided numerous opportunities and insured that they had little trouble setting up client networks. Only a few Scots actually became members of the Jamaican bar, however; the vast majority were hindered by having to learn the English law. Those who did made very tidy sums indeed, for almost every white man and woman in the island had some interaction with the civil courts. Thomas Gordon, an attorney in Jamaica, admitted, "In spite of the great disadvantage of being a Scotch man I have made very genteely by my profession."[43]

Many sojourners who had trained in Scottish law discovered only after they arrived in the island that they had new apprenticeships to serve before being allowed to practice their avocations. Rather than retrain, most of these people quickly turned to estate management. Proliferating absenteeism made the profession increasingly popular; estate managers virtually ran the Jamaican plantation society and economy. A manager not only had to manipulate accounts and payments but also had to influence his employer's opinion. By examining the careers of several men involved in some aspect of law or management or both, the way in which Scots used these occupations to their own benefit can be described and their relative successes and failures demonstrated.

Thomas Gordon described the process that prospective members of the bar underwent. "Barristers here (even the Attorney General)," he wrote, "have not occasion for Clerks & by a late rule of Court none can be admitted Attornies except such as have been so in England or Ireland unless they serve under Articles to some of the Practisers here for five years." He continued to warn that "one year is dispensed with & one year only in favour of those who have served out their time with a writer to the Signet in Edinburgh."[44]

For this reason, very few Scots lawyers set up shop in the colony before 1767.[45] Those attorneys who came to the island expecting to join the bar

[43]Thomas Gordon to Archibald Grant, 27 June 1752, Grant of Monymusk, GD 345/1162/4/7, SRO.

[44]The exact wording of the statutes regulating the legal profession can be found in *The Laws of Jamaica* (St. Jago de la Vega, 1792), v. 1, p. 278, and v. 2, pp. 34–35, 121. In 1763, the law apparently changed the court ruling that Gordon mentioned, so that only one additional year (not four) was required of Scots who were Writers to the Signet in Scotland before being admitted to the courts in Jamaica. Thomas Gordon to Archibald Grant, 29 July 1753, Grant of Monymusk, GD 345/1162/5/28, SRO.

[45]The colonial laws limiting the legal profession of English lawyers appear to have been overturned by Westminster. The Jamaica Assembly passed a new act in 1773, with very strict

often returned to Scotland when they discovered the obstacles that the assembly had placed in their paths. In 1753, Archibald Grant of Monymusk sent a Mr. Fordyce to Jamaica to earn his fortune as a lawyer, probably in exchange for a vote from Fordyce's father. (Grant was running for Parliament.) When Thomas Gordon could procure for Fordyce only a clerkship that paid £90 a year, and none of his other connections could get him anything at all, Fordyce decided to cut his losses and return to Scotland where he would earn full lawyer's fees without having to retrain in English law.[46] Those with adequate qualifications in Scotland generally found the frustration of an additional clerkship quite unbearable.

Mr. Blair, another of Archibald Grant's clients, "changed the Path of the Law for that of Agriculture," in 1756. He found planting far more lucrative, especially after tallying the costs to complete a second extended apprenticeship.

> After remaining in an Estate of Servitut [sic] four years with an allowance hardly sufficient to support the necessaries of Life he would probably have been double that term before he could have got a comfortable maintenance & all the time exposed to all Temptation.[47]

Being "exposed to all Temptation" caused many Scots to act in order to extricate themselves quickly. Few in Jamaica wanted to be there for a long time; anything that added to that time invariably was to be avoided. Only a few had the patience to tackle the discrimination and become lawyers in the colony. In 1767, James Gillespie related to Archibald Grant that he had chosen to complete his second apprenticeship:

> Until six months ago, I was not admitted an Attorney at Law of the Courts here, owing in a good measure to the severity of our Law in that respect; and was even under the disagreeable necessity of serving another four years Apprenticeship.[48]

restrictions on who could practice. This time, however, it did not discriminate against the Scots (*Laws of Jamaica*, v. 2, p. 121). Perhaps this represented an acknowledgment that the Scots were no longer second-class partners in the empire.

[46]See Thomas Gordon to Archibald Grant, 29 July 1753. For reference to electioneering, see Alexander Grant to Archibald Grant, 17 May 1753, GD 345/1162/5/40x, SRO. Ninety pounds a year was quite a good salary by Scottish standards, but it would have been worth considerably less when transported to Britain. Its full value could only be enjoyed by staying in the island.

[47]Thomas Gordon to Archibald Grant, 6 January 1756, Grant of Monymusk, GD 345/1164/3/38, SRO.

[48]Mr. [James] Gillespie to Archibald Grant, 7 October 1767, Grant of Monymusk, GD 345/1171/1/128-129x, SRO.

Though little had changed in the twelve years between Gordon's and Gillespie's letters, Gillespie obviously believed he had invested too much time and effort getting to Jamaica. To go back to Scotland would have meant facing the same uncertain prospects that he had left. To remain, however, allowed a clear possibility of acquiring his fortune. He was willing to bet that the restrictions on Scottish lawyers would work to his advantage. The expanding Scottish population in the island did have legal needs and, he thought, they would be willing to choose a fellow Scot to serve them.

The island had not earned its reputation as an incredibly litigious place for nothing. Contemporaries believed Jamaica's legal profession to be extremely large. When Gillespie counted them in 1767, Jamaica had more than 70 practicing lawyers and about 20 barristers. He reckoned it had more "disputes in Equity than all the other North American or Island Colonies put together, belonging to the Crown of Great Britain. . . . [F]or some Courts past," he observed, "2000 Civil Actions have been issued from One Court, and we have four of these Courts in the Year." Jamaicans rarely paid their debts; "few are without being sued."[49] Scots who were able to circumvent legal requirements for their qualifications, or who underwent a retraining in English law, or who came out to Jamaica expressly to learn the profession had numerous opportunities to do very well indeed.

Archibald Sinclair advised Sir Robert Gordon to train his son William to be an attorney in England. Knowing his countrymen's predilections for dealing with each other whenever possible, he thought that the advantages to be gained in a profession with so few Scots would make the extra time and effort worthwhile. In 1760, William's father sent him to Alexander Grant, an erstwhile merchant and the cousin of Archibald Grant of Monymusk, in order to learn to be a Caribbean planter. William fell out with Grant, who was then warring with his partner, another cousin, Sir Alexander Grant [of Dalvey], the London merchant. William Gordon arrived with a letter of recommendation from Sir Alexander.[50] His cousin then sent him to Sinclair, a retired Jamaica merchant and now estate manager, who advised the younger Gordon to return quickly to Britain. If William were a Scot trained at London in the English law, Sinclair maintained that he could "make a Good Figure & a Competent Fortune at our Barr, where there is at present but one Scotch Lawyer (& he is near Sixty years of age). . . . Almost every man in this Island has more or less Concerns . . . to be transacted in the Courts of Law or Chancery."[51] What is more, he suggested, doctors and overseers

[49]Ibid. See Sheridan, *Sugar and Slavery*, p. 371, for similar conclusions about an earlier period.
[50]Lewis Gordon to Sir Robert Gordon, 9 June 1760, MS La. II. 498, EUL.
[51]Archibald Sinclair to Sir Robert Gordon, 25 June 1760, MS La. II. 498, EUL.

operated chiefly in only one parish, whereas lawyers drew their clients from across the island. Mr. Sinclair did not mention other professions; no Scot did. For them the choice was simple: medicine, law, planting, or trade.[52]

As might be expected from contemporary description of the problems they faced, examples of Scottish lawyers or attorneys actually making good at this profession are rare. One about whom we know something is John Grant. He learned to practice law in England sometime in the 1760s, perhaps after several years at Glasgow University. After working as a lawyer and managing Jamaican sugar estates, he became the island's chief justice in 1784.[53] From the information that has survived about John Grant's career, we know that he had many prominent clients (in both Scotland and England) when he served as an attorney. Among them were John Fuller, Hugh Tolson, Ludovick Grant (for the late Sir Alexander Grant), and Richard Beckford.[54] Upon taking his seat at the head of the high court, he parcelled out his attorneyships to his brother Francis, whose life forms the principal subject for the next section. The position of chief justice paid very little, but Grant did earn a number of commissions and salaries which were associated with it.[55] He obviously acquired enough to be able to extract his money from Jamaica and purchase Kilgraston estate, in eastern Perthshire, in 1785. He left the island in 1791 to retire to his newly purchased estate and died, having become a Scottish landowner in his own right, in 1793.[56] Justice Grant was more of an excep-

[52]Religion could also be included in these categories. Lists of Anglican parish clergy do exist in the PRO. I have not checked them for Scots because I have been unable to locate more than a handful of surviving letters from ministers. The only quantity of personal correspondence I have found belonged to the Reverend John Pool, who was rector in Westmoreland, Jamaica from 1747 to 1766, at Kingston from 1766 to 1768, and at St. Andrew, from 1768 to 1782. (See Frank Cundall, *Historic Jamaica* [London, 1919], pp. 165, 207, 347.) Pool was an Englishman who spent a substantial part of his time managing the estates of absentee planters. His correspondence with Roger Hope Elletson and George Brydges, Duke of Buckingham, can be found in the Stowe Papers, volume 14 (1&2), STG Box 25; and elsewhere at the Huntington Library, San Marino, California.

[53]Colonial Office Records in the PRO indicate that John Grant had a rather volatile career before becoming Chief Justice. In 1779, Governor Dalling removed Grant and three other associate justices from the island's highest court because he did not like the way they behaved. They brought the matter to the government in London and were ultimately reinstated. For the voluminous records, see CO 137/38, CO 137/39, and CO 138/24, PRO, Kew.

[54]These powers of attorney can be found in Powers series 83/72, 83/223, 83/242, and 84/8, JA.

[55]See Addison, ed., *Matriculation Albums,* and Sir William Fraser, *The Chiefs of Grant* (Edinburgh, 1883), v. 1, p. 528, for biographical information on John Grant. For a discussion of the Chief Justice position, see Long, *History,* v. 1, pp. 70–76.

[56]See John Grant to Charles Gordon, 28 November 1785, MS 1160/6/36, Gordon of Cairness, AUL, and John Grant to Charles Gordon, 17 July 1787, MS 1160/6/47, AUL. Grant's death notice is in the *Caledonian Mercury* of 6 April 1793.

tion than a rule; he struck the right balance between gaining money in Jamaica and working toward an independent existence in Scotland.

ESTATE MANAGEMENT

Another avenue, perhaps the principal one, that Scots with either legal or mercantile experience used to move closer to financial independence was the position of estate manager or estate attorney.[57] Estate managers, usually with more than one property under their direction, performed a remarkable variety of duties. They not only hired and fired overseers, bookkeepers, and other white personnel, but they also decided, whenever they were allowed to, how many slaves to purchase and how to use them to insure maximum productivity. They were responsible for buying plantation supplies, keeping everyone well fed, and selling the crops, or arranging for their consignment. They had to advise the owner of what needed to be invested in order to raise production levels, as well as whether or not the crop matched expectations. They were also responsible for making sure that governmental regulations were honored and the proper forms filed in Spanish Town. Sometimes owners would disagree with their managers and order them not to undertake a particular project. When this happened, the manager was bound to respect his employer's wishes. Such requests, however, frequently arrived after the manager had already carried out his plans.[58]

The managers, like the Chesapeake tobacco factors, often had all the advantages of running their own estates without the added responsibility of actually owning them. They were employees, yet many of them acted like owners. Slow communication between Britain and the island meant that they often did what they liked without fear of reproach. In such a manner, they could arrange to save their earnings (by keeping or making them as liquid as possible) much more regularly than an owner who was dependent upon a favorable climate, as well as a manager, for accruing wealth. These managers also held a great deal of patronage in their possession. While, of course, they had to honor the owner's requests, they were usually allowed a good deal of leeway to fill any vacancies with candidates whom they wanted (or needed) to

[57]See Richard Pares, *A West India Fortune*, p. 24, for a discussion of the concentration of attorneyship amongst a "knot of businessmen . . . who made [it] almost a profession."

[58]In the Jamaican slave registration returns for 1817, St. Ann's parish had forty-eight attorneys. Twenty-one managed more than one property, seventeen of these were responsible for either two or three, and four attorneys had an average of seven properties. Since an attorney had to pay some attention to each estate, he could not handle too many at once. Attorneys formed partnerships to increase the number they could manage. Another way to increase income was through extramural activity, pilfering and embezzling.

assist. In short, this position probably provided the greatest chance for success as the Scots defined it, independence away from Jamaica. Because they worked on other people's property, shrewd managers would have been more sensitive to problems that they might encounter later, on their own properties.[59]

Nearly every family whose private correspondence has survived has one or more estate managers in it; the profession held enormous promise. For the purposes of the present study the career of Chief Justice Grant's younger brother Francis provides a fine illustration of an estate manager's opportunities, travails, and ultimate success.

Grant's friend, and fellow Scot, Charles Gordon, arrived in Jamaica to settle his deceased merchant uncle's affairs in the early 1770s. Becoming frustrated by his difficulty in wading through the usual Jamaican quagmire of credit, debt, and security, he left the island for a North American tour in late 1773. At that time, he appointed John Grant his attorney. Grant purchased the Georgia sugar plantation in Trelawny Parish in 1778 for £26,000. It then produced 140 hogsheads of sugar per year, though Grant reckoned that it could produce 200. He offered his "bargain" to Gordon, who agreed to accept the property and return to the island. Missing Scotland, however, Gordon left Jamaica in 1781 for good. He appointed John Grant and his brother Francis to act as his attorneys. Gordon also gave complete charge of the estate to Francis, employing him as the manager.[60]

Francis Grant soon became insecure about his own abilities to manage Georgia. Even though he had several other estates in his charge, he questioned his own skills because neither praise nor reprimand was forthcoming from Gordon. Charles Gordon was a horrible correspondent. He wrote to no one except his friend the chief justice, and even then only infrequently. Francis had nothing to worry about. At first he was reluctant to assume the role which was being offered him on a silver platter, but he soon learned to seize his opportunities.

Gordon thought Grant was a good manager. He did not like to worry about Jamaica, and Grant's detailed letters made him believe that everything was under strict control. In a rare burst of correspondence, Gordon wrote to his employee. "I do assure," he told Francis, "that while I am possessed of

[59]Elsa Goveia in *Slave Society in the British Leeward Islands at the End of the Eighteenth Century* (New Haven, Conn., 1965), p. 204, talks of a "leveling down" of the white upper class. Those who remained in the island were not as well off as the absentees (otherwise they would not have still been there), though they acted as if they were. This new upper class admitted the absentees' managers and attorneys.

[60]Absentees frequently appointed friends and neighbors to be their managers. See Pares, *A West India Fortune*, p. 20.

the Estate I do not wish to see it managed by any one Else."[61] Several months later, he confided his faults to John, "Your brother has wrote me very frequently . . . I must own that I have been very much to blame in not writing him oftener. . . . I am sorry that he should have placed that to the account of neglect which disposed from my confidence in him."[62] But even while Gordon apologized for his errors, and continued to accept Grant's decisions without question, Francis vented his disaffection:

> So total a Silence to a Correspondence which you acknowledge to have been very regular on my part, could not fail to wound the feelings of a Man even of less Sensitivity than I. . . . it is too much to be near two years without answering one, & to know you were during that Very period corresponding with another [Grant's brother John] on business, which it was naturally connected with my province as your acting attorney to be made acquainted with.[63]

Grant should have been thankful that he had as much autonomy as he did; a number of estate owners became so frustrated with the problems of their plantations that they constantly meddled in managerial affairs, making life all the more difficult for the manager. Gordon's inattention, no doubt, arose from his mounting British debts and his desire to sell the Jamaica plantation to pay them. Like all sojourning Scots, he wanted his money out of the island, but insisted on earning a profit in the process. As a result, he demanded that he be paid with British security. Chief Justice Grant reminded him of Jamaica's way of doing business.

> English security is not to be expected. There is scarcely a man in Jamaica who can command it. But I conceive should a purchaser come in the way who could lay down about a fourth of the price, and get a mortgage on the Estate together perhaps with other property of his own, you might be as safe as with English security.[64]

In the same letter, he implored him to correspond with his brother Francis, who remained the person in charge of the estate. For his part, Francis had now formed a deep affection for Georgia and he let its owner know.

[61]Charles Gordon to Francis Grant, 6 May 1784, MS 1160/5/86, Gordon of Cairness, AUL.
[62]Charles Gordon to John Grant, 23 August 1784, MS 1160/5/86, Gordon of Cairness, AUL. This sort of correspondence should have been the other way around according to Pares. Grant appears to have been an honest attorney.
[63]Francis Grant to Charles Gordon, 10 August 1784, MS 1160/6/32, Gordon of Cairness, AUL.
[64]John Grant to Charles Gordon, 12 May 1784, MS 1160/6/31, AUL.

Perhaps by saying so, he hoped to get Gordon to write more. "I confess I feel an attachment," he wrote, "which I have not in the same degree for any of my other concerns & therefore I have a desire of giving it as much as possible of my personal attentions."[65] He began to split his time between his own house in Montego Bay and Georgia, in nearby Trelawny parish.

Like all managers, Grant never hesitated to ask for more money, despite knowledge that Gordon was trying to sell the estate. In February 1787 he wrote Gordon for permission to purchase twenty additional slaves. "I shall never ask you for another as long as I live," he penned the owner.[66] He correctly believed that more slaves and new buildings and works added to a Jamaican estate's value; what he failed to realize was that Gordon could not locate a satisfactory buyer for the estate even at a much lower value. By plowing more money into his Jamaican property, Gordon made it increasingly unlikely that he would be able to extricate himself without a loss. Grant's request unwittingly points to the contradiction that hurt so many sojourners. In order to increase an estate's profitability, money had to be invested in it. But once invested in the soil, capital could not be easily extracted from it and removed to Scotland.

Charles Gordon, subscribing to the commonly held belief that more labor automatically meant more profits, approved Grant's request for added strength. His approval, without any questions, was a bit unusual. A decade earlier, G. O. Kinloch responded to a similar request from his manager James Wedderburn by saying that he did not "find from the Circumstances of the Case that it will be prudent . . . to Launch out in the Purchase of 30 more Negroes this season, I reather choice to work carefully those that I have."[67] For Francis Grant, Gordon's acceptance of his judgments allowed him to continue to play the part of an independent planter.

If Grant had to deal with the absentee plantation owner on one side, he also had to deal with the plantation staff on the other. In 1781, he wrote Gordon that, "I see dayly too many Instances of Carelessness & bad management in your Overseer [a Mr. Allan], he is by no means the Man you took him for."[68] Gordon, in a rare burst of intervention, gave Allan a second chance. Typical of estate managers who did not wish to answer for their actions, Francis Grant had his lapses as well. "I cannot be particular as to every improvement or alteration on the face of this Estate since you saw it, nor do I conceive such a detail to be very necessary, but upon the whole, I can assure you that it is in a thriving way—more so than you had a right to

[65]Francis Grant to Charles Gordon, 28 September 1784, MS 1160/6/34, AUL.
[66]Francis Grant to Charles Gordon, 12 February 1787, MS 1160/6/43/1-2, AUL.
[67]G. O. Kinloch to James Wedderburn, 6 February 1773, GD 1/8/36/3, SRO.
[68]Grant to Gordon, 23 September 1781, MSS 1160/6/15/1-2, AUL.

expect when you left it."[69] Francis Grant could get away with this largely because Gordon was so lax in exercising his prerogatives. In 1783, Georgia still only produced 142 hogsheads of sugar, a measly two more than when it was purchased half a decade earlier. All of Francis Grant's efforts left it well short of the 200 his brother had predicted when he offered Gordon the estate.

Production soon improved dramatically. By 1788, Francis Grant had become extremely proud of his efforts. He had obviously paid the estate more attention, even without Gordon's instructions. He viewed it as a barometer of his success as a manager.

> It is certainly a better property than when you knew it. [E]ven the cultivated land . . . is improved. . . . It is also pretty nearly compleat in Buildings & enclosures, nor is there much of anything wanting except Negroes to bring it forward to 300 hhd & to keep it up afterwards. . . . I shall not be greatly surprised if it reaches that crop next year."[70]

Charles Gordon did not seem to be bothered, despite increasing financial difficulties at home, when the estate failed to match the manager's new expectations of 300 hogsheads. He was unusual in this respect, for most other estate owners became "convinced from long observation, that middling estates in this country [Jamaica] are very unproductive and precarious, more particularly so to the absentees. Such Estates only answer when the Proprietors live on them with frugality and industry, and even then, most . . . of this class are distressed."[71] But the managers prospered, regardless of the estate's position.

There were two ways in which attorneys could be paid. The first involved a straight salary, with perhaps some perquisites such as food and drink. In this case, the attorney earned the same amount, which was often substantial, from year to year, regardless of the amount of work he did or whether or not the estate fared well. The second, and probably more common, means of payment was through commission. In this case, estate managers received roughly 6 percent of an estate's produce. This arrangement, in theory, encouraged them to pay more attention to a crop by making them dependent upon it for their own living. In practice, however, many estate managers were emboldened to keep plantation supplies for themselves and skim money from the plantation accounts for their own use. In either case, however, the plantation attorney would do well.[72]

[69]Grant to Gordon, 20 November 1782, MSS 1160/6/25/1-3, AUL.
[70]Grant to Gordon, 4 July 1788, MSS 1160/6/58/1-2, AUL.
[71]G. Cuthbert to Mr. Fotheringham, 19 June 1785, GD 121/3/80, SRO.
[72]See Goveia, *Slave Society*, pp. 204–6, Pares, *A West India Fortune*, pp. 19–22, 141–49, and

By December of 1788 neither Gordon nor Grant had found a buyer for the property. No one was willing, or able, to give British security. Grant continued to berate Gordon for being such a poor correspondent, especially since he was so attentive to his employer's requirements. "In place of growing a getter Correspondent as you have long ago promised me," he complained, "I really think you are becoming worse & worse every day; but I shall get no good of scolding you. . . . You are too old to mend."[73] Grant began to realize that Gordon's inattention gave him unbounded authority to act. Others noticed as well.

It was at this moment that young Archibald Stirling, a junior member of a family in comfortable circumstances, arrived in the island with a letter of recommendation to Francis Grant. Grant also managed brother John Stirling's property, Hampden estate. Archibald, whose Uncle Archibald left him some property in St. Mary's parish, seemed impatient to assume its control. He resented the restrictions that his relatives had placed upon him and lashed out at Grant, their representative.[74] He found him, because he managed so many estates on Jamaica's west side, to be opinionated and difficult. "Mr. Grant . . . feels himself a man of consequence in this side of the Country & has a great deal of the hauteur of a highlander; consequently [he] expects little attentions which a man in a middling sphere would look over."[75]

By using his training and skills to acquire the management of several estates, Francis Grant had become independent. He ran Georgia estate without supervision. His employers on at least seven other estates were far away; though they supervised his actions more closely, the physical distance between them ensured a significant time delay.[76] He had achieved all of the advantages that accompanied owning property, without incurring many of the risks that proprietors had to take. All he needed was to have "his" estates create enough income for him to retire. In the truest sense, Grant had very nearly achieved what his countrymen desired. Though he served at the

Craton and Walvin, *A Jamaican Plantation*, pp. 145–46 for their descriptions and analysis of this problem. A corrupt estate manager and overseer at the Hope Estate in St. Andrew's, Jamaica are revealed in the letters to and from Roger Hope Elletson, 1767–1775, Stowe Collection, volume 14, HL.

[73]Francis Grant to Charles Gordon, 9 October 1789, MS 1160/6/68/1, AUL.

[74]There is a copy of the power of attorney appointing Grant as the Stirling estates' attorney dated 14 May 1790, in Powers 111/77, JA. It is also likely that there was an earlier power of attorney enrolled before 1780.

[75]Archibald Stirling to his father, 5 November 1789, T-SK 11/3/127/1, SRA.

[76]Among the plantations Grant managed were Glasgow estate (John Gordon, Bristol Merchant, owner), Dundee estate (Stothert of Cargen, owner), Baulk (Scrymgeour, owner), Content (owned by James Stirling), Hampden (Stirling owned), Georgia (Charles Gordon, owner), and Friendship (Stirling owned).

pleasure of others, they were far away and dependent upon him for their information. He controlled them rather than the other way around.

As if to prove his ambition and demonstrate his success at his profession to the rest of the island and to Scottish society, Grant wrote Gordon in the autumn of 1791. He offered to buy Georgia from him, despite his own plans to return to Scotland in two or three years' time. Grant even offered British security.[77] By December, when the crop appeared to be very short, he realized how much he would lose and wrote Gordon that "I sincerely hope it [Georgia] is not mine."[78] In February of the next year, he found out that Gordon had declined to sell it to him. Grant was so relieved that he responded to his employer by telling him he would never again contemplate owning a sugar work. The tumultuous winter of 1791–92, when Grant had to wait for mail from Scotland to learn whether or not Gordon accepted his offer (and, thus, whether or not he owned a plantation) can easily be envisioned. He remained unusually lucky in his escape from massive debts and continued to be comfortably settled and, in a very real sense, independent.

No more of Grant's correspondence has been located. When his brother John died in Scotland, Francis returned home to inherit the estate. He lived there until his own death in 1818, at the age of 73. His successful career suggests the manner in which Scots estate managers operated. In general, they had charge of more than one estate. Most had legal experience; they often had been trained as merchants and attorneys. By handling all of the plantation's business and selectively communicating information, they could frequently play the part of independent country gentry. Perhaps most important, if they could keep their own money out of Jamaica property, they could actually achieve what they and their countrymen sought. If, like Gordon, the owner was willing to give his manager authority to act, the role became that much easier. There was, after all, virtually no supervision.

MERCHANT PLANTERS: WELL-CONNECTED "SONS OF FORTUNE"

The Stirling family, from Perthshire in central Scotland, began with more wealth than many others who were bound for colonial sojourns. The family patriarch, James Stirling of Keir (d. 1749), and his wife had, however, contributed twenty-two children to the world. One Perthshire estate, no matter how far it stretched, was not enough to support them all. Several of Stirling's younger sons went abroad to make a fortune; some went to India and others to the West Indies. When the patriarch died, the estate passed from hand to

---

[77] See Grant to Gordon, 2 August 1791, MS 1160/6/73, AUL. That Grant could offer British security indicated that he was removing his earnings from the island as he received them, rather than investing in Jamaican properties.

[78] Grant to Gordon, 6 December 1791, MS 1160/6/77/1-2, AUL.

hand until it finally rested with Archibald, the fourth eldest son, in 1759. Because he had not anticipated succeeding to the lands of Keir and Cadder, he had earlier lived in Jamaica as a merchant and continued to invest his profits in his younger brothers' East Indian ventures. Archibald despised the West Indies; he returned home as quickly as possible after he had made some money in trade. It was this money, coupled with the profits gained from his Indian investments, which supported (or nearly so) his younger brothers' Caribbean adventures.

Robert Stirling, one of the younger brothers, struck out for Jamaica in 1742. Trying to earn enough to elevate himself to the much more prestigious rank of planter, from which, he believed, one could easily retire to Scotland with a guaranteed income, he traded on behalf of a merchant house. He was impatient, however, and despite six years work and savings purchased an estate on credit. His family obliged by providing a source of British security, which was more common in 1748 than 1787 (though it should not be considered usual).

> I am extreamly obliged to him [brother Archibald] for his kind offer of lending me five hundred pounds Sterling which I shall accept of & must say it comes very opportunely at this time as I have lately made a purchase of an Estate [Frontier in St. Mary's parish] here that stands me in very near £8000 Stg so that you may imagine I have occasion for the asistance of all my friends.[79]

Robert believed the estate would generate £2200 currency income that year (approximately £1570 sterling), if the property could make one hundred hogsheads of sugar and between forty and fifty puncheons of rum. If it did, and continued to do so, it would allow him to pay off all of his debts within four or five years and return home to his family to "live off the produce of it."

In 1749, when their father died, Robert wrote Archibald that he would not be able to come home that year as he had originally intended. His problem was money. He needed more in order to create the profitable sugar estate which he envisioned.

> You must have known then that the late purchase I have made & some disappointments we have met with in trade has occasioned me to be in debt to some people that are pressing for their money. . . . [A]dvance me about fifteen hundred pounds which with the five hundred I have already had will be two thousand Pounds Stg. for which I will give you a Mortgage on my Estate here.[80]

---

[79]Robert Stirling to his brother, March 1748, T-SK 11/2/38, SRA.

[80]Robert to Archibald, 1 July 1749, T-SK 11/2/64, SRA. Sheridan describes this very technique; *Sugar and Slavery,* p. 276.

When he consented, Archibald had no way of realizing that he had involved himself and his family in these estates for the next century.

Each year Archibald asked when Robert was coming back and each year he found out that the departure had been delayed for another year because of an inability to extract enough money from the plantation to insure a comfortable Scottish existence. "I cannot put my affairs settled yet in such a manner as I would have them," he pleaded, "& find after a man has been here in Business for some Years it requires a most unspeakable time to wind up his Affairs to a proper Conclusion which I am resolved to do before I quit the Island that I may not be obliged to return again."[81]

By 1753, Frontier managed to produce only eighty-eight hogsheads of sugar and fifty puncheons of rum. While he claimed to clear about £2000 currency, the property's production was still more than twelve hogsheads below desired levels. Robert's debt had not subsided either. Things never got any better for him; still he maintained the posture that he was doing well and would soon be home.[82]

Robert's family grew tired of his broken promises and repeated requests for money. They told him so, which really bothered him. "I have the character at Home," he wrote Archibald, "of not being very moderate in my desires, yet I hope when it pleases God I get there to convince you all that I can Live very happily on a moderate Income."[83] Here was one Scot with a reputation for enjoying luxury who claimed that he had moderate habits. In all likelihood, Stirling was no more a conspicuous consumer than any one else in his position. His sense of guilt, brought on by his family, indicates a desire, common to many Scots, to extract himself from Jamaican society. It indicates as well the problems faced by many sojourners. To be independent at home might entail a cut in the standard of living enjoyed abroad. But to remain in the island would mean giving up the sojourn and becoming an immigrant. The number who chose the latter path, thus admitting that they enjoyed the way that they lived in Jamaica, was surely significant.

For all their complaints about his consumption patterns, Robert's brothers never hesitated to use their financial involvement to insure that he provided proper patronage opportunities. They often sent friends and relations out on fortune-gathering sojourns. The extremely large size of the Stirling family made it imperative that able children go off to learn a useful business and attempt independence. Robert described the route that any who came recommended to him would almost certainly follow, before becoming an overseer.

[81]Robert to Archibald, 12 March 1750, T-SK 11/2/68, SRA.
[82]Robert to Archibald, 30 September 1753, T-SK 11/2/81, SRA.
[83]Robert to Archibald, 12 March 1750, T-SK 11/2/68, SRA.

A Young man . . . must expect to go through a good deal of drudgery work at first. He will be about 2 years or 18 months at least before he can be presumed to be well enough acquainted with the business to take upon him the charge of a Plantation as an Overseer, in which time he lives on the Estate under the Character of Bookkeeper to it, altho that is the least part of business he has to do, which is chiefly to take care of the Stores & receive in & deliver out everything belonging to the Plantation & to attend the Negroes. . . . He has generally about £20 or £25 per Annum wages, besides such fare as the Plantation affords. . . . When he is deemed sufficiently qualified to be an Overseer his friends get him into the first vacant birth of that kind . . . the salary is from £80 to £100, £150, & some £200 per Annum according to the size of the Plantation and the generosity of the Employer.[84]

But patronage, however essential for a big family, did not refill the family coffers. Archibald Stirling grew increasingly impatient at his younger brother's failure to pay back his debts. Money simply had to reverse its flow and return to Britain. To expedite the process, Archibald sent James Stirling, another brother, to Jamaica in 1753, in order to collect some of the family debts while earning a living as a merchant. He failed.

In 1757, Robert and James jointly purchased another plantation, called Hampden in St. James's (later Trelawny) parish. James had obviously forgotten his instructions to get money out of the colony, not put it in. Archibald advanced more money from his pockets, probably on James's advice. And then James decided that he liked neither planting nor Jamaica. He quickly sold his shares to his brother, on condition that he be allowed to buy them back at any time, for a £300 annuity and returned home in 1761.

By 1763, four years after assuming the family title, and still not having been repaid, Archibald completely lost his temper and accused Robert of renouncing his transient status and becoming a stereotypical Jamaican planter:

Yours of January the 14th . . . is the only one you have favour'd me with for now upwards of three Years, and as it is going on to six since you remitted me a farthing, it is not surprizing there should be a coolness betwixt us neither can there be a doubt . . . on which side the blame is chargeable, for how can you imagine I can afford to let such a sum . . . lye dead in your hands. . . . what title have you to expect that I should be obliged . . . to make an annual sacrifice of so much merely to support that idle Vanity you seem to have of having large possessions.[85]

[84]Robert to Archibald, 9 June 1750, T-SK 11/2/69, SRA. Young men sent from Glasgow to the Chesapeake received virtually the same deal fifteen years later. Low wages and exhausting travails were commonplace. Nonetheless, if these wages had been paid in a form that was easily extracted from Jamaica, they would have amounted to tidy sums indeed.

[85]Archibald to Robert, 31 March 1763, T-SK 15/11/1, SRA.

Robert had reason to worry; his brother, his most gentle creditor, was unhappy. If he had been at home, he would have been in deep trouble. But he took comfort for he knew that his other creditors could not easily attack him to recover their debts if he was in Jamaica. As a general rule, legal action was to be avoided for as long as possible. Creditors hoped that by extending the terms of agreement, the debtors would pay within new restrictions. This hope often proved false, wasting time and usually resulting in a lawsuit anyway. If the creditor had brought immediate action, even in Jamaica's overcrowded courts, at least the delay would be the system's fault and the system could ultimately make good on its obligations. Robert again postponed his voyage home, for the last time.

He died in 1764, a financial failure. He owed £92,000. Of course, he was owed £68,000, mostly from his merchant career. His brother James returned to take control of the joint property and settle the family's affairs. James wrote to Archibald, in 1765, that the debts which Robert had left behind were "a prodigious Sum to be sure." Yet he still believed that "there is enough to pay every body if the Creditors will give time which they will be obliged to do."[86] James began to realize that he might be in Jamaica longer than he anticipated and that he might well have to leave before he could finally sort matters out.

Family members in Scotland continued to use James, as they did Robert, to introduce acquaintances to the right people, so that they could get rich quickly. James was not particularly delighted to oblige unless it was on his own terms. With single-minded determination, he wanted to transact business and exit the island. Finding positions for those who came recommended took time away from these aims. No wonder that he sent some "clients" back. "I have been endeavouring to gett Miller a place in town to no purpose & he wont goe to the Country on any Acct," he complained, "where I could have got him a bookkeepers place the first day he landed." He warned his family. "[W]hen you recommend any again ask them if they will go into the Country which if they are willing to do I may be of service to them but not otherways."[87]

James also encountered problems in ridding himself of the estates. He overestimated yields and the estates underproduced; the pattern continued. Revenue was always less than projected and made the property less attractive to purchasers. "I expected to have made at Hampden 250 hhds at least Rum in proportion but we made only 206 & some of that very bad & at Frontier I

[86]James to Archibald, 4 June 1765, T-SK 22/3/5, SRA. The idea of time is fascinating. People would make bonds with enormous penal sums and not pay them off. Delaying tactics were extremely common. Though there were many lawsuits, little seems to have been done to rectify the larger problem of deficit spending. See Sheridan, *Sugar and Slavery*, pp. 274–78.
[87]James to William, 4 June 1764[5?], T-SK 22/3/7, SRA.

expected 130 hhds but I don't think we shall reach 80 and the Quality of the Sugars bad."[88]

James decided he had enough. He thought in 1765 and 1766 about selling everything and immediately leaving the island. There was not, however, enough cash in the country to buy him out without huge losses. The family assets could not be liquidated. This was precisely the situation in which Scottish transients found themselves time and time again.

But neither was James completely honest. The very same day he told Archibald that he could not afford to pay anyone "one shilling," he wrote brother "Willy" with plans to build a new sugar works at Frontier, in order to increase profits. Where James planned to get money for a new works is unknown. Most likely, he reinvested any debts he did collect into the plantation while telling Archibald that they could not be collected. He did not entirely misrepresent affairs to his brother; any payments he received, if they followed the pattern, would have been worth much less in Scotland.

Sometime in 1766, James received an offer for Hampden. He wanted to accept the £42,000 bid but decided to wait until Archibald, as the other executor of Robert's estate, had a chance to respond. Urging Archibald to accept, and reciting in detail the story of the late slave rebellion near the estate, he concluded that "you . . . will see how precarious our lives and fortunes are in this Country and what good reason I have to want to be at home again." The offer for Hampden seemed more appealing because it would have been purchased by a gentleman in London, giving a reasonable settlement, and money in sterling. James hesitated a bit because he thought the estate's value to be closer to £50,000. The buyer thought that price "dear but people who knew the property thought otherwise. However to satisfy the Creditors, secure the payment of your demand in Great Britain & to be an inducement . . . I offerd it for £42,000 which he agreed to & every body thought he had a prodigious Bargain."[89] Before Archibald had a chance to respond to the offer, Robert's creditors refused to accept the payment schedule and forbade the sale of estate. They thought they could get more out of it by continuing to demand the proceeds of the sugar consignments to Britain. The deal was off. James returned home exasperated.

In 1774, Robert Stirling's estate, ten years after his death, now owed between £30,000 and £40,000 sterling, a sizable increase. Even after James's elaborate efforts to eliminate the problem, mounting interest added up. Archibald grew angry with the state of things and wrote to his cousin, Patrick, who was now managing the estates. "I am most heartily tir'd of it and with too good reason, for within these six years past you have repeatedly

[88]James to Archibald, 27 August 1765, T-SK 22/3/9, SRA.
[89]James to Archibald, 8 July 1766, T-SK 22/3/21, SRA.

assur'd me (& certainly there could be no better authority) that against Crop 1772 every farthing of Robert's debts would be paid & a free property left to the heir," he grumbled. "Now crop 1773 is come to hand yet that property is still indebted 'twixt 30, and 40,000£ Sterling," he roared with absolutely no patience. "Your seasons I observe are promising, but I suppose some devilry or other will happen to blast your hopes as usual."[90] While Archibald increasingly came to loathe sugar estates and the mentality required to make them profitable, the estates themselves continued to be the prizes to which most of the island's adventurers aspired. Having a profession or trade which earned a profit was not enough; wealth, success, and independence were measured in land and slaves. Archibald warned Patrick:

> Sugar Estates, tho' under the best management, are so little to be depended upon that no person in my situation ought to risque his money in such undertakings, least by biting at the shadow he shou'd chance let go the substance.[91]

Not many Scots knew they were biting at shadows and letting go of substance when they switched from trade or profession to planter. Many gave up lucrative businesses which, with hard work, provided a steady income. Francis Grant came very near to making this mistake and was delighted to learn that his offer had been rejected. But eighteenth-century British and Scottish culture defined the ideal life as one of leisure, with land to support a family's needs. Because of the shortage of land in Scotland, many Scots sought the quickest way to acquire it. Education and a professional career simply became the means to reach the conclusion. In the end, the difficulties encountered could make sojourners into permanent emigrants.

Archibald Stirling displayed his intense hatred for the way he believed sugar planters to behave. "Except the Dons in Leaden Hall Street," he scrawled, "I don't think there is such a set of Ideall folles under the Sun as Sugar Planters. They are in a constant State of Delusion, by which means they not only deceive themselves, but mislead without any intentions their Constituents at home, which I dare say is often of bad consequence."[92] But he did nothing to prevent his relatives from striving to earn their independence in the colony. Even if he did not like involving his money in a plantation, he did realize that prospects for those without sizable estates in late eighteenth-century Scotland were bleak indeed. The colonies provided at

---

[90]Archibald to Patrick Stirling, 8 April 1774, T-SK 15/11/107, SRA.
[91]Archibald to Patrick Stirling, 19 October 1772, T-SK 15/11/66, SRA.
[92]Archibald Stirling to William Innes, 29 September 1773, T-SK 15/11/87, SRA. Leaden Hall Street, London, is where many West (and East) Indian merchant firms had their offices.

least an opportunity to do well. For all his raving to the contrary, these chances mattered a great deal.

> I am quite averse to involving my patrimonial Estate any deeper in quest of precarious riches in a distant Country where appearances are so exceedingly deceitful or rather bewitching that the best inform'd of you all are not proof against the infatuation.[93]

Impatient with others' feeble efforts, Archibald assumed Robert's debts as his own in 1777. He believed that he could make the estates profitable without leaving home simply by using his relatives already in the island as his servants. He wrote to his nephew, the manager for Frontier estate. "As to the Hampden consignments I will come under no obligation, I look upon that as my own property. The Frontier that of the Creditors."[94] He managed through juggling books, making deals, and paying off creditors—principal without interest—to clear most of the estates' debt.[95]

Archibald died on 21 November 1783. He had tried to keep his Jamaican and Scottish properties separate from each other. He remained adamant that the Scottish estate and its revenues should not support the Jamaican properties. His British property was worth a substantial £107,131.18.1 against debts of nearly £33,000 in 1780; it was no wonder that he wanted to preserve such a large sum from the pitfalls of the Jamaican economy. The Court of Session, Scotland's highest court, ultimately ruled that it was all his property, and should be considered one estate.[96]

Because Archibald had no children of his own, he named his three closest relatives as his trustees: his brother William, his cousin John (of Kippendavie, whose family also had Jamaican property), and his cousin David Erskine. William's eldest son James received Keir and Cadder (the Scottish lands) which, by 1793, had been valued at £135,473.4.8 less debts of only £4500. After ninety-nine years, or as long as the trustees decided, Hampden was to pass to William's second son, John, and his descendants. If John had no heirs, then they would pass to the other sons and heirs in descending order of their birth.[97] This was a rather substantial legacy; in 1780, Stirling had Hampden valued at around £35,000 with 300 slaves, after its debts were

[93]Archibald Stirling to Patrick Stirling, 16 July 1774, T-SK 15/11/f.114, SRA.

[94]Archibald to John Stirling, 21 April 1777, T-SK 15/12/17, SRA.

[95]By this point, the interest exceeded the principal and Stirling agreed to pay off the original sum borrowed. Creditors would readily have accepted this solution, especially if the debt was so overdue and the alternative was legal action with only the hope of payment as the outcome. Cash in hand was always preferred to court orders and costs.

[96]See Copy of the Court of Session decision, 1787, T-SK 15/48/4, SRA.

[97]See the Last Will of Archibald Stirling, 25 August 1783, T-SK 15/23, SRA.

paid. Less hefty, though with potential, Frontier estate passed to Archibald, William's third son. In 1780, after all its debts were subtracted, it was only worth £5000, even with two hundred slaves living on the property. Archibald Stirling had made Hampden profitable, at least on paper, and the loss on Frontier, still substantial, was not nearly so great as when he assumed control of the property.

The next generation was eager to see its new possessions. Archibald's nephews had all inherited his penchant for improvement; they wanted to increase their wealth and protect their social standing. The younger Archibald, who had been given Frontier estate, arrived in April 1789 to learn how to be a Jamaican planter and then take over his property. Francis Grant, Hampden's manager, introduced him to the Scottish community in the island's west end. Young Archibald received a warm welcome everywhere he went. When Grant procured him a position at Glasgow estate, he seemed quite happy, despite a struggle with mosquitoes, to settle in and learn his business.

Meanwhile, his older brother John, who had been given Hampden, arrived in Kingston on 13 September 1789. John and Archibald were not reunited until 14 October, when John went to visit his younger brother in the west end. Francis Grant supervised both lads and their training. The Stirling trustees in Scotland continued to dictate policy for their estates, managers, and wards; Grant was careful to follow their instructions. He did, however, intercede when one or another of the boys took offense at some of the restrictions placed upon them.

Good news from the two lads already in the Caribbean encouraged the family to send young Robert out in 1791, to follow in his brothers' footsteps. Grant soon procured him a position at Content estate in St. Ann's. Archibald left Glasgow estate that year and moved to Friendship, another of the Grant-managed properties. John, meanwhile, assumed quasi-control of his inheritance and continued to scheme to improve his estates. He sounded remarkably like every other ambitious Scot of the past five decades, including his uncles. He wrote the trustees for permission to purchase land.

> The value of lands has risen amazingly since your Mr. J.S. left the country & they are becoming more valuable every day. . . . It was never my intention to purchase more than 200 to 250 acres, but then they cannot be procured . . . at less than £7 Curry if even at that.[98]

His request was denied. Given that Hampden's crop was only reckoned at 215 to 220 hogsheads of sugar for 400 slaves, family reticence to invest more

---

[98]John to John William Stirling, 16 April 1791, T-SK 11/3/147, SRA.

money in a property with such a checkered past is easily understood.[99] The struggle had moved on into the next generation. As soon as the new arrival saw the property, visions of expansion consumed any self-restraint. Independence, wealth, and status were measured in property. These Scots failed to see that the property had to be in Britain. The Stirling family's younger brothers of fortune in 1750 and 1790 looked remarkably alike. So they would look until well into the next century.

[99]Even so, the plantation had been markedly built up since 1780 when it had only 300 slaves. This growth would seem to fit with the expansion of the Jamaican economy in the years after the American Revolution.

3

TOBACCO TRANSIENTS: SCOTS IN THE CHESAPEAKE

The Chesapeake region early developed an economy based upon the production of a staple crop. As in Jamaica, the Europeans cultivated and settled only a small portion of Virginia's and Maryland's available land; all three colonies had substantial frontiers. Also like Jamaica, this pair of mainland colonies underwent a significant period of growth and development after 1740. In both cases, Scottish sojourners actively contributed to and benefited from this expansion. But here the similarities stop.

The staple crops were tobacco on the mainland and sugar in the island. Jamaica's population achieved a black majority as early as 1664. But even after the American Revolution, the Chesapeake still had only a few pockets where the number of blacks exceeded the number of whites.[1] By the beginning of the eighteenth century, Chesapeake-born white men and women outnumbered immigrants to the colonies. The natural rate of increase among creole families continued to accelerate.[2] This expanding population, with its established ties to Virginia and Maryland, certainly contributed to the development of social and cultural institutions such as churches and schools which Jamaica almost completely lacked.

Historians have repeatedly remarked that the island colony had virtually no schools until late in the eighteenth century. Maintaining their ties to the

---

[1]Orlando Patterson in *Slavery and Social Death* (Cambridge, Mass., 1982) believes the number of blacks on the island in 1658 to have been 1400 (against 4500 whites). By 1664, 8000 blacks lived in Jamaica along with 6000 whites (p. 477). Richard Sheridan (*Sugary and Slavery*, p. 211) noted that the census of 1673 returned 7,768 whites and 9,504 blacks. For the Chesapeake, see Allan Kulikoff, *Tobacco and Slaves* (Chapel Hill, N.C., 1986), pp. 332, 340. For the actual numbers of the Chesapeake populations see U.S. Bureau of the Census, *Historical Statistics of the United States, Colonial Times to 1957* (Washington, 1960), p. 756.

[2]See Kulikoff, *Tobacco and Slaves*, pp. 42–43.

metropolis, parents—who viewed themselves as sojourners—sent their white offspring to be educated in Britain. Virginia and Maryland began the same way. Literacy remained low there until at least the middle of the eighteenth century. In 1724, only one school teacher could be found for every one hundred white families. But as the century progressed, and the population grew, basic education became more widespread. Schools, though they were often little more than vocational workshops, provided at least rudimentary instruction for the free white population.[3]

In the Chesapeake, established Anglican churches were intended to sit at the center of each community. The law required regular monthly attendance, though it was not often enforced. Participation in all organized religion, particularly the established church, declined through much of the century, even among members of the gentry where its support was strongest. Dissenting sects increasingly appeared after 1750. Though they often succeeded in persuading many people to join them, churchgoers still remained in the minority. But even this much could not be said of Jamaica. Though the parish was the colony's official governing unit, the island sorely lacked churches. Religious participation in any form was minimal. Even the Anglican clergy were absentees![4]

Though the Chesapeake's white population had long been naturally reproducing itself by 1740, migration to the colonies from abroad also contributed to regional population growth. Such immigrants surely comprised a significant portion of the additional 46,719 white Marylanders and 138,991 white Virginians who appeared in the colonies' populations between 1740 and 1770.[5] They gave up whatever they had in the old world (or in other colonies) in the belief that they could achieve something better in Virginia and Maryland.

A number of Scots went to these mainland societies between 1740 and 1776. But many of them do not really qualify as immigrants. Like their countrymen in Jamaica, they wanted to return home. They too believed that they could endure the new world only for as long as it took them to acquire

[3]For Jamaica, see Ragatz, *Fall of the Planter Class*, p. 21, and Brathwaite, *Creole Society*, pp. 268–70. For the Chesapeake, see Kulikoff, *Tobacco and Slaves*, pp. 195–98 and Rhys Isaac, *The Transformation of Virginia* (Chapel Hill, N.C., 1983).

[4]For the Chesapeake, a good discussion of religious life can be found in Kulikoff, *Tobacco and Slaves*, pp. 232–40. For Jamaica, see Ragatz, *Fall of the Planter Class*, p. 19 and Patterson, *Sociology of Slavery*, p. 40. Edward Brathwaite (pp. 23–25) comments upon both the Church of England's official role in the island and the white population's general lack of religion. During the period of his study (1770–1820), there was "something like one Church of England clergyman per 1,500 white inhabitants" (p. 25).

[5]For a description of Germans settling in the frontiers of western Maryland, see Aubrey Land, *Colonial Maryland* (Millwood, N.Y., 1981), pp. 199–204. One wave of immigrants came from Britain in 1773–1776. Bernard Bailyn in *Voyagers* identifies them, pp. 204–39, 266. The statistics come from *Historical Statistics*, p. 756 (and my calculations upon them).

the independence they sought. By 1740, the transatlantic tobacco economy had begun to recover from the frequent slumps and depressions it suffered during the eighteenth century's first decades.[6] Plentiful and cheap land made tobacco a growth industry.

Scottish sojourners seized the opportunity. Until the 1740s, most tobacco planters sold their crop under the consignment system. English merchants sent factors or "supercargoes" to the Chesapeake with goods that the planters had requested. After delivering their wares, the factors and supercargoes collected tobacco and returned with it to London or Bristol in order to sell it. Once a buyer for the crop had been found, the merchant house deducted shipping, freight, insurance costs, and commission (as well as the cost of any goods received) from the proceeds. If any money remained, the planter received a credit in the merchant's account book. The costs of shipping and goods, however, frequently exceeded the price that the tobacco fetched at market. In this case, the firm debited the planter's account for the difference. This process repeated itself each year. Under this system, the tobacco producer, rather than the merchant or the purchaser, assumed the costs of getting the tobacco from the colonies to market.[7]

Such conditions really suited only one group: the English merchants. The merchants made a profit regardless of either the shipping costs or the crop's selling price. The larger, more established tidewater tobacco planters could much more easily afford to shoulder the consignment costs since they had a larger margin of disposable income. Because they did not live as close to the edge as many of the region's smaller planters, they could better withstand fluctuations in the tobacco reexport market, although they did not like this system. Many of them suspected—as did smaller planters—that the merchants with whom they dealt at London were not completely honest and that the price of the goods they received had been inflated and the prices they finally got for their crops were too low.[8]

Scottish merchants, by contrast, had financed limited trading missions to the Chesapeake since 1707. They bought tobacco outright and resold it on

[6]Paul Clemens, in *The Atlantic Economy and Colonial Maryland's Eastern Shore: From Tobacco to Grain* (Ithaca, N.Y., 1980) describes the cyclical nature of the tobacco economy in Maryland's Eastern Shore, and Kulikoff, *Tobacco and Slaves*, pp. 78–117, provides a good general description of the economic activity during the period. He argues that the prolonged depression of the 1720s and 1730s increased movement to the frontier and increased agricultural diversification, at least in the interim.

[7]This system also operated in Jamaica's sugar economy. See Sheridan, *Sugar and Slavery*, pp. 269–80.

[8]There is a substantial literature on this topic, as well as on the innovations the Scots introduced. See, for example, J. H. Soltow, "Scottish Traders," p. 84. Jacob Price has, by far, contributed the most to our understanding of this system. See his *France and the Chesapeake*, v. 1, pp. 658–71 and "The Rise of Glasgow in the Chesapeake Tobacco Trade, 1707–1775," pp. 193–94.

European markets. At first, each venture, run by a consortium of local merchants, hired a supercargo to go to the Chesapeake and exchange goods directly for tobacco.[9] He would then return to Scotland with the tobacco and, after spending some time at home, go back to the colonies for the next trading trip. Under this system, the Scottish merchants assumed all risks. The planters received a fixed price for their crop (payable in goods); they did not worry about shipping or commission charges. But because the time between voyages varied, the planters could not count on selling their crops to the Scots.

This direct trade system particularly suited changing Chesapeake society. After 1720, increasing population forced both settlement and cultivation to move inland into the piedmont, away from the crowded tidewater areas. Planters in newer areas of settlement still grew tobacco. But their plantations were smaller and they needed to produce enough other crops to feed their families, so they each produced less tobacco. The thought of having to pay increased shipping costs, simply because they lived farther from the point of collection, irritated them. Nor could they easily afford to be put in a situation where they did not know how much they would receive for their crops until several months after they consigned it. By paying a set price for tobacco, assuming transportation risks, and later introducing permanent stores (which could offer credit from one year to the next) in new settlement areas, the Scots successfully cornered a sizable part of the growing tobacco market.[10]

Scottish merchants had two important natural advantages over their English competitors that allowed them to operate such a system profitably. Geography played a crucial role. The route between the Chesapeake and the west of Scotland, passing north of Ireland, often took two weeks less than from London (where cross-channel winds frequently prevented ships from sailing). The shorter time required to cross the Atlantic guaranteed that more voyages could be completed, and thus more tobacco collected, in a fixed period of time. More significantly, the developing economy in Scotland's western lowlands ensured low operating costs. Wages remained lower than in other parts of Britain and, just as important, labor was plentiful. The Glaswegians could offer higher prices to planters than any of their English competitors.[11]

[9]This system was also in limited use by merchants in some of the English outports. See Price, *France and the Chesapeake*, v. 1, p. 662; Soltow, p. 85. One supercargo who went on several of these ventures is discussed in Edith E. B. Thomson, "A Scottish Merchant in Falmouth," *Virginia History Magazine* 39 (1931): 108–17, 230–38.

[10]See Price, *France and the Chesapeake*, v. 1, pp. 658–71, and Devine, *Tobacco Lords*, p. 57.

[11]See Price, "The Rise of Glasgow," pp. 187–88, and Devine, *Tobacco Lords*, p. 58. Devine also explains the ways an underdeveloped country was able to provide the capital for such trade. In effect, it amounted to a shrewd and well-timed use of credit (pp. 89–99).

Supercargoes crossed the Atlantic in ships filled with goods for the colonial residents. They served as the merchants' representatives by collecting tobacco in exchange for manufactured goods. Their employers did not consider it essential for them to remain in the Chesapeake when not purchasing tobacco: therefore many returned to Scotland after each ship was loaded. In an attempt to secure more business, and easier access to their customers, during the 1740s, some of the merchant groups paid their supercargoes to stay in the colonies and open permanent stores. Most of these were in the piedmont, generally along the principal rivers. This arrangement gave the Scottish firms easy access both to the spreading colonial population and to the natural shipping routes.

The first strand of resident Scottish factors went along with this plan principally because they saw in it a way to earn money in a hurry. As remuneration, they generally earned a commission of five percent of the total value of the tobacco they received and ten percent of the total value of the goods they sold to planters. Being paid in such a fashion encouraged them to be industrious by developing additional business when they were not busy collecting tobacco; attracting more customers would substantially contribute to increasing their personal fortunes. During the 1740s and 1750s, many people who would, within a decade, become "tobacco lords" spent time in the colonies acting in this capacity. They effectively utilized the direct purchase method. When they could, many of them traded on their own accounts.

Family members sent them goods which they were then able to sell, off of their employers' books. It seems likely that they amassed considerable wealth as a result of these enterprises. Though virtually none of the private correspondence from their colonial sojourns has survived, the final results of their efforts remain clear. The Scottish share of the British tobacco trade doubled from 10 percent to 20 percent between 1738 and 1744 and reached 30 percent in 1758. In that year, the Glasgow trade passed both London and the English outports to become the single most important market for tobacco.[12]

Just as the Scottish ventures proved successful at procuring business for Glasgow firms by offering high prices, ready goods on easy credit terms, and freedom from the perils of consignment, they benefited the factors in the colonies. These men accrued considerable individual wealth and then began

[12]See Soltow, "Scottish Traders," p. 85, and Price, "The Rise of Glasgow," p. 197, for a description of the establishment of permanent stores in the Chesapeake and their locations. Soltow also describes the experiences of one of the earlier factors who traded to the West Indies on his own account. Devine, *Tobacco Lords*, p. 9, remarks that all of the notable figures in the post-1760 trade had spent some time in Maryland or Virginia as supercargoes or factors. Unfortunately, Devine has been unable to document what portion or amount of the tobacco lords' wealth was earned in the Chesapeake. Price, "The Rise of Glasgow," has provided the figures for Glasgow's share of the market (p. 180).

to return home. And, motivated by their own success, they plowed a significant portion of their individual profits back into the tobacco trade. They knew firsthand that the Chesapeake frontier extended even farther west of their stores. They had witnessed, if not encouraged (by the prices they paid), a continuing increase in tobacco cultivation.[13] As a result, the pronounced Scottish presence as traders became institutionalized by 1760.[14]

A second wave of Scottish sojourners, lasting from 1760 until the American Revolution, now flocked to the Chesapeake. They sought to emulate the success of their employers who had been to the colonies earlier. Ambitious young men from the west of Scotland perceived that their opportunities were better in the Chesapeake than at home. Sharing the same goals as both their predecessors in Maryland and Virginia and their contemporaries en route to Jamaica, most wanted only to improve their position at home, not give it up for something else.

The second group of transients did not meet with as much success as their predecessors had. Despite the booming tobacco economy and the expanding Scottish share of the market—it had increased to over 50 percent of British imports between 1768 and 1771—those who labored to collect the crop in the colonies did not usually get to share the profits. Like many who achieve power and wealth, the former factors—the tobacco lords—had consolidated their positions of control. In 1728, ninety-one people or firms entered tobacco at Port Glasgow or Greenock. By 1773, with the total value of commerce nine or ten times greater than in 1728, only thirty-eight firms entered tobacco. And many of these firms were simply assorted permutations of an even smaller number of people. Though these merchants had been paid with commission to encourage their entrepreneurial spirit, they paid poor salaries to their employees. (Still, they were generally better than what was on offer at home.) While the tobacco lords had been allowed to carry on their own trades in the 1740s and 50s, their employees faced mounting restrictions on such endeavors. All of these changes combined effectively to decrease the ability of individuals to satisfy their ambitions through working in the Chesapeake.

This second wave of sojourners faced two other problems, both of which can be attributed to their predecessors' success. First, the Scots so dominated the expanding tobacco market that hostility and resentment were easily

[13]Here, Jacob Price's *France and the Chesapeake* relates how the French market, which purchased much of its tobacco from Glasgow, expanded, also driving up prices. Additional description of the resurgence of tobacco in the two decades before the American revolution can be found in Kulikoff, *Tobacco and Slaves*, pp. 141–57. Paul Clemens, *From Tobacco to Grain*, notes that while both tobacco prices and production rose, production per capita decreased from 186 pounds in 1712 to 155 pounds in 1773 (pp. 111–19).
[14]See Price, "The Rise of Glasgow," p. 191, and Devine, *Tobacco Lords*, p. 72.

directed against them, when problems hit the internal British credit market in the early 1770s and they believed it necessary to begin calling in planter debts. As contemporary Jamaican observers Edward Long and Lady Nugent remarked approvingly on the Scots' industry and success, contemporary observers in Virginia and Maryland did just the opposite. Landon Carter commented that an editor whom he did not like was "a Scotchman and will be a villain." Scots were not only identifiable by their accents; they were merchants and factors, associated with plunging planters into debt and trying to accrue fortunes at every one else's expense.[15]

The second, and related, problem was that their employers did not appear to appreciate the changes in the region's economy. Increasingly diversifying after 1760, it moved away from tobacco and toward grain.[16] In 1740, Scottish traders had been wonderfully adept at capitalizing on the economic growth in the region; by 1770, they failed to change with it. They had become so successful at trading tobacco that they neglected everything else.

Scottish Customs Records for 1774–75 reveal that Scots imported only £19.12 worth of flour from Maryland (less than one percent of imports totaling £84,234.10.10) and only £2832.1.3 worth of grain from Virginia (amounting to 0.83 percent on a total of £341,407.6.6). The Virginia Shipping Returns, which recorded where products loaded on a ship actually went, are irregular after 1740 and end in 1770, leaving it extremely difficult to make a more detailed inference about the course of Scottish trade until the Revolution. Scotland's Exchequer Records, however, are complete and list the contents of each ship clearing the country's ports. Surveys of the years between 1770 and 1775 reveal that merchants imported nothing but tobacco (on the order of 97 percent), and some wooden products such as staves, hoops, and masts, from the Chesapeake.[17]

Chesapeake grain exports, which were increasingly important to the colonial economies during this period, went to the Caribbean or to London, and from there to southern Europe. Perhaps because both Scotland and its chief reexport market, northern Europe, produced enough of their own grain to

[15]Jack P. Greene, ed., *The Diary of Colonel Landon Carter of Sabine Hall, 1752–1775* (Charlottesville, Va., 1965), 15 April 1776, p. 1018. There is absolutely no indication that remarks of this sort circulated in Jamaica. Probably Carter's perception of Scots came close to matching the way many people who were indebted to them felt. The Scots were easily made scapegoats.

[16]Thomas Preisser's dissertation, "Eighteenth-Century Alexandria, Virginia, before the Revolution, 1749–1776" (William and Mary, 1977), provides a useful discussion of the shift away from tobacco and toward grain. Paul Clemens, *From Tobacco to Grain*, has a good chapter, entitled "Agricultural Diversification," on the reasons for the gradual deemphasis of tobacco, and why grain replaced it. Also see Kulikoff, *Tobacco and Slaves*, pp. 120–21.

[17]See "Scotch Importation of Foreign Goods & Merchandize" RH 2/4/12, SRO. (Photocopy of Customs 14, Volume 1B at the PRO, Kew). Also see the Virginia Shipping Returns (CO 5/1445–1450) at the PRO, Kew, and Scottish Exchequer records (E 504/15) for Greenock and (E 504/28) for Port Glasgow, both at the SRO.

satisfy local needs, the Scots stayed away from it. Whether this was the case, or whether something else accounted for the lack of interest, those who actually worked in the colonies found their hands tied by the tobacco only policy. Just as the Scots earlier acquired the tobacco trade, other merchants based in Philadelphia and Baltimore now made the switch from tobacco to grain.[18] To add insult to injury, "foreign" merchants were kicked out of the Chesapeake with the outbreak of hostilities between British and colonial forces. The American Revolution effectively ended the Scots tobacco trade and the period of long sojourns in the region.

THE CALEDONIAN PRESENCE

As in Jamaica, the number of sojourners identified by the sample of correspondence is relatively low. And, once again, the small size of the group belies its significance. Scottish merchants in the Chesapeake were part of an extremely important transatlantic venture. Without their presence, the tobacco trade between Britain and the colonies would have looked tremendously different. Understanding their experiences and motivations helps us to understand better the nature of the Atlantic world in the eighteenth century.

The 139 Scots in the correspondence sample presented in Chapter 1 came from the same places in Scotland. More than 80 percent of this sample grew up in either Glasgow or the surrounding western regions. They were also trained to do the same thing. Most of the group partook of Glasgow's commercial relationship with Maryland and Virginia.

The absence of a more diverse group of sojourning Scottish professionals in Virginia and Maryland can be explained simply by realizing that greater opportunities to earn a quick fortune existed elsewhere. For example, Jamaica and South Carolina were far less healthy (especially for Europeans) and more labor intensive (for slaves) than the Chesapeake. Medical services would surely have been much more in demand, and thus more profitable there. In all of the mainland colonies, the importance of education increased during the eighteenth century. More trained people were educated at home. Colonists on the mainland could thus fill many of the roles that the Scots occupied in Jamaica. Finally, many Scots in Jamaica capitalized on the high rate of absenteeism by becoming attorneys. In the Chesapeake, certainly the

[18]See David Klingaman, "The Significance of Grain in the Development of the Tobacco Colonies," *Journal of Economic History* 29 (1968): 268–78, and Paul Clemens, *From Tobacco to Grain*, esp. pp. 176–201. Clemens has noted that Spiers, French, and Co., a Glasgow tobacco house, opened a direct grain trade between Maryland's Eastern Shore and Southern Europe, which would explain their absence from Scottish records. I have been unable to find any indication that other firms did the same.

larger planters always lived in the colony. They developed and participated in political institutions in Virginia and Maryland, not Westminster. This difference in focus effectively limited opportunities in that particular category.[19]

THE CAREERS

The first generation of Scottish merchants left very few usable records. As a result, we know far more about the concentrated Scottish involvement in the Chesapeake from around 1760 until the Revolution. During the War for Independence many records were destroyed, further hampering efforts to reconstruct individual lives over a longer time period. For sojourners, the conflict between Britain and America proves to be the pivotal event in their collective careers.[20]

THE MERCHANT ASSISTANT

During the period between 1760 and 1776, Scots and tobacco became inextricably linked, at least in the public mind. When Robert Carter's tutor, New Jersey-born Philip Fithian, observed in 1774 that "all the Merchants & Shopkeepers . . . through the Province are young Scotch-Men" he was not wildly exaggerating.[21]

According to J. H. Soltow, "Legend held that the road to wealth and success in business began with employment as a storekeeper for a tobacco firm."[22] With that hope, Alexander Wilson went to Alexandria, Virginia, in 1768. The son of Glasgow University's astronomy professor, he had appren-

---

[19]The differences could also be the result of a bias in the sources. Certainly, family and business papers in Scottish archives are less likely to include the records of permanent immigrants to the American colonies than those in American record offices. It is, therefore, worth noting that two other scholars—both of whom have worked with Scottish and Chesapeake archives—arrived at similar conclusions. William Brock in *Scotus Americanus* remarked, "Apart from the Highland migration, Scottish movement was likely to follow the channels of trade" (p. 170). Charles Haws, in the conclusion to *Scots in the Old Dominion, 1685–1800* (Edinburgh, 1980), reckoned that "perhaps the development of this [tobacco] trade . . . was the greatest overall contribution that the Scots made to Virginia. It was certainly the area where the greatest number of known Scots were discovered" (p. 109). Haws goes on to observe that Scottish involvement, in medicine and education, was significant, though more for quality than quantity.

[20]Thomas Devine's *Tobacco Lords* suggests a steady increase of trade from 1740 until the Revolution. The late 1760s and early 1770s saw the entrenchment of the larger Glasgow companies in their final forms. See chapter 5(a), pp. 72–81. For the actual trade statistics see Price, "New Time Series for Scotland's and Britain's trade with the Thirteen Colonies and States, 1740–1791," pp. 307–25.

[21]H. D. Farish, ed., *The Journal and Letters of Philip Vickers Fithian, 1773–1774* (Williamsburg, Va., 1957), p. 29.

[22]Soltow, "Scottish Traders," p. 87.

ticed himself to Glassford and Henderson, a large Glasgow-based tobacco concern then operating in the colony.[23] After a six-week Atlantic passage and a brief tour of both the Potomac's shores, he settled in to learn his business. Writing his parents in April 1769, he described the duties that people in his position were expected to perform. "When a new Asistant comes to a store, " he explained, "his business is to sweep the store out every Morning, see that all the goods are in their proper places, the oldest assistants business, is to see that the Books are carefully posted up every Night, and in the daytime, all 3, 2, or 1 just according to the number that there is in the Store, waiting upon the planters."[24] Wilson's experience was fairly typical. During the months when tobacco was actively being purchased, he claimed to work in the store from sunrise to sunset. He would not have been well paid for his travails. Wages began at around ten pounds sterling per annum, increasing by only five pounds per year.[25] The immediate ambition of these men, which few ever attained, was management of their own store and a successful private business on the side. The final measure of success, which even fewer attained, was a comfortable independence in Scotland.

Wilson is important to scholars because his correspondence with several of his friends in the colonies, all of whom came from near Glasgow, has survived. Glaswegians transplanted to the Chesapeake encouraged their colleagues at home to join them. Sandy Miller, one of Wilson's few "mates" still left in Glasgow, wrote at the end of 1769 and indicated his determination to take up residence on the Atlantic's western side. "I little thought . . . when I parted with you last to have the pleasure of following you so soon," he reflected, "you must know that on account of a great number of my comrades having gone abroad (none of whom I so much regretted as you[)] I grew tired with Glasgow and resolved to go to Virginia . . . to be in the same

[23]Glassford and Henderson figure prominently in Devine, *Tobacco Lords*, and Jacob Price, *Capital and Credit*, esp. pp. 28–29. It was one of the largest firms in northern Virginia and Maryland. A prodigious sample of the company's books can be found in the Manuscript Department, Library of Congress.

[24]Alexander Wilson to his parents, 7 April 1769, Letterbook, p. 4, TD 1/1070, SRA.

[25]James McLeod earned fifteen pounds per annum in 1773 at Osborne's (James McLeod to Donald McLeod, 15 September 1773, p. 3, McLeod of Geanies papers, MS 19297, NLS). His brother William, who was apprenticed to Spiers and Company, only earned five pounds after two years of service (William McLeod to his father, 1 June 1772, McLeod of Geanies Papers, MS 19297, NLS). Thomas Devine considers the wages of storekeepers, though not of apprentices, to have been very good by eighteenth-century Scottish standards (*Tobacco Lords*, p. 84). The storekeepers sat at the top of their pay scale; most people in the tobacco business earned considerably less, and many of them could not collect their salaries. In 1755, James Robb wrote his employer Patrick Mitchell that he had not received his first or second year's wages. Mitchell responded that he would allow him five pounds for the first year, ten for the second, and fifteen for the third. (See James Robb to Patrick Mitchell, 10 November 1755, and the reply, 29 October 1756, Mitchels, Johnston & Co Papers, T-MJ 422/6, SRA.)

employ with you."[26] Members of Glasgow's upwardly mobile classes encouraged their sons to cross the sea as part of a continuing educational process in which they had a chance to improve their fortunes. Like Sandy Miller, they were aware of limited opportunities at home and saw that a number of their colleagues had already left for the Chesapeake. Most of Wilson's compatriots thus arrived at the same conclusion as William Steuart who, in 1771, wrote his cousin Charles that "I am a Convert to the Scots maxim of seeking, as the last resort, in a more distant region or scene of business that fortune which shall be denied me at home."[27]

The opulent lifestyles of the merchants who lived in Glasgow provided visible reinforcement of this maxim. They had, after all, achieved their wealth in the Chesapeake. Alexander Wilson had a very short American career; it was unhappily curtailed by recurring kidney stones. He returned to Scotland in 1771 after "2 years 6 months and 22 days." Though he spent only a limited time in the colonies, Wilson's later letters reveal a good deal about the way in which he spent it and the ways which his apprentice friends in Alexandria continued to prosecute their business. Like many eighteenth-century men, he was determined to enjoy himself. "Don't forget the Girls," he wrote Sandy Miller,

> Give me a particular account of them. Pray have you as many fine ones and as many daft hickups with them as you used to have in Maryland. For my part, I can truely say that I never saw, nor don't suppose I shall ever see again, such merry and such agreeable times as I did the little while I staid in Virginia.[28]

Despite Wilson's professions to his parents that he worked every day but Sunday and barely went out, he appears to have regularly gotten around Alexandria society. While he blamed his illness on too much physical exertion and told his parents that it resulted from heavy lifting, he addressed the reader of his letterbook, admitting that his strains came from skating on the Potomac and dancing, "which I allways faithfully attended."[29] He always regretted leaving the American girls with whom he could "do anything you have a mind" for the "dull doings indeed" of his countrywomen.[30] Professions of apprentices working from sunrise to sunset must, as a result, be questioned. Young and certainly active, Alexander Wilson returned home without acquiring the fortune he had sought.

[26]Sandy Miller quoted in Alexander Wilson to his parents, 17 December 1769, Letterbook, f. 14, SRA.
[27]William Steuart to Charles Steuart, 13 July 1771, Steuart Papers, MS 5040, p. 129, NLS.
[28]Wilson to Sandy Miller, 25 November 1775, TD 1/1070, SRA.
[29]Wilson letterbook, f. 15, TD 1/1070, SRA.
[30]See Alexander Wilson to Sandy Miller, 29 July 1771 and 25 November 1775, TD 1/1070, SRA.

Not surprisingly, none of Wilson's friends achieved their ambitions in the Chesapeake either. One completed his apprenticeship and then went to Jamaica. He decided that he could achieve independence faster in the Caribbean. Another Alexandria compatriot crossed the Potomac to work in Maryland, where he died in 1773, after struggling to succeed on his own. A third left Alexandria after his term expired and moved to Osborne's, another tobacco intake center (along the James below Richmond), before he died in 1775. Robert Donaldson, Wilson's closest friend at Alexandria, experienced an intense frustration with business as the Revolution drew nearer. He wrote Wilson that he had "no Friends—no money—in such an emergency one must put up with many things they otherwise would not. However, I'm determined to do something for myself soon."[31] He returned to Glasgow during the early part of the war.

Before he left the colonies, Donaldson encountered considerable anti-Scottish, anti-merchant feeling. Writing to Wilson in 1774, he commented on the decline of business and the ascent of troubles. "We Scotchmen have hardly anything to say now. A multitude of Irishmen that lately arrived here from I believe every corner of the Globe have totally eclipsed us."[32] Though Alexandria's business increased, the Scots' share of it did not. No doubt this failure, in part, was caused by their reluctance to move outside of tobacco. As early as 1769, Alexandria had become an important shipping point for grain. When Wilson arrived, he observed seven merchant stores, only four of which purchased tobacco. The others bought grain. But his countrymen refused to purchase anything but tobacco in significant quantities.[33] If the Scots in the colony began to feel their own decline, the English and American residents were eager to accelerate this process. Promoting ethnic rivalries could only benefit the dominant population by removing those to whom they were indebted, they believed.

O. Poor Paddy a while ago at the celebration of his anniversary was in the morning found hanging in the Stocks, with his coat button'd behind and a String of potatoes round his neck by way of beads. A thousand to one but St. Andrew suffers some indignity of a similar nature. Tho' it happened that no Scotchmen were concerned in it.[34]

---

[31]Robert Donaldson to Alexander Wilson, copied in Wilson's letterbook, 23 May 1774, TD 1/1070, SRA. The mobility of assistants in the tobacco business after several years is quite striking.
[32]Ibid.
[33]See Alexander Wilson to his parents, 17 December 1769, TD 1/1070, SRA. For details of Alexandria's changing trade patterns, see Preisser, "Eighteenth-Century Alexandria."
[34]Donaldson to Wilson, copied in Wilson's letterbook, 23 May 1774, TD 1/1070, SRA.

In Osborne's the following year, William McLeod remarked that "A man's being a Scotchman is sufficient to condemn him upon the slightest information. They being looked upon as the greatest enemys to America."[35]

Wilson's short colonial career illustrates some important points. He came from Glasgow's middling ranks as did his friends. He went to the Chesapeake to improve his standing at home. Part of a Glasgow venture, he followed the accepted path, trying to earn a fortune through trade. Finally, he showed not only a consciousness of Scottish identity but also observed that others perceived that identity, thereby reinforcing it. Wilson, however, left the colonies and returned home before gaining the charge of his own store. It is therefore necessary to examine another career for details of life one rung up the tobacco industry's corporate ladder.

THE TOBACCO FACTOR RUN AMOK

James Lawson and his brother-in-law John Semple created a tobacco partnership sometime during the 1750s.[36] Lawson, who lived in Glasgow, at least in theory directed Semple, who lived in Maryland. They had agreed to purchase Maryland tobacco, import it, and then sell it in the Glasgow markets for reexport. From 1748 until the mid 1750s Semple and James Jamieson, a prominent Glasgow tobacco merchant, had engaged in trade in the colonies.[37] Lawson soon learned that Semple had a habit of disregarding his partners' wishes and doing what he thought best. If this were not bad enough, he was sloppy. Jamieson maintained that Semple had "not kept accompt of Charges upon the Saint Mary's Store nor of . . . [his] household expences nor . . . a regular Cash accompt and . . . [his] Private Goods was intermixed with the Companys Books" during his tenure with that firm. And Jamieson threatened legal action.[38]

But Semple was, after all, in the Chesapeake and his partners were in

---

[35]William McLeod to Donald McLeod, 8 September 1775, p. 48, McLeod Papers, MS 19297, NLS.

[36]The exact terms of this partnership are not known; the legal documents which detailed them have probably been lost.

[37]See James Lawson to John Semple, 25 December 1758, Court of Session Extracted Processes, CS 96/1197, and 26 March 1760, CS 96/1197, SRO, for details of the difficulties surrounding the dissolution of the Semple-Jamieson venture.

[38]James Lawson to John Semple, 25 December 1758, CS 96/1197, SRO. Jamieson constantly complained to Lawson about Semple's failure to remit. In fact, he threatened legal action several times. Lawson began to become less sympathetic as his brother-in-law ignored the problem. "Mr Jamison & Son are in the outmost rage & Swears They will now prosecute you to the last cost what it will. . . . I cannot help saying you are to blame." To Semple, 26 March 1760, CS 96/1197, SRO.

Glasgow. He did not like taking orders through the post.[39] This situation closely parallels that of Jamaican estate managers, who often did what they wanted, sometimes disregarding their employers' wishes. Lawson knew all of this about his brother-in-law; even so, he consented to continue the partnership. He believed that the tobacco colonies held great amounts of wealth for those who could extract it and get it home. Living in Glasgow, he could see the apparently increasing fortunes of those with Chesapeake interests and connections. Perhaps this example spurred him on, actually allowing him to trust Semple's judgment. Lawson continued to invest money as his partner requested it. He offered only suggestions and always deferred to Semple's judgment.

> If you are to fix a new Store what would you think of fixing one on the Virginia Side in the neighbourhood where Mr. Galloway of Ayr has his store on. I am of Opinion that would answer but no doubt you are the best judge where is the most proper place which I leave entirely to yourself.[40]

Semple, predictably, considered that Lawson was giving him free rein to do whatever he wanted. For the next five years he took the company's money and small profits and bought himself a house, an iron forge, and anything else he thought necessary to live a comfortable life. Whatever money he had not managed to spend, he put back into the partnership that allowed him to enjoy this lifestyle in the first place. For the time being, he had achieved independence, albeit in Virginia and not his native country. But he failed to realize that he had done so on borrowed time and money. In the short term, Lawson's capital and seeming deference permitted Semple the opportunities he wanted.[41]

By 1762, Lawson had grown quite tired of his neverending problems with his brother-in-law, and rebuked him.

> Really John you have by far too much hope for a cautious Merchant and too little caution for our small Capitols. . . . [A Purchase of a forge] may be a good bargain for People who act cautiously and have a good stock to follow it out But I think it is a rash Step in you to engage in to such a multiplicity of

[39]Glasgow merchants who assumed quite dictatorial positions while leaving their employees little or no room for independent action are discussed in Devine, *The Tobacco Lords*, pp. 83–87.

[40]Lawson to Semple, 21 February 1760, CS 96/1197, SRO.

[41]Richard Pares has indicated that this sort of behavior was characteristic of most estate managers and attorneys when they were left to their own devices (*A West India Fortune*, pp. 19–21, 142–49.) The difference between Semple and many West Indians was that Semple would be caught (though not made repentant).

Works . . . when you knew my pinch for want of money to pay our debts here.[42]

The letter had no effect. Semple continued to ignore his partner and do what he wanted. He bought the iron forge at Occoquan, Virginia on someone else's credit.[43] The similarity to Francis Grant, the Jamaica estate manager, is more than superficial. Grant acted as if he were a property owner rather than a property manager. In this way, he acquired the independence he sought, at least temporarily. So too did Semple. The differences came in what they did with their earnings. Grant remitted his to Britain; Semple invested his in Chesapeake property. As a result, Grant did well and Semple ultimately failed. Lawson was not playing his absentee part very well; because he controlled the bulk of the capital he wanted to dictate policy to his partner, who wanted to make a fortune in a hurry and was not averse to free spending. The conflict between the frugal and the profligate deepened, as it did on many a Jamaican plantation. Even the sums of money involved began to approach Jamaican levels. In late 1763, Lawson reckoned Semple to have spent £18,000 currency (around £14,000 sterling) on all of his purchases.[44]

Things became so bad that Lawson in 1762 sent Alexander Hamilton and Alexander Lithgow to Virginia, ostensibly as new assistants. In reality, they were spies on Semple. Each took over the management of one of Lawson and Semple's stores and attempted to collect the firm's debts. But Lawson soon began to complain about Lithgow wanting too many goods to sell when he was supposed to be going out of business. The Chesapeake environment, with its booming tobacco industry, and the Scots' desire for profit corrupted even the best laid plans. In 1764, after two years with small improvement, Lawson resolved to go to the colonies in order to take control of his business, dissolve the partnership with Semple, and recover what he could.[45]

---

[42]Lawson to Semple, 19 July 1762, CS 96/1198, SRO. Semple also planned to open two new stores to purchase grain. Lawson rebuked him and he backed away from this plan. In the long run, and with much hindsight, it might ultimately have saved the business to have acquired these stores and become a grain exporter.

[43]The source of this capital is unknown. It did not come from Lawson. At least part of the partnership's proceeds was invested in it, though the total amount is unclear. It also seems that Semple had several other investors giving him capital in Glasgow, though their identities remain obscure. It is certain, however, that by 1773, Semple owed Philip Lee over £3000 sterling, as a mortgagee of his forge. See Philip Lee to Arthur Lee, 20 July 1773, MSS 1, Lee Family Papers L51, 243–257, Virginia Historical Society, Richmond.

[44]See Lawson to Alexander Hamilton, 3 September 1763, CS 96/1199, SRO. For the conversion rate, see John J. McCusker, *Money and Exchange in Europe and America, 1600–1775* (Chapel Hill, N.C., 1978), pp. 211–12.

[45]See James Lawson to Alexander Hamilton, 13 January 1763, and Lawson to Alexander Lithgow, 13 January 1763, CS 96/1199, SRO. For Lawson's complaints against Lithgow, see Lawson to Lithgow, 9 May 1763, CS 96/1199, SRO.

Lawson had to withdraw from active trading in Glasgow late in 1762 because he claimed that he was dunned for payment whenever he was seen in the Glasgow streets. He became very bitter toward his brother-in-law and partner. "Your avarice for this World is beyond all bounds of Reason, God only knows how you'll extricate yourself," he chastised Semple. In 1765, Lawson was presented with a bill for £1900 payable to Lord Baltimore, a bill that Semple had drawn, which Lawson had never authorized.[46] It was the last in a series of bills that Lawson had refused to pay and which his partner continued to draw. He dropped everything and went immediately to the Chesapeake to find out just what his renegade relation had been doing with their money. Soon after arriving, he discovered that Semple had collected the firm's debts and reinvested them in his own business, the forge with which Lawson had refused to become involved.

Like many going to settle business accounts and estates in Jamaica, Lawson insisted that he was only going to stay in Maryland for a year and collect what he could of the £10,000 sterling which he reckoned his partner then owed him. Semple, in a futile bid to preserve his lifestyle, did his best to make matters difficult. When one of Lawson's agents went to settle a particular account, Semple would soon appear and offer the planter more time and lower interest. He believed this tactic would protect his own business and keep his customers loyal. He was absolutely right. By pandering to the planters, the Scottish merchant could be reasonably sure of keeping their business. When this willingness to compete and to accommodate was withdrawn as a result of the credit crisis of 1772, Scottish losses and unpopularity significantly increased.

Like many of his Jamaican counterparts, Lawson wanted to avoid lawsuits at any cost. He believed litigation could drag on for years and cost a good bit of money; the courts would not be the remedy to force his renegade partner to remit. As a general rule, this belief was correct; yet it seems with hindsight that had he immediately instituted legal proceedings against his brother-in-law, he might have been able to escape the colony much sooner than he did, with more to show for his efforts. He might also have been able to avoid much of the litigation with which he was faced upon his return to Scotland. He remained in the Chesapeake for nearly ten years, from 1765 to 1774.[47]

For almost a decade, Semple avoided Lawson but continued to make debt collection difficult. Lawson lived at the firm's store in Port Tobacco and Semple traveled between his forge at Occoquan and a house at Bladensburg.

[46]Lawson to Semple, 6 September 1763, CS 96/1198, SRO. See also Lawson to Semple, 21 January 1764, CS 96/1198, SRO.

[47]I have been unable to locate any records in the county courts of Virginia that indicate Lawson prosecuted Semple. The records for Prince William and Stafford counties are incomplete; it remains possible that legal action could have been taken.

Despite repeated promises to settle the books, which caused Lawson to assure his wife of his imminent return, the two met perhaps once a year. Each year promises were made and each year Semple broke them. He had succeeded in creating a comfortable life for himself, albeit on money not his own, and he did not want to be bothered with satisfying his creditors. It might have meant the loss of all he had worked so hard to achieve. He believed, like Jamaican planters and managers, that more time and investment would produce enough income to pay everyone off with very hefty profits. Lawson continued to plunge farther into his partner's quagmire. He saw only one way out and that meant staying in the Chesapeake. "Were I to leave this in the present Situation," he penned one of his creditors, explaining his delay, "without having a settlement with Mr. Semple the life I could afford you & my family would be shame poverty & misery for, John would take every shilling belonging to this concern and apply it to his own purposes. This I have too good reason to know."[48] Nevertheless, he still expected to go home in the spring of 1768; he was six years premature.

Each year his wife received at least one letter that read something like this:

> Mr. Semple has not come over to finish our settlement, I daily expect him and am in hopes he will at last perform his promise. If he does not come here in one or two weeks hence I am of opinion the Glasgow ships from this River [Potomac] will be all gone So as it will oblige me to stay till the Spring as I am not fond of takeing a winter passage.[49]

Lawson had a particularly difficult time expressing his frustration and representing his partner's misdeeds to his wife because she was Semple's sister. He did not want to upset her by being away for long nor did he want to upset her by explaining why he was away in the vivid detail which he allowed his other correspondents. His young children grew up, for all intents and purposes, with a father they barely knew. In 1769, Lawson wrote one of his Glasgow merchant suppliers requesting that he send out a new wig. Lawson gave explicit instructions that the merchant not tell Mrs. Lawson. On the same day, Lawson informed his wife that he would certainly be home that autumn. Obviously, he deliberately misrepresented his situation to his wife. He could not decide what to do, but he knew he could not easily go home without being attacked by his creditors. He had fallen into the same dilemma faced by Robert Stirling in Jamaica fifteen years earlier. Both had huge debts at home and could avoid payment by staying out of Scotland. Such a solution, however, had a substantial drawback. It insured that the comfortable

[48]James Lawson to John Pagan, 7 March 1767, CS 96/1200, SRO.
[49]James Lawson to Nancy Lawson, 30 October 1767, CS 96/1201, SRO. The reader should note Lawson's desire to travel directly from the Potomac River to Glasgow.

Scottish independence was postponed and made more elusive. James Lawson was stuck between being creditor and debtor. If he went home, he would be dunned. If he stayed, he would have to dun and meet uncertain results.

By 1772, when Lawson wrote his usual unhappy letter home, he lamented that his wife (who was now ill) had not come to Maryland. He claimed to have thought that he would have returned long before then. "Had I known the time I have been detained here," he wrote Nancy Lawson, "I would have endeavoured to have had you . . . here some years ago." He disliked the Chesapeake, both because of the weather and the problems he encountered trying to settle his business with Semple. He continued, "I never did nor never will blame you in the least for any difficultys your Brother has brought upon me."[50] The tone of his letter suggests that he might not have been entirely truthful.

Other creditors had already pounced upon Semple in January 1771. They had him put into prison bounds at Dumfries, Virginia. Semple was not allowed to leave the town at all, though he was not confined to any particular space within it.[51] There he remained until his death in 1773, because his creditors refused to allow him out. He would not agree on a plan of repayment with those to whom he owed money and he refused to settle the estate. He had insisted that they invest more money to keep his forge running and then that they be allowed to keep its profits in payment. Suspecting that such a scheme would not prevent Semple from keeping the income himself, they refused. For this particular Scot, time had run out.[52]

Lawson finally left Virginia in 1774, still a mortgagee of the forge. He had, in fact, leased it from Philip Lee in an effort to get it running again so that it could pay off his debts.[53] The situation bears a striking resemblance to that of James Stirling who had two years earlier left Jamaica without settling his brother Robert's estate. The system where residents of the colonies loaned each other money kept the colonies' internal economies operational; it also ultimately defeated the Scots merchants. It is not a little ironic that they were

[50]James Lawson to Nancy Lawson, April 1772, CS 96/1203, SRO.

[51]The court records for this period are again missing, so it is not known which of Semple's creditors instituted the action. Semple received some moral support, though not from anyone to whom he owed money. In a letter to Semple, William Allason, a Scottish merchant, wrote, "I am now & have long been very sorry for your confinement, what purpose it will answer some individual Creditors I don't know, tho I imagine they have an early Payment in view." (William Allason to John Semple, 28 April 1772, Letterbook, 1770–1789, f. 143, Acc. 13, VSL.)

[52]See, for example, Lawson to Alston and Morton, 12 July 1771, CS 96/1203, SRO. Col. Philip Lee foreclosed on the forge (he held the first mortgage for £3000) and resolved to sell it (he owed money himself) unless he was paid off. See Lawson to Alston and Morton, 14 January 1773, CS 96/1203, SRO, and Philip Lee to Arthur Lee, 20 July 1773, MSS 1, Lee Family Paper L51, 243–257, VHS.

[53]See Philip Lee to Arthur Lee, 20 July 1773.

among its chief participants. Stirling had tried to collect his brother's debts for several years; incredibly, Lawson believed he had done the right thing by chasing Semple for nearly a decade. When he returned to Glasgow, he wrote his creditors of his plight. Had he not gone, he wrote, his creditors would not have gotten "2/6 in the pound and by my going out I am in hopes to be able to pay them 20/ in the pound exclusive of Interest which I flater myself you will be satisfied with more especially when you consider I have spent Nine years of my life to procure that sum without doing any other thing for my self."[54] He failed to mention that he wrote this letter from jail. Immediately upon his return, he was taken into custody. John Hamilton, one of his creditors, had assigned the £1600 debt to a Mr. Tait. Tait obtained a judgment from the Scottish Admiralty Court against Lawson while he was on his passage back to Glasgow. Lawson, upon disembarking, was immediately sent to the Edinburgh Tollbooth; he remained imprisoned from 10 August to 15 September. Tait had convinced the court that Lawson was intending to dodge all his creditors and return to the Chesapeake.[55]

Records indicate that Lawson was released from jail because the Court of Session, Scotland's highest court, overruled the Admiralty Court's decision. It is unclear what finally became of him.[56] What is certain, however, is that Lawson curtailed the freedom and independence (not to mention the blank checkbook) of his partner in the colonies simply by showing up. After scheming and using his position to advance himself rather than his business, Semple died in disgrace. Lawson, for his part, lost ten years of his life chasing him down with very small return. This particular case ended in failure before the Revolution even began. An attempt to move away from tobacco into iron or grain could not succeed without proper management and capital. Scots like Lawson were not willing to advance the latter, and Semple did not use the former. John Semple's case represents only one end of a broad spectrum of possible behavior.

THE OBEDIENT AND DEPENDENT FACTORS

Commenting extensively upon the degree to which the Glasgow tobacco houses dominated the Chesapeake's tobacco trade, existing scholarship ex-

[54]James Lawson to Thomas Philips and Company, September, 1774, CS 96/1203, SRO.
[55]See James Lawson's suspension, AC 8/1861, SRO.
[56]Scottish courts kept together all of the documents that had been submitted as evidence. Along with the court's decisions and legal opinions, this was known as a process. Evidence from each process, for preservation purposes, was later removed and kept separately. These are known as the extracted processes. The Court of Session process from which these letterbooks have been extracted has been lost. In other records, there are some references to a Mr. Lawson going from Glasgow to Virginia after the end of the war, but it is unclear that this is the same man.

amines business and management styles from a macroeconomic perspective. In other words, profitability, the Glasgow organization, and Glasgow's innovations and contributions to Britain's trade have dominated discussions of the commercial connections between Scotland and the Chesapeake. All of these topics are important, but they do not tell us much about what life was like for the dutiful factors in the colonies.[57]

For them, Glasgow loomed somewhere over the horizon. Factors had to reconcile their own ambitions with those of their employers. They often discovered that the men who had already made their fortunes and who dictated the rules from Glasgow no longer understood daily life in the Chesapeake. The tobacco lords' notions, based upon personal experiences of at least a decade before, often created problems for their employees. It was one thing to impose policy from a Scottish merchant house; it was quite another to have to implement it along the isolated stretches of the Chesapeake backcountry.

After Glasgow had secured its position of primacy, most trading concerns exerted extremely tight control over their factors abroad in order to ensure greater profitability. Alexander Henderson became the chief factor at John Glassford's new Colchester store in 1758. His brother, Archibald, later a partner in the firm and a tobacco lord in his own right, began the store.[58] From the very beginning, Alexander Henderson found himself at odds with his employers. They had authorized him to pay no more than twelve shillings six pence per hundredweight of tobacco. Yet his competitors, employees of other Glasgow firms, offered planters nearly twice as much—twenty-two shillings per hundredweight. Glassford's did not want him to offer credit; their competitors had authorized its use. A planter would neither sell for a low price when better ones were on offer nor turn down the prospect of goods on credit. Demand was high, and if a factor could not offer competitive prices, the planters would not do business with him. Henderson apologized to Glassford's: "I am sorry . . . to tell you that I can buy but very

[57]For the best work on this subject, see Devine, *The Tobacco Lords;* Price, *Capital and Credit, France and the Chesapeake,* and "The Rise of Glasgow," as well as Soltow, "Scottish Traders". Having read these, however, I found myself needing to put things back onto a more human scale. I wanted to know how instructions were received, how behavior was affected by the external control imposed upon the factors, and how the men in the Chesapeake actually lived.

[58]See Devine, *Tobacco Lords,* pp. 70, 74, for example. It has not been possible to trace the entire careers of the Henderson brothers. This sketch aims to illustrate some of the more common problems. The tobacco company's newer stores tended to be located at or above the fall line. Glassford's had stores in thirteen Maryland locations and five Virginia locations. With the exception of Norfolk, Virginia, and Leonardtown, Maryland, all appear to have been in newer areas of settlement. (See the Inventory to the Library of Congress collections for a complete list of all locations.) Price, in *France and the Chesapeake,* v. 1, pp. 666–67, notes as well that the Scots did not give up their outlets in the tidewater area because the French preferred this region's tobacco.

little Tobacco this year, I do not think I'll get above sixty Hogsheads." But there was little he could do short of disobeying his orders.[59] Glassford's in Glasgow complained to him about low yields; but he continued to observe their instructions on how much he could pay. "I cannot say that it looks more favourable," he wrote, "the country is so much overstocked with goods at present & is likely to continue so for some time, that I'm afraid it will not be in my power to make you but a triffling remittance this year."[60] Henderson knew however that he was going to have to ignore the company if he was to gain any share of the market. He let the company know that "I am still as low or lower than my neighbours, and must give these prices or shut up store."[61] By the end of the year, after being reprimanded by the company, he let loose his feelings.

> I find you require a certainty of speedy payments that the trade shou'd be carried on without any bad debts which in my humble opinion are next to impossibilities. In the small course of my knowledge, I never found a trade free from a risque of bad debts nor can any man affix a certain time when he may be in Cash for Goods deliver'd here, so many accidents might interpose to disappoint him.[62]

By 1760, the Glaswegians had no choice but to accept their operative's pleas, consent to pay more, and realize that they would have to offer more credit if they wanted to maintain or increase their share of the market.

Like many Jamaican managers, Alexander Henderson knew that his salary as a factor would not sustain his ambition to become independent.[63] Just as estate managers recognized their limited opportunities and worked for more than one estate to increase their income (with very little added risk), tobacco factors developed ways to raise additional revenue. Alexander Henderson, like many other tobacco factors, organized his own trading business, using his skills and connections to earn extra money selling goods independent of his firm. Thus, they not only became dependent upon their employers for instructions in their principal business but also extremely dependent upon prevailing market conditions in their personal ventures.

The tobacco houses in Glasgow generally frowned upon such activity and

[59]Alexander Henderson to John Glassford, 10 June 1758, Letterbook, f.1, TD 168, SRA (photocopy of original in Alexandria Public Library, Alexandria, Virginia). Jacob Price in *Capital and Credit*, pp. 125–26, quotes Henderson's brother describing how factors had no choice but to offer more credit to get as much tobacco as possible. Competition was fierce.

[60]Henderson to Glassford, 23 February 1759, p. 15, TD 168, SRA.

[61]Henderson to Glassford, 5 June 1759, p. 19, TD 168, SRA.

[62]Henderson to Glassford, 29 December 1759, p. 36, TD 168, SRA.

[63]His salary was around £100 per annum by 1762. See Henderson to Glassford, 20 September 1762, p. 92, TD 168, SRA.

tried to limit it; they believed it undercut their own business. Alexander Henderson explained his reasons for wanting to trade on his own account and argued that if he was not allowed to continue in his quest for riches, he would leave the firm.

> I must be looking out for . . . some advantageous Business [which] might offer in less than that time [his six year contract], which perhaps I could make shift to get into, which if prevented by any engagement with you, might be of the worst of Consequences to me.[64]

The company responded by offering him an additional ten pounds a year in wages on condition that he decline to set up his own business. But he insisted on trading independently. His employers agreed to his demand only when he consented to give them two years notice before leaving the firm permanently.[65]

By 1762, Henderson began to tell the company that it made things much more difficult for itself by not heeding his advice. The firm had not sent the proper goods to him, and he was having a hard time meeting its quotas for tobacco acquisition. "You cannot expect," he reprimanded his employers, "that I can either make a cheap or an extensive purchase, while I am so ill and irregularly supply'd with good's (pardon the freedom with which I write to you for my Reputation is at Stake as well as your Interest) when I send a Scheme for goods I expect it will be comply'd with."[66] His problem was common; it runs through the pages of virtually every surviving factor's book.[67] The constant conflict between factor and merchant did little to advance business. Henderson, like most experienced factors, believed that he understood local conditions better than his Glasgow employers. The two groups were completely dependent upon each other, one for capital and goods, the other for honest reports of the situation.

A comparison with Jamaican estate managers is well warranted. Like the factors, the managers rarely worried about possible conflicts of interest when they managed more than one estate. Their employers, however, sometimes

---

[64]Henderson to Glassford, 29 December 1759.

[65]Such a business could be organized as follows. Friends who worked as clerks to merchant houses in Glasgow (houses that had little or no business in the Chesapeake) or family members sent goods to the factor to sell on his own. The profits were then split between the Chesapeake Scot and his accomplice in Glasgow. In this way, the merchant houses could be bypassed. Shop assistant James McLeod ordered £67 worth of goods in 1774 (James to Donald McLeod, 13 February 1774, MS 19297, p. 5, NLS). Unfortunately, I have been unable to locate any indication of how successful this or any other side business was.

[66]Henderson to Glassford, 20 September 1762.

[67]Some examples can be found in James Robinson's Letterbooks, 1767–1773, TD 167/1, SRA; John Hook's Letterbook, 1763–1772, MS 22174/a, VSL; and Alexander Hamilton's Letterbook, 1773–1790, Mic. M 23, EUL.

complained that they paid more attention to one estate than another. Employers and employees often clashed even though they depended heavily upon each other.[68] In the final analysis, however, those on the spot either in Jamaica or the Chesapeake had the ability to do as they pleased. If they acted openly, they could very possibly be dismissed; if clandestine, they stood to profit until their employer took action against them, which might never occur.

Henderson reiterated his desire for greater control over the company's daily affairs. And when another firm offered him a hundred pounds a year to work for them, he threatened to leave Glassford's unless they matched the offer. This they did. Though a hundred pounds a year amounted to a substantial wage by either Scottish or Chesapeake standards, it did not compare favorably with what Jamaica merchants or managers could earn in a good year. Even if Henderson spent very little of it (his room, board, and washing would have been gratis), he would have had to work for many years to earn enough to purchase a Scottish estate or even a share of the merchant house's business. These low wages drove the factors to want to run their own businesses. Managing their own projects prevented them from devoting full attention to their employer's business, which brought chastisement from home.

The Glasgow tobacco merchants were not terribly interested in helping their employees accomplish what they themselves had achieved. This is not a little ironic, as many of them had been in the colony before the 1760s when their innovation and entrepreneurial spirit brought them fortunes. By restricting these qualities amongst their employees and dictating what they could and could not do in their free time, the Glasgow merchants ensured that their factors would remain in dependent conditions. Even so, many employees believed they could advance. After all, they had the example of their firm's proprietors to reassure them. The promise did not match the reality.

The case of James Robinson, who trod the same path as Henderson a decade later, reveals that his employers, Cunninghame and Company, tolerated even less than Glassford's.[69] Robinson, a schoolmaster's son, brought £33.2.0 worth of his own property with him when he went to Virginia in

---

[68]This seems to be a fairly typical clash between employee and employer. The aims of labor and capital had become different. Labor wanted to achieve the wealth and status of capital. And capital understood two things. First, if labor achieved the same level of wealth, capital would need to acquire more in order to maintain their positions of control. Second, restricting labor's access to advancement too much would create even greater antagonisms.

[69]For a printed collection of the letters to and from Robinson see T. Devine, ed., *A Scottish Firm in Virginia, 1767–77: W. Cunninghame and Company* (Edinburgh, 1984). This publication of the Scottish History Society is divided into two parts: Correspondence of James Robinson with the company and Correspondence with the factors in Virginia (the smaller section).

1761. Apprenticed for three years to the Cunninghame company, he later (sometime before 1768) became the company's chief Virginia factor, based in Falmouth. Because he had to deal more regularly with his employers, he became increasingly intolerant of their policies which, he thought, were based less on Chesapeake reality than upon Glasgow desires.[70]

To the people he supervised, Robinson enforced the company line. But in his interactions with Glasgow, he was every bit as combative as Henderson had been ten years earlier. He showed no enthusiasm when he had to terminate a new employee because the man decided to get married. And he was careful to demonstrate that the decision to do so was not his own; rather it was the company's.

> Your agreement with the company continues untill the first day of October 1769. But they have wrote that they cannot agree to be served by a married man, if a single one can be got, thinking the former must often be necessary called from their business by his family affairs.[71]

Paternalistic to extremes, yet unwilling to bend any rules, William Cunninghame and Company constantly made hard and fast, almost arbitrary, decrees like this one. Anyone who deviated at all from total devotion to the firm was sacked. This included men who married (perhaps to improve their fortunes), men who set up their own businesses (for obvious reasons), and men whose stores did not reach expected profitability levels.[72]

"Frugality or good management is extremely necessary at all times but more so at present," Robinson passed on the company line, "when there appears a certain prospect of a considerable Loss."[73] Robinson's warning to an errant factor did no good; the company continued to complain about low profits. The firm did not understand the changes that had taken place in the rural economy after the founders had left the colony.[74]

Frequent changes in point-of-purchase management could not have helped business. New faces, belonging to people with Glaswegian accents,

[70]"Contract between Wm. Cunninghame, et al. and James Robinson," 24 August 1761 (TD 82/13, SRA), and "Inventory of James Robinson for Virginia Shipt," 22 April 1761 (TD 82/11, SRA). Cunninghame's stores were all situated at or above the fall line (see "General Inventory of Stores," GD 247/59/Q1, SRO).

[71]James Robinson to Bennett Price, 11 September 1768, Letterbook, p. 7, TD 167/1, SRA (photocopy of original, GD 247/8/58, in SRO).

[72]The firm instructed Robinson to eliminate one of these people, and set up the scene so that the real reason for sacking their man would be obscured. See William Cunninghame to James Robinson, 8 January 1772, GD 247/P/2/1, SRO. Also see Devine, *Tobacco Lords*, pp. 82–87.

[73]James Robinson to John Turner, 22 April 1769, p. 13, TD 167/1, SRA.

[74]There is evidence that William Cunninghame had spent substantial time in Virginia before the tobacco boom of the 1760s, see Devine, *Tobacco Lords*, p. 87.

inevitably aroused the local population's suspicion. So too did the Scots' efficient operations. There can be no doubt that those whom the Scots had supplanted stirred up the colonists by pointing to the vast amount of debts held by "foreign" merchants. Because the firms also tended to keep their operatives apart from the local community, Scots factors became increasingly unpopular with the settlers. Robinson instructed a new factor, "Live on good terms with your neighbours in Town. . . . Too great an intimacy with any of them may be attended with bad Consequences, secrecy in . . . Transactions of Business . . . is what I would strongly recommend."[75] He advised his charges to keep their promises to the customers; this would win their trust and secure loyalty. He neglected to tell this particular factor to stay within the company's prescribed spending limits.

Robinson saved that line for others. "Frugality or Oeconomy is Generally the offspring of a Sound Judgement. . . . Not the Smallest Extravagance can or will be allowed of, especially ordinary expences."[76] Those sojourners who reported to him were stuck in the middle, just as Robinson was. Did they listen to their employers, who controlled their wages, or did they respond to the market, without which the wages would not be paid? The Glasgow merchants knew their own reexport markets and what they could afford to pay for tobacco without losing profitability. They were often involved in trade wars with each other.[77] All of this made little difference to their employees, who were concerned with their own careers. As a result, loyalties were often divided.

Cunninghame's became incensed with one of their factors when they found out that he had developed his own business enough to acquire individual property. In July of 1774, as the tobacco markets became increasingly difficult, the Company wrote John Johnston, reprimanding him for "purchasing the Plantation, building the Store House, Dwelling House, and other out Houses." They continued to chastise him, making the way in which they perceived their employees apparent. "We allow none of our Servants to enter into any engagements they cannot immediately fulfill and we look upon it as reflecting on our Credit. . . . You are unworthy to eat our Bread."[78] Rather than terminating this man, they referred his case to Robinson. They minced no words about their dislike for Johnston when they accused him of being "a common lyar having advanced several falsehoods to us."[79] Robin-

[75]James Robinson to John Likly, 6 October 1771, pp. 61–66, TD 167/1, SRA.
[76]James Robinson to Francis Hay, 13 October 1773, p. 86, TD 167/1, SRA.
[77]A description of one such price war can be found in James Robinson to Cunninghame and Company, 1 June 1772, TD 167/2, SRA. This particular problem over prices was not new; one or two merchants always wanted to undercut their competitors and gain more of the available business.
[78]Cunninghame and Company to John Johnstone, 15 July 1774, GD 247/59/Q, SRO.
[79]Cunninghame to James Robinson, 22 July 1774, GD 247/59/Q, SRO.

son was instructed to keep him under tight control, even though he lived miles away, or face the consequences himself.

Factors and storekeepers were the middlemen between the company and the planters, and their chief factors—like Robinson and Henderson—were in the middle between the company and the rest of their factors. In this role, Robinson, who was extremely attentive to his correspondence, was not exempt from corporate criticism. "It will give us much pleasure, " the company suggested,

> your being much more Cautious in making out your Schemes in future, and of your putting in practice your Intention of taking a rough Inventory of all your Goods on hand prior to your making out such orders. . . . We herein do positively discharge you from making any Contract with any man whatever for more than his Current Crop at any certain price.[80]

No one was exempt from Glasgow's demands. Day to day management became extremely difficult because external interference was so regular and common. As times worsened, so did the interference. Even so, Scots continued to come to Virginia as tobacco factors and storekeepers, right up until the Revolution. Many came after it was over, to assist in attempts to collect the debts. All of these people believed that they had the opportunity to improve their wealth and status. Of course, this image of the hard-working employee saving enough of his high wages to purchase an estate was perpetuated by the tobacco lords themselves and bore little resemblance to reality.[81]

Instead, most men encountered an environment where they had to choose between the wishes of their employers and their personal ambitions. Often, no matter how they chose, they would lose. Their wages were not high enough to meet their expectations of earning a quick fortune and the restrictions enforced by their employers slowed down their personal pursuits. Fortunes could not be quickly made, at least not for those who played by the moguls' rules.

OTHER PROFESSIONALS

Scottish sojourners who did not engage in commerce also went to the Chesapeake, though in far fewer numbers than their "merchandising" coun-

[80]William Cunninghame to James Robinson, 18 July 1774, GD 247/59/Q, SRO.
[81]The road to wealth for some was certainly this way. Devine reckons debts owed to the Glasgow houses at the time of the Revolution to be over £1,000,000. See *Tobacco Lords*, pp. 59, 113–20.

trymen.[82] They did not wear their transiency as visibly as the factors did: they accounted for a smaller percentage of their chosen occupations and they associated more freely with those in other ethnic categories. As a result, many eluded the vilification of Scots before and during the American Revolution. Even so, they shared the same aims as their countrymen. They wanted to earn enough to afford a comfortable existence at home. In order to do so, they sought to use their educational background and professional training as fully as possible.

John Ravenscroft was born in 1749; his father died soon afterward. In the following year, his mother, Ann Stark Ravenscroft from Amelia County, Virginia, married George MacMurdo, a Scottish merchant. When his health failed in 1752, she accompanied her new husband to Scotland. George MacMurdo certainly had not acquired the fortune that he had intended when he left the colonies for his native country. Bringing Ann's three-year-old son John with them, however, the couple did not go to Scotland empty-handed. Ann had also been left some Virginia property—three plantations, thirty slaves, and some cattle. When the MacMurdos departed the Chesapeake, the estates annually yielded them around £200. This income allowed MacMurdo to lease a farm upon his return to Dumfriesshire in order to provide for his ever-increasing family.[83] They produced ten children; the family's resources began to be strained. Mrs. MacMurdo did not, however, have to worry about her firstborn son.[84]

John Ravenscroft's father had left his infant son some property, the proceeds of which provided for his Scottish upbringing. While not nearly as large as estates in Jamaica, they were not insubstantial. In 1761, Black Water plantation had been let for £13.7.6, while Maycox plantation hired out at £30

[82]I am not alone in making this claim. According to Brock, *Scotus Americanus*, the majority of Scots in Virginia were "either men engaged in the tobacco trade or episcopalian clergymen" (p. 30). He does not make a distinction between sojourner and immigrant. I did not find records for any but immigrant clergymen. Among them is the diary of the Rev. Robert Rose, who *emigrated* from Scotland to Virginia in 1724 (*The Diary of Robert Rose: A View of Virginia by a Scottish Colonial Parson, 1746–51*, ed. Ralph Emmett Falls [Verona, Va., 1977]). The original is at the Huntington Library. A description of the life of the Rev. John Buchanan, who was born in 1743 near Edinburgh and lived in Richmond, can be found in George Wyllie Munford, *The Two Parsons* (Richmond, Va., 1884).

[83]Sir John Sinclair in *A Statistical Account of Scotland* (Edinburgh, 1793) reports that houses in some parishes of Dumfriesshire let for annual rents of around £1 a year (v. 4, pp. 216, 457, 519). The highest rent in one parish was £220 for an enormous sheep farm (v. 4, p. 517). One of the parish ministers calculated that it would cost annually £10.6.8 for a man to live adequately with a wife and four children in his part of Dumfriesshire. Thus, £200 per year seems to me to be a very reasonable living expense for a large family in this part of Scotland.

[84]See the "History of MacMurdo" in a letter to Mr. Tod (n.d. [post 1780], MacMurdo Papers, Acc. 7199/4/4, NLS), a fairly complete synopsis of the main genealogical developments in this family.

annually. Ravenscroft's other income that year amounted to "£92 besides what can be made by the six hands upon the plantations, perhaps £50 or £60 more."[85] His mother's brother, Bolling Stark, managed the properties, kept accounts for the estate, and transmitted the money to Scotland at fairly regular intervals.

Though not a Scot by birth, Ravenscroft was raised as one. His guardians, uncle and stepfather, decided that it would be best for him to learn a profession in Scotland and then return to Virginia. They believed his social stature would be noticeably increased as a result. He could use the income from his land to support himself while building up his business. He would then be able to use the proceeds from that trade to improve his property. It seemed both simple and logical. When John was only twelve, uncle Bolling related his plans for John to MacMurdo. Bolling Stark well knew what the costs would be. "Give my love to Johnny," he wrote, "& tell him I beg he will apply closely to his Studies and if Physick is not very disagreeable should be much pleased to have him brought up that way." Of course, he added, "if he prefers anything else let him follow the bent of his own inclination." Anything else was the English law.[86]

After several years of thought, young Ravenscroft decided that indeed he did want to be a physician. The Chesapeake did not have the problem with an overabundance of [Scottish] physicians that Jamaica did. Instead, the mainland colonies had a problem convincing those who sought independence to go there and not somewhere else. Demand still exceeded supply as late as ten years after Ravenscroft had made his decision to become a doctor. A Maryland tobacco factor wrote, "There is not any business followed on this Continent, which in the end would prove more advantageous than the practice of Physic & Surgery." Even so, he cautioned, "like all other Employments it must be attended with the utmost care, dilligence & attention. A regular education is necessary."[87] Uncle Bolling, increasingly hurt by economic problems in the Chesapeake, began to have second thoughts about educating John to become a physician when he discovered the expense involved in medical education. "I have come to the following resolution," wrote Stark,

> that is to allow him £150 Sterling per Annum, the first £150 to become due next October. . . . If you will undertake to superintend his Education upon

[85]See Bolling Stark to George MacMurdo, 15 June 1761, MacMurdo Papers, Acc. 7199/3/1, NLS. There appears to have been some trouble in procuring the estates' proceeds from the agent, who had difficulty collecting from the tenants.

[86]Bolling Stark to George MacMurdo, 15 June 1761.

[87]John Campbell to William Sinclair, 26 July 1774, Sinclair of Freswick Muniments, GD 136/416/1, SRO. Campbell went on to condemn medical "practitioners" in Maryland and Virginia for not being properly trained. He did not consider two years at the medical colleges of New Jersey or Philadelphia a suitable education.

these terms, I shall take it as a very particular favor but if you chuse to be excused from the trouble, your recommendation of a Gentleman properly qualified would be very obliging. But if no such can be had . . . he must be sent out to Virginia immediately . . . and I'll endeavour to get him into some genteel business, which may be attended with no more expense than his estate will bear.[88]

Ravenscroft matriculated at the medical college at Edinburgh in 1765. He believed his family coffers to be much fuller than they actually were and for the next several years bitterly complained about his uncle's failure to remit on his account. His stepfather appointed George Muir, in Edinburgh, to see that the scholar received proper maintenance. But the two never got along. Muir perceived John to be far too free-spending and Ravenscroft thought Muir haughty and stingy. "I don't know whether it be Law or the will of the father that puts in the wards power to change his Guardian. If it be in my option & I have attained that age he shall be no longer my Guardian."[89] Ravenscroft spent so much time complaining about being ill-provided for that it is impossible not to wonder how he had any time left to study medicine.

Part of John's education included spending time in London. Here he observed cosmopolitan practitioners and had his first chance to see the great English metropolis. He was not impressed. Quite the contrary, he yearned for his "native" Scotland.

How much the young people are altered here from Scotland. They never almost think of sitting down to drink. If you speak of Brandy, good lord they cry, I wonder you are alive. . . . I believe they think [they are] made of gold for they can't speak without Guinea Guinea at every word.[90]

While he continued to write home for money every other month, his experiences in London made him realize just how badly he had behaved toward his guardians. He knew then that he would have to do something for himself soon; his dependent situation made him hanker for financial and personal independence. He returned to Edinburgh, graduating in 1770. He then faced a new dilemma.

Many of his medical friends and colleagues were about to undertake the grand continental tour. Ravenscroft found this a very attractive proposition. But Bolling Stark, who had grown tired of his prodigal nephew, urged him to

[88]Bolling Stark to George MacMurdo, 28 December 1764, Acc. 7199/3/1, NLS.
[89]John Ravenscroft to George MacMurdo, 13 June 1766, Acc. 7199/3/3, NLS.
[90]John Ravenscroft to George MacMurdo, 22 August 1768, Acc. 7199/3/3, NLS.

return to Virginia. Stark refused to put out any more money. And Ravenscroft agonized.

> You know my impatience to be over there [Virginia] & at the same time my readiness to delay that. . . . I must own Frugality is not my cardinal virtue but I imagine I will be wiser on that head when engaged in my own affairs & my attention taken up with practice as a Physician, then in this part of the world where Pleasure is so easy to be purchased.[91]

With his very Scottish ambition firmly developed, he set off for Virginia in 1771. Happy to arrive in a country where he thought his prospects good, with an excellent chance to acquire his independence, he soon changed his mind. He wrote to his mother, "I was joyous with getting of[f] the sea & every object gave me pleasure, but too soon the novelty was over. . . . These Virginia Estates are the devil."[92] He so hated the country that he quickly sold off his properties. He kept one estate to support himself. Doctors did not do as well here as they did in Jamaica. "Were I to swelter through . . . in practising Physick," he explained, "perhaps I might book 400£ & one half never paid."[93] Virginia was much too different from Scotland where "pleasure could be so easily purchased." His constant complaining made him realize that he could not stand to be in the colony any longer. His medical practice did not earn him a fortune as fast as he desired. Four hundred pounds (or, more properly, half of that) was simply not enough. Even when coupled with the revenue from his estate, it still fell far short of what he hoped to make. Ravenscroft, far more indolent and pleasure-seeking than many other of his countrymen, returned to the "Land of Cakes" in 1774 and became a property-owning physician there.[94]

[91]John Ravenscroft to his mother, Ann MacMurdo, 26 April 1770, Acc. 7199/3/3, NLS. Ravenscroft's medical class numbered twenty-two, seven of whom came from the colonies.

[92]John Ravenscroft to his mother, 15 December 1771, Acc. 7199/3/3, NLS. His half-brother George MacMurdo, who went to Virginia in 1770 as a merchant's apprentice in order "to rise in the world by means of the American trade," had earlier let his mother know that he didn't like Ravenscroft's estates. "Mecocks is a very sickly unhealthy place. . . . It did not at all answer my expectations" (George MacMurdo to his mother, 10 November 1770, Acc. 7199/4/1, NLS).

[93]Ibid. In the 1780s, Alexander Maclarty hoped to earn twice as much in Jamaica as Ravenscroft could expect in Virginia, again supporting the notion that there were more lucrative places for doctors to go than the Chesapeake.

[94]In vernacular use during the seventeenth and eighteenth centuries, the land of (oat)cakes refers to Scotland. See William George Smith, ed., *The Oxford Dictionary of English Proverbs*, 2d edition (Oxford, 1948). Smith provides two contemporary illustrations: one in *The Lauderdale Papers* (1669) and the other in Edward Burt, *Letters from a Gentleman in the North of Scotland* (1730). I have also found the term used in Robert Burns, "On the late Captain Grose's Peregrinations through Scotland" (1789), and Robert Fergusson, "The King's Birth Day in Edinburgh" (173?). Burns's use would have made the term even more popular.

He apparently did not do particularly well in Scotland either. He spent far more than he earned. Ravenscroft sold his estates in Virginia before the war, but only received 40 percent of the price before the hostilities broke out. As a result, his Scottish purchases were never completely paid off. In 1783, Ravenscroft's widow filed a claim for temporary support to the Loyalist commission. She testifies that she was £800 in debt—living in "great distress"—with an income of only £25 per year.[95]

In 1774, John Campbell did not reckon the Chesapeake or anywhere in North America, a particularly good place for Scots to settle permanently. While he acknowledged that possibilities for physicians and other skilled sojourners existed in Virginia and Maryland, he was unenthusiastic about the prospects for emigrants. "You mean people possessed of some property at home," he wrote clarifying his definition, "rather discontented with their situation, who would wish to convert what little they have into some of the fruitful acres of the West. . . . This they will not find it so easy to do at this time." Campbell found the Chesapeake "a happy Country to those who can make use of its advantages but . . . the natives . . . are Lazy & indolent & consequently for the most part are greatly indebted to British Merchants. I have often remarked that our Countrymen do well."[96] Campbell, thus, shared Ravenscroft's opinion that pre-Revolutionary Virginia and Maryland were not terribly enticing places in which to settle or to sojourn. Both men agreed that Scots, generally reckoned by their non-Scottish neighbors to be the heartiest and most industrious, could do well but that their hard work and diligence would result in a better return elsewhere.

Fewer records of Scottish professionals survive from Virginia and Maryland than from Jamaica. Ravenscroft is only one of a small number of Scottish physicians in these colonies about whom something is known.[97] Another in Virginia at the same time was Dr. James Currie. His Chesapeake sojourn came before Currie had trained as a physician. His career, nonetheless,

[95]The commissioners rejected her claim (LT, 5/122, NYPL). There is no record of a compensation claim. It is possible that one of Ravenscroft's children returned to Virginia after the war. See John S[tark] Ravenscroft to Mr. Radford, 15 February 1802, BR 262(51), HL. The letter is about a sale of pistols.

[96]John Campbell to William Sinclair, 26 July 1774, Sinclair of Freswick, GD 136/416/1, SRO.

[97]There is also the case of Dr. Alexander Hamilton, the Maryland physician, whose journal of a trip up and down the eastern seaboard has been published. See Carl Bridenbaugh, ed., *Gentleman's Progress: The Itinerarium of Dr. Alexander Hamilton* (Chapel Hill, N.C., 1948). Of Hamilton's medical career surprisingly little information has survived. The records of the Tuesday Club, a group of Annapolis men who met regularly from 1745 to 1755 (MS 854, MdHS), have been published by Elaine Breslaw, *Records of the Tuesday Club of Annapolis, 1745–56* (Champaign-Urbana, Ill, 1988). These records provide some information about the club's members, many of whom appear to have been Scottish. Also see Charles Haws, *Scots in the Old Dominion*, pp. 38–52, for a list of some of the most notable Scots medical people.

provides an important illustration of how those Scots who chose to leave the Chesapeake and return home often improved their situations more easily in Britain during and after the war than they could have done by remaining in the colonies.[98]

The son of a Dumfriesshire minister, Currie arrived in Virginia during 1771, aged fifteen and a grammar school graduate, to fulfill a five-year shop assistant's contract. Though he initially went to Glasgow in order to become a physician, the city's involvement with the Chesapeake, and the general excitement there because of it, convinced him (as it surely must have convinced many others) to head to Virginia instead. In his journal, which begins in 1776, just as he is leaving the colonies, he contemplated his five years in Virginia, finding "the good & ill balanced." He remembered the "many gloomy hours . . . labouring under the effects of pain & sickness, a hard usage . . . and the misfortune I had, of living with a man, from whom nothing could be learned that belonged either to the man of business or to the gentlemen." He also recollected that "my situation had been much more agreeable than that of other young fellows in my way."[99]

He returned to Glasgow in 1777, intending yet again to become a physician. He then anticipated setting out for the West Indies to earn the fortune that had eluded him in both Virginia and in his native country. Though he wanted to attend the University of Edinburgh, medical degrees from Glasgow University took one year less to complete. He enrolled there and graduated from the medical college in 1780.[100] He got as far as London on his journey to the Caribbean but then suddenly decided to stay in England. He apparently received an irresistible opportunity to practice medicine in Liverpool. After sojourning there for half a decade, Currie realized what a person required in order to acquire the independence which was so much pursued (and so elusive) in the colonies. He shared his newfound knowledge with his cousin, Dr. James Currie, a physician in Richmond, Virginia. It is the only precise definition of the term we have.

£4000 Sterling will make a bachelor independent; and for the love of God, if you can by any means squeeze this sum out of the wreck of your fortunes,

---

[98]Currie is perhaps better known as the editor of *The Works of Robert Burns, with an account of his life and a criticism of his writings. To which are prefixed some observations on the character and condition of the Scottish peasantry* (London, 1800), for many years the standard edition.

[99]"Manuscript Journal kept by Dr. James Currie during a voyage from Nixonton, North Carolina to the Island of St. Martin's, 1776," p. 3c [21 September 1776], MS 920 Cur 69, Liverpool Record Office.

[100]See *Dictionary of National Biography*, v. 5, p. 341, and William Wallace Currie, ed., *Memoir of the Life, Writings, and Correspondence of James Currie, M.D., F.R.S.* (London, 1831), vol. 2.

endeavour to insure it, by placing it out on some security in Britain where the principal will be safe, and the interest paid every half year.[101]

Cash or reputable securities in Britain mattered most. The Glasgow tobacco merchants knew this a decade earlier; so too did Jamaican planters. But the alluring appeal of colonial property overcame them. Buying it did not mean that they mentally gave up the sojourn; they perceived it simply as an investment. Few realized that the value of the investment depended upon things located outside Britain, thus making it less secure. Currie's advice to his cousin would have helped many in similar situations in both the Chesapeake and Jamaica. "If you get property in land," he wrote, "it pays no interest; if in debts, you have neither principal nor interest, and if in houses, though you may have appearances of both today, yet you cannot be secured against the treachery or the accident that . . . may consume your property to ashes."[102]

After practicing medicine along the Mersey for twelve years, James Currie realized his ambition; he purchased a Scottish estate. He had achieved what all of his countrymen had wanted to do without going to the colonies to do it. Indeed, his time in Virginia probably slowed him down, though it provided him with a good deal of insight into what was wrong with his countrymen's quests in that colony.

Despite his long residence in England, Currie never lost his Scottish identity, and he despised those who had.

> I like nothing so little as the awkward attempts of a Scotsman to be an Englishman. . . . I love Scotland dearly, I like her green Vales, her clear streams, her black mountains. As I travel north, I always watch the moment, and mark the spot . . . where Burnswark rises above the English horizon, and presenting itself the first object in Scotland, recalls . . . the idea of my native country.[103]

Sentimental about the place of their birth, but unconvinced that their country offered them enough socioeconomic mobility, many middling Scots looked everywhere else for opportunities. Currie's extensive sojourn had served him well, in both knowledge and fortune. Most Scots, however, were not so fortunate.

---

[101]James Currie to James Currie [Richmond], 1 July 1787, printed in W. W. Currie, *Memoir*, v. 2, p. 5. Currie was referring to the Richmond fire in that year. He could have substituted hurricanes in Westmoreland, Jamaica.

[102]Ibid.

[103]James Currie to Miss Ann Duncan, 1794, Currie, *Memoir*, v. 2, p. 321. Burnswark is a famous hill near the main road between Carlisle and Glasgow.

Nor did doctors and merchants have a monopoly on colonial sojourns. Records from a few other Scots professionals in the Chesapeake survive; these suggest that teachers, too, viewed the colonies as places to use their education to acquire the independence they could not discover in their native country. Philip Fithian commented in 1773 that most schoolmasters and tutors in Virginia were Scottish.[104]

John Harrower's story is well known and is worth presenting here if only to demonstrate that some Scots tutors and school masters were not sojourners. They intended to remain in the Chesapeake, and earn their living there without returning. Forced to leave his native Shetland Islands in December 1773, because he had no money, no job, and no means to support his family, John Harrower made his way south, "in search of business," along the east coast of Britain. He intended to go no farther than Holland. When he found himself penniless in London on 26 January 1774, he indented himself to go to Virginia in return for bed, board, washing, and a five-pound lump payment. After his passage, Colonel Dangerfield, who lived seven miles south of the Rappahannock River, purchased his indentures. Dangerfield needed a tutor for his children; Harrower filled the requirements.[105] From May 1774 until sometime in 1777, he acted as the plantation tutor. He ate with the family and soon became a part of it. Allowed to supplement his income, he accepted private pupils, charging them each four shillings (sterling) per quarter for their lessons.[106]

Harrower's story is remarkable, certainly, but of his background, ambitions, and aims little is known. Despite an apparently good education, he had been deprived of a living in his native country. Unlike many sojourners, Harrower did not choose specifically to go to Virginia; he was driven there by hunger. As a result, his experiences more closely fit the mold of the highland emigrants than the temporary transients. Once he got to the colony, any thoughts he might have had of eventually returning to Shetland evaporated. His letters to his wife reveal that he wanted her to join him:

> I yet hope (please God) if I am spared, some time to make you a Virginian Lady among the woods of America which is by far more pleasant than the roaring of

[104]Farish, ed., *Fithian*, p. 29. Fithian also notes an increasing tendency for the creole population to supply its own teachers.

[105]See *The Journal of John Harrower: An Indentured Servant in the Colony of Virginia, 1773–76*, ed. Edward Miles Riley (Williamsburg, Va., 1963). Riley identifies Harrower as a merchant in Shetland before he left (p. xiv). Bailyn, in *Voyagers*, calls Harrower "a peddler of stockings and small household goods" (p. 277). Harrower, like many Scots and unlike many indentured servants, was literate. He wanted to be a schoolmaster and the captain of the vessel encouraged this pursuit (see *Journal*, p. 39). Harrower did not go to Glasgow to seek employment when he left in 1773. If he had, despite being an outsider, he could perhaps have procured an assistant's place in one of the merchant houses, on either side of the Atlantic.

[106]*Journal*, p. 56.

the raging sea round abo' Zetland. . . . But this I must do by carefullness, industry and a close Application to Bussines.[107]

Receiving this letter, Mrs. Harrower consented to leave Shetland and make her way to Virginia as soon as a suitable opportunity arose. She appointed her brother, a merchant ship's captain, to handle the arrangements. Unfortunately for her, her husband died before she could leave. Colonel Dangerfield then offered to send her seventy pounds, toward her and her children's support. John Harrower was certainly not a sojourner. Yet he resembled that group in one respect. He saw an improved future for himself through "carefullness, industry, and a close Application to Bussines."

Few other schoolmasters' records survive, despite the seeming preponderance of Scottish tutors. David Duff, from northeast Scotland, migrated to Maryland and taught school on the Eastern Shore for a number of years. It is unclear whether he went, like Harrower, as an immigrant or, like many other Scots, as a sojourner. Claiming to have missed the only ship from Glasgow to Maryland in 1771 by four hours, he took passage to Virginia.[108] After arriving at Norfolk, he immediately went to Port Tobacco in search of a job. He was offered a teacher's position there for thirty pounds a year, hardly the kind of money which would allow an independent estate in any country, though some tobacco factors received even less. He turned it down and crossed Chesapeake Bay. At Oxford, Maryland, he secured a position as a private tutor. He earned sixteen pounds per year plus bed, board, and washing, but also had the opportunity to teach other children. He believed he would earn as much as forty or fifty pounds that year.[109]

Like Harrower, Duff decided to stay in the colonies and build a new life there. When he wrote to James Grant in 1780, he had been settled for three years as a schoolmaster in Dorset, Maryland. Considerably advanced in salary and status and now at a place called Eden, he lived on a plantation, which belonged to the school, and had just purchased another house. He

---

[107]*Journal*, p. 76. This perspective is unique among all the evidence I have examined. It seems to me that Harrower's preference for America can be easily explained by considering that he was forced out of his own country by poverty and lack of opportunity. While many men left Scotland for the latter reason, none of the other sojourners, to my knowledge, had to endure the poverty that Harrower did. His journey to the colonies was anything but pleasant. But once there, he was able to earn a reasonable living doing something he enjoyed. Therefore, he certainly asked, why go back?

[108]There is no date on this letter. However, the survey of newspapers described in Chapter 1 reveals that no fewer than five ships intended to go to Maryland that year. Perhaps he missed the last ship.

[109]David Duff to James Grant, n.d. [Docketed: 1772], Grant of Grant Muniments, GD 248/349/5, SRO. Duff's salary was far greater than Harrower's, indicating the high cost exacted from indentured servants.

even hired someone else's slave to do his farming. Each scholar paid him four pounds the first year, six pounds the second, and twelve the third. When he asked for one hundred pounds per year per scholar, probably as a ploy to get a raise, his "proposal was treated with ridicule, but I agreed for as much of this country produce as greatly exceeds that sum."[110]

Duff and Harrower certainly were different from the other Scots traveling from Scotland to the Chesapeake. Both came from the "greater" northeast, neither was really a merchant, and both settled permanently in the colony. With the exception of their education and occupations, neither fit the usual Chesapeake model as it has been here described. Yet, the little that is known about them suggests that while Scots going abroad chose certain places depending upon their education, skills, and socioeconomic background, exceptions did exist.

JAMAICA AND THE CHESAPEAKE: COMPARISONS AND CONCLUSIONS

Scots sojourners in the Chesapeake exerted far more influence than their relatively low numbers might at first suggest. Though they amounted to only a small fragment of the total population, their effects upon it were significant. Because they increasingly controlled the tobacco trade after 1740, they were blamed for many of the problems facing the colonists. Nonetheless, Chesapeake residents were dependent upon them for imported household and personal goods. As important, Scottish sojourners point us toward Atlantic history. One group of people with truly transatlantic links—living in two worlds—had influence in both of them. The Chesapeake region provided an outlet for the ambitions of Scotland's middling classes. The Scottish presence in Virginia and Maryland, at least before the war, allowed a higher quality of life for those who had business interactions with them.

When compared to their Jamaican counterparts, they show similarities. Both groups saw the new world as a means to achieve something better in the old.

As a tangible entity, the sample of Scots entrepreneurs presented in this chapter was far less diverse, both in terms of geographical origin and occupational category, than its Jamaican counterpart. Because most transient Scots in the Chesapeake were employed by Glasgow merchant houses who viewed the colonies as their own wealth-generating provinces, members of this group were paid less, had fewer opportunities for advancement, and had

[110]David Duff to James Grant, 20 May 1780, GD 248/228/1/94, SRO. A David Duff graduated from King's College, Aberdeen in 1770. It is unknown whether this is the same man.

much stricter control placed upon them than their Caribbean counterparts. Wages in Virginia, albeit with a lower cost of living than Jamaica, lagged significantly behind those in the island. A bookkeeper to an island plantation earned sixty pounds sterling a year to start while many shop assistants in Virginia were paid less than twenty-five pounds sterling a year. Chesapeake Scots after 1760 had considerably less opportunity to earn enough to change their status. It also took them longer.

They had, however, the examples of the big tobacco lords who had been over before them as motivation. But these very merchants, through their restrictive employment practices, prevented their employees from achieving the same level of success. Later sojourners in the Chesapeake were closely supervised from across the Atlantic. As a result, they had few opportunities to misbehave, take risks, and make their fortunes. The Scots in Virginia and Maryland would have much preferred to have behaved like Francis Grant in Jamaica.

4

WEBS OF PATRONAGE:
SCOTTISH NETWORKS IN
JAMAICA AND THE CHESAPEAKE

The Scots confronted an alien environment when they arrived in the Western Hemisphere; they could not have entirely comprehended local cultures and customs. The hybrid creole population in Virginia and Maryland greatly outnumbered Europeans. And because the dominant influences of both Chesapeake colonies had identifiably English roots, the Scots stood out even more. Something similar took place in Jamaica, though much less cultural development—let alone creole cultural development—had occurred before the end of the eighteenth century. The Scots, therefore, needed to develop some sort of strategy for survival.

Immigration historians often assume that most people who move to an alien culture gradually acculturate and assimilate. They take on more and more of the characteristics of the society in which they find themselves.[1] This accommodation, in effect, makes life easier for members of the minority group by proving that they do not harbor hostile feelings. It has the added benefit of demonstrating to others their intention to remain permanently. People who do not plan on staying, like the "professional" Scots, frequently find themselves in complicated positions. Because they look backward to the old world rather than forward to the new, they call attention to themselves as outsiders. Their neighbors, members of the host society, view them with suspicion.[2]

[1]For a general treatment of the process of acculturation and assimilation, see Oscar Handlin, *Immigration as a Factor in American History* (Englewood Cliffs, N.J., 1959), and *Boston's Immigrants: A Study in Acculturation, 1790–1865* (Cambridge, Mass., 1941). More recent scholarship has argued that acculturation did not universally take place. The best summary of the changes in the literature of migration is found in Ewa Moraska, "The Sociology and Historiography of Immigration," in *Immigration Reconsidered*, ed. Yans-McLaughlin, pp. 187–238.

[2]This theory of host-society hostility is put forward in Bonacich, "A Theory of Middleman

"Sketch of Bridgetown in Barbados, 1813" drawn by Robert Johnston, a Scottish sojourner in Jamaica, while en route from Scotland to Jamaica, pen and ink drawing, 1813. Powel Collection, R. Johnston, Drawings, The Historical Society of Pennsylvania.

In order to counter such hostility in the host society, Scottish transients did what many groups in similar situations have done over the course of the last two centuries—they turned to each other for support. Scots, both in Jamaica and the Chesapeake, generally resided near each other. Moreover, they established business and community networks among themselves. On the most basic level, association allowed them to reinforce their own cultural values. But, like many groups in more recent history, their choice of professional and merchandising occupations dictated that their contacts could not be so exclusive as to isolate the Scots from those who lived permanently in that society. Indeed, the Scottish sojourners needed the business of the population at large if they hoped to fulfill their own ambitions. They walked a thin line; they could not afford to alienate potential customers yet they did not want to become assimilated into their hosts' society.

Scottish networks had several functions. First, they facilitated patronage in both Jamaica and the Chesapeake. By ensuring that the ethnic group's

Minorities" and Jonathan H. Turner and Edna Bonacich, "Toward a Composite Theory of Middlemen Minorities," *Ethnicity* 7 (1980), esp. 151–52. They argue that the more ethnocentric the culture and distinct the group as it moves into a society with a high concern about national integration, the greater the chance for host-society hostility.

members, young and old alike, had the right credentials and the requisite connections, the webs suggested and provided career paths, occupational alternatives, and even friendships. They were not, of course, created to regulate non-business relationships (as they often did) but rather to facilitate the fulfillment of the sojourner's professional aims and ambitions with a minimum of difficulty.[3]

In the second place, the networks provided a focus for ethnic solidarity. They fostered a sense of belonging in those who had not previously demonstrated any feelings of collective consciousness while simultaneously reminding those who had that they shared not only a common past but also the same agenda for the future. The sojourning Scots' neighbors perceived them to be members of an alien culture, and that perception provoked the group into maintaining an image of distinctiveness. They lived up to the stereotype.[4]

Rather than striving to overcome society's inherent prejudices against outsiders, the Scots attempted to play them to their own advantage. By doing so, they appeared to accept their prescribed position in the social order. They could then devote most of their energy to achieving their economic goals precisely because they were not perceived as a threat. In other words, sojourning Scots moved closer together because their English neighbors already perceived them to be a distinct group. As Ned Landsman has argued,

---

[3]The best discussion on migrant networks I have seen is Charles Tilly, "Transplanted Networks," in *Immigration Reconsidered*, pp. 79–95. For a useful bibliographical introduction to the social science literature on patronage, as well as for a model that supports some of the arguments in this chapter, see S. N. Eisenstadt and Louis Roniger, "Patron-Client Relations as a Model of Structuring Social Exchange," *Comparative Studies in Society and History* 22 (January, 1980): 42–77. Another useful discussion of patronage networks can be found in Eric R. Wolf, "Kinship, Friendship, and Patron-Client Relations in Complex Societies," in *The Social Anthropology of Complex Societies*, ed. Michael Banton (London, 1966), pp. 1–22. Charles Camic, in *Experience and Enlightenment*, pp. 206–7, discusses patronage in the context of Scottish professionalism and the enlightenment at home. He believes that nothing accentuated dependency more than patronage, which was supposed to eradicate it.

[4]By far the most useful models, which persuasively suggest that such behavior was characteristic of sojourners, can be found in Bonacich, "Middleman Minorities" and Bonacich and Turner, "Toward a Composite Theory of Middlemen Minorities." For a description of stereotypical images and the ways members of ethnic groups lived with one another, see Mary E. Wilkie, "Colonials, Marginals, and Immigrants: Contributions to a Theory of Ethnic Stratification," *Comparative Studies in Society and History* 15 (April, 1977): 67–95. For defining groups within a society, see Adrian C. Meyer, "The Significance of Quasi-Groups in the Study of Complex Societies," in *Social Anthropology*, pp. 97–121. For the English attempt to eradicate strong Irish identity, which initially brought the Irish closer together, see Nicholas Canny, "Identity Formation in Ireland: The Emergence of the Anglo-Irish," in *Colonial Identity in the Atlantic World, 1500–1800*, ed. Nicholas Canny and Anthony Pagden (Princeton, N.J., 1987), pp. 159–212.

"the initial impact of the American experience was to create a common ethnic identity among the Scottish settlers."[5]

While the Scots' behavior was similar in both colonial areas, the nature of the networks and the outcomes they achieved in Jamaica and the Chesapeake form a contrast. Scottish domination of the Chesapeake tobacco trade coupled with their pro-British stand made them fiercely unpopular as the events which led up to the American Revolution unfolded.

Edna Bonacich described a theory which is in large part applicable to the Scots. She argued that such "middlemen minorities" often act as a buffer between the aristocracy and the bottom ranks of society. Things would generally go well for the sojourners until the need for a scapegoat arose. The carefully constructed place of the middlemen made them perfect targets. This happened in the Chesapeake. There does not appear to have been any such crisis of confidence directed at those Scots who lived in Jamaica.

Finally, these Scottish networks maintained clear and direct lines of communication with relatives, friends, and acquaintances at home. In the words of Edna Bonacich,

> sojourners have little reason to develop lasting relationships with members of the surrounding host society. But they have every reason to keep deeply alive the regional and broader ethnic tie, for these relationships will persist in the future towards which the sojourner points.[6]

Maintaining strong ties to home allowed the Scots to reinforce their belief that their colonial experiences were temporary. Such links, also useful for continuing patronage, provided a constant source of new labor from Scotland. This self-perpetuation eradicated any need to assimilate, or otherwise deviate from a plan, in order to become part of the dominant culture. Connections came from "the Land of Cakes" and not from the colonies themselves.[7]

[5]The Scottish community in eighteenth-century New Jersey is described in Landsman, *Scotland and Its First American Colony*, pp. 141–62; the quotation is from p. 174. Bonacich has found that members of such groups demonstrated "a resistance to out-marriage, residential self-segregation . . . the maintenance of distinct cultural traits." Communal solidarity was important to the group's economic success. See "Middlemen Minorities," p. 586. This behavior is common among sojourners, at least as they are portrayed in Paul C. P. Siu's "The Sojourner." Thomas Sowell, in the *Economics and Politics of Race* (New York, 1983), esp. pp. 24–26, describes Chinese transients living in other societies. They became subjects of awe, for their diligence, and resentment, for their apparent success.

[6]"Middlemen Minorities," p. 586.

[7]Of course, the tendencies described in the first three chapters for sojourners from Glasgow and the west to go to the Chesapeake and transients from elsewhere to choose Jamaica must be remembered here; Scottishness was the lowest common denominator within the colonies; it did not seem to operate in that way within Scotland.

Scottish transients, who went to Jamaica in ever-increasing numbers between 1740 and 1800, generally lived near each other. Their close physical proximity suggests the existence of several unofficial neighborhoods for Scottish fortune hunters. Apart from an obvious presence in Kingston (a mercantile mecca), the Scots generally resided in the newer (in 1750) and less developed areas in the island's northern and western parishes. Among those parishes with the highest percentage of Scottish names were West-moreland, Hanover, and St. James (in the west) along with Trelawny (created from St. James in 1773), St. Ann's, and St. Mary's (along the north coast).[8] Such settlements made network interaction extremely simple, given eighteenth-century visiting practices, and facilitated the cause of patronage.[9]

Similarly, in the Chesapeake, because of the Scots sojourners' monolithic presence in the tobacco industry, high concentrations of Scots have been found in the tobacco warehouse towns, and in the many (James, Potomac, and Rappahannock) river towns where Glasgow merchants had their stores. There was, as well, an increasing tendency during the period for some Scots to move to the back country. While some of them went as employees of newly opened Glasgow stores, many of these people were not sojourners at all; rather they had immigrated to the mainland colonies.[10]

A strong case could be made that classical eighteenth-century patronage emanating from Scotland created the areas with high concentrations of sojourners. These Scots were told where to go before they ever left home. It can also be demonstrated that the networks in the colonies themselves generated patronage, and drew Scots into them after they had arrived in the new world. Transients who arrived without definite positions could frequently be accommodated in one of these networks. Likewise, those who became dissatisfied with their prearranged appointments could make use of the webs to change their situations. In both cases, the simple fact of ethnicity acted as the minimum requirement for gaining access.[11]

[8]See the discussion below as well as Barry Higman, *Slave Population and Economy in Jamaica, 1807–1834* (Cambridge, 1976), pp. 18–25.

[9]The 1754 Landholders list for Jamaica suggests that certain parishes had a higher concentration of landowners with Scottish names. Matching this information with the addresses from which much of the surviving correspondence came confirmed my choice of these six parishes for analysis. For an excellent examination of visiting practices in Virginia, see Michael Zuckerman, "Fate, Flux, and Good Fellowship: An Early Virginia Design for the Dilemma of American Business," in *Business and Its Environment: Essays for Thomas C. Cochran*, ed. Harold Sharlin (Westport, Conn., 1983), pp. 161–84.

[10]There are virtually no letters (in either Britain or the United States) and only imperfect public records from which to gather information about the lives of these individuals. As a result, all that can be said with any certainty is that some people who had Scottish names lived in the back country, outside the main areas of this study. I am unable to say anything about Scottish communities of the more permanent (immigrant) type.

[11]See Landsman, *Scotland and Its First American Colony*, esp. pp. 142–47, for a discussion of

Of the sojourners who lived near each other, many shared either a common family member or business acquaintance. Some, however, simply came from the same geographical region in Scotland. The plethora of Grants (from Northeast Scotland) in Trelawny and St. James, Jamaica, and the high number of Glasgow Scots in Alexandria and Port Tobacco persuasively prove this point. All it took to gain a place in a colonial Scottish network, apart from ethnicity, was knowing someone, or someone who knew someone, in the desired place of residence. People came to know other people through kinship, business relations, and simple physical proximity. Being a Scot was all that was necessary to gain access to the networks, but very specific rules came into play inside them.[12]

Members of the immediate family came first. They were followed by extended family, generally second and third cousins. After them came personal acquaintances from the same town or region, who were, in turn, followed by members of their families. Patrons looked first to family. If no one could be found who could satisfy the particular needs, they helped those further down the list, always paying particular attention not to help anyone out of turn.

THE DATA FOR JAMAICA

As I have noted, it is simply impossible to identify every Scottish sojourner, or even every Scot, who lived in the island during any individual year. It is, however, entirely possible to estimate the distribution of such people in a number of years throughout the period. Several means to do so can be utilized. The first is the 1754 list of Jamaica landholders in the Public

---

similar Scottish behavior in the early part of the eighteenth century. Landsman argues that Scots only moved to places where other Scots lived and that they depended upon old world connections.

[12] Allan Macfarlane, in *The Family Life of Ralph Josselin* (Cambridge, 1970), explains how visiting patterns and interpersonal relationships defined community. Lorena Walsh's excellent paper "Community Networks in the Early Chesapeake" shows how physical proximity created interpersonal relationships and expanded a person's world of friends and acquaintances. Charles Camic in *Experience and Enlightenment*, ch. 7 (pp. 205–7) describes the ways the Scottish middle classes used patronage to achieve better employment and further personal goals. And Edna Bonacich, in "Middlemen Minorities," comments on the characteristics of sojourner networks. The next most popular places for Scots to go (after Jamaica and the Chesapeake) were the East Indies, and in the West Indies, Grenada, St. Vincent's, and Tobago, all of which were added to the British Empire in 1763. The account books of Alexander Houston & Company, a Glasgow concern trading extensively in the sugar economy, reveal that their main business was in these islands, and a somewhat smaller business with the Scottish residents on the far eastern side of Jamaica. See Houston & Company Records, MS 8796, NLS.

Record Office.[13] The identifiable Scots numbered 140 out of a total of 1564 names.[14] These 140 landholders held 213 tracts of land. Of these 213, 31.5 percent were located in three adjoining parishes, St. James, Westmoreland, and Hanover, in the island's west side. In terms of the total acreage privately held, St. James parish ranked fourth, Westmoreland third, and Hanover twelfth, out of a total of nineteen. All three parishes produced impressive quantities of sugar.[15]

The colony's sixth and tenth most settled parishes, St. Mary's and St. Ann's, along the island's north coast, had approximately the same number of Scots landowners as the island's most heavily settled parishes, St. Elizabeth's and Clarendon, along its south coast. Because more people lived in the south, the concentration of Scots would have been more significant in the north. Table 4.1 depicts the actual rankings of each parish.

All of the parishes that had a high number of Scots in 1754 could be characterized as growth areas in 1774, and continued so, even as late as 1832. Each had a diversifying, though still staple-producing, economy. As might be expected, the heaviest emphasis fell upon sugar production, though estates that produced other crops were not at all uncommon. Edward Long has provided the only systematic analysis of the differences and similarities between the various late-eighteenth-century economies. He described St. James parish in 1774 as the leading sugar producer, "the most thriving district of the Island." He also remarked that its western neighbor, Hanover parish, "bids fair to vie with those esteemed the richest in Jamaica." This ranking is even more impressive after one realizes that it had achieved this status since its creation in 1723. Long observed that since its inception in 1736, St. Mary's parish had grown exceedingly fast. But even so, in 1774, only one-fourth of its areas had been placed under cultivation.[16]

Barry Higman has thoroughly studied similar interparish variations during the first part of the nineteenth century. In his book, Higman explicates some

[13]See CO 142/31, PRO, Kew. I counted each Scottish name and omitted those which may be either Scottish or English. The names and number of Scots on the island can not be taken directly from this list. Many absentees were also listed. Also, a small (perhaps insignificant) number may have been second or third generation (none earlier, because the Union of Parliaments and Scottish authority to settle in the island, did not take place until 1707).

[14]Sheridan, in *Sugar and Slavery,* estimates that fully one quarter of the landholders were Scottish, pp. 369–70.

[15]See Add. MSS 12,434/11–12, Long MSS, British Library. In 1739, Westmoreland had the second highest number of sugar works (after Clarendon), Hanover the fifth, and St. James the twelfth. By 1768, St. James was the leading sugar producer, Westmoreland and Hanover were third and fourth. See ADD. MSS 12,435/31–32, BL. Trelawny parish, created in 1773, would have been included in the St. James's parish statistics.

[16]Edward Long's *History of Jamaica* contains a description of the economy and the "state of the parish" for each of the island's divisions. See esp. v. 2, pp. 78–79, 206, 212, 213, and 219, for some of his remarks about the parishes under discussion here.

Table 4.1. Scottish landowners in Jamaica, 1754

Parish	Number of Scots	Rank	Acreage held (rank)
Kingston	0	19	19
Port Royal	1	18	18
St. Catherine	13	8	8
St. Andrew	18	3	7
St. David	5	14	16
St. Thomas in the East	15	5	5
Portland	3	16	17
St. George	5	14	14
St. Elizabeth	16	4	2
Vere	14	6	13
Clarendon	11	10	1
St. Dorothy	2	17	15
St. John	7	13	11
St. Thomas in the Vale	10	11	9
St. Mary	14	6	6
St. Ann	12	9	10
St. James	29	2	4
Hanover	8	12	12
Westmoreland	30	1	3

Source: "Jamaica Landholders in 1754," CO 142/31, PRO, Kew.

of the regional differences within the island's agricultural and economic structures. Planters expressed "fairly strong preferences" when choosing where to buy their land and what crops to produce upon it. According to his findings, Westmoreland parish, in 1832, was the sixth most important sugar producing parish. It supported, as well, a significant, if small, number of cattle pens and pimento walks. So did Hanover, though its sugar production exceeded that of Westmoreland, its southern neighbor. Trelawny parish was the island's leading sugar parish in 1832, and especially in the eastern regions, also had a number of estates with pimento walks. Here, pens were all but insignificant.[17] St. Ann's, in the middle of the island's north coast, produced impressive amounts of sugar, and was probably the most diverse of the parishes as well. It had a minor coffee-growing area, but also ranked first in the cultivation of pimento and second in the ratio of livestock to slaves in 1832. In addition, Jamaican residents had discovered that the lands in St. Ann's hills were particularly suited to cattle penning. St. Mary's parish, which borders St. Ann's on the east, produced the third highest amount of

[17]Higman, *Slave Population*, pp. 18–25. Edward Brathwaite has also, in *Creole Society*, p. 122, indicated that in 1820 the eight most densely populated parishes included the six discussed here as well as St. Elizabeth's and St. Thomas-in-the-East. Higman's discussion, to my mind, is much more precisely determined.

sugar in the island. It appears to have done so with even more brutality than normal in the colony. Among all of the island's sugar cultivation regions, St. Mary's had the lowest rate of natural increase amongst its slave population. In 1832, St. James's parish, which had been the leading sugar producer in 1774, still had many sugar plantations, more than fifteen other parishes in fact, though their productivity was not so great as in other parts of the island or even as great as it once had been. Clearly, its soil had begun to tire after decades of monoculture. That Trelawny parish was separated from St. James in 1773 surely removed many of the sugar plantations from its jurisdiction, also contributing to its declining position relative to other parishes.

Each of these six parishes, by 1800, also had more slaves in them then almost all the others. Of the group, Trelawny stood first (27,827), which was not a surprise, given that it had more sugar estates than any other parish. Westmoreland had the fewest number of slaves (20,864) and ranked seventh (out of twenty) among all the island's parishes. The other four, of course, all ranked higher than Westmoreland. By 1810, in each of these parishes, except St. James, more slaves were reported than had been a decade earlier. The Scots showed clear preferences for these growth regions. They chose the areas that underwent some of the island's most profound expansion in the second half of the eighteenth century. These locales all had a large, and rising, number of opportunities, especially in sugar production.[18]

These parishes also comprise two adjacent geographic areas; they can be used as a sample to examine the structure and function of Scottish networks (which, no doubt, existed wherever the Scots settled) in Jamaica. The next chronological opportunity to measure Scottish habitation patterns comes in the form of a highly detailed map drawn in 1761.[19] It plots a substantial number of the island's landholders and named plantations on a map with a scale of roughly one mile to an inch. The Scots in Westmoreland, Hanover, St. James, St. Mary's, and St. Ann's parishes have been identified, again using simple surname analysis. In cases where the map provided only a

[18]For further information on the differences and similarities between the six parishes, see the tables in Higman, *Slave Population*, pp. 53, 255. His information for the first part of the nineteenth century can be extrapolated back into the eighteenth century. Coupled with the sources in the Long manuscripts cited above, it makes evident the growth of these regions across the period.

[19]Thomas Craskell, *The Map of the County of Cornwall and Island of Jamaica and the Map of the County of Middlesex and Island of Jamaica* (London, 1763) (LC: G4963.C6 1763 .C7 Vault and CO 700/[Jamaica]/Maps 17–19, PRO). The areas I have chosen to examine not only had a higher concentration of Scottish landowners in 1754 but also have left consistently more qualitative evidence about their residents. These were the areas with more Scots living in them. Surviving material from parishes that have not been included (and for which there is less source material to study) indicates that similar, if smaller, communities and networks had also formed there. See, for example, the Houston and Company Records (St. Thomas-in-the-East parish) at the National Library of Scotland.

Table 4.2.   Scots v. non-Scots, 1761

Parish	Scots	Non-Scots	% Scottish
St. Ann's	24	84	22.2
St. Mary's	14	95	12.8
St. James (incl. Trelawny)	28	100	21.9
Westmoreland	20	82	19.6
Hanover	16	75	17.6
TOTALS	102	436	19.0 avg.

Source: Thomas Craskell, "The Map of the County of Cornwall and Island of Jamaica," and "The Map of the County of Middlesex and Island of Jamaica" (London, 1763), Map Division, Library of Congress.

plantation name, I have taken the Jamaican Crop Accounts (or Accounts Produce) for 1760 and attempted to identify the estate's owner, its attorney, or both.[20] The number of Scottish names and estates on the map is compared with the number of non-Scottish names and estates in Table 4.2. It can be easily seen that the Scots constituted significant minorities in all of these parishes, and that the number of Scottish estates had increased substantially since the 1754 survey.

Within the five parishes, the Scots demonstrated a remarkable tendency to reside in fairly close proximity. Where either the owner or the estate manager of a property included on the Craskell and Simpson map has been identified as Scottish, the estate has been plotted with a dot on Map 1, Scottish residences in 1761. In all of the parishes but St. Mary's (which seems to have had few of its plantations represented in the Crop Accounts), many Scots lived near their countrymen. They had easy access by road to their neighbors. As a result, they could readily transact business. Of course, they also had many English neighbors, who naturally outnumbered them (and have not been plotted on Map 1). Even so, the concentration of Scots in these areas is anything but a coincidence. Such clustering is characteristic of both settlers and sojourners from the same ethnic group.[21]

Unfortunately, no comparable sources have yet been found which can provide information on Scottish settlement patterns for any year in the

[20]The Jamaican Crop Accounts can be found in the Jamaica Archives, Series 1B/11/4. They are indexed, usually either by name of plantation or name of owner (it did vary from year to year and plantation to plantation). The series is nearly complete from 1755 virtually through the nineteenth century. Unfortunately, many attorneys and managers did not file the required papers until ten years after they were required to do so, if they bothered with the bureaucracy at all.

[21]The literature here is particularly large. For example, see Bonacich, "Middlemen Minorities," for the sojourner case, and Sowell, *Economics and Politics,* pp. 54, 69, 77, and 148–56, for some basic examples and a brief overview of the immigrant tendency to settle in the same places.

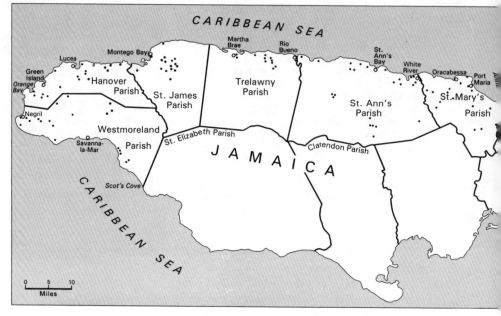

Map 1. Scottish residences in Jamaica, 1761

period from roughly 1765 to 1800. The next opportunity for a geographic analysis comes at the turn of the nineteenth century. Based upon James Robertson's exquisite 1804 map of the three counties of Jamaica, Map 2 (Scottish residences in 1804) demonstrates a greatly enlarged Scottish presence. This increased concentration occurred precisely in those areas of the island which had significant Caledonian concentrations forty years earlier. The number of Scots in each of these parishes, as opposed to the number of non-Scots in these parishes, is displayed in Table 4.3. The percentage of Scots as a proportion of the total population, which ranged from 23.3 percent in Westmoreland to 35.5 percent in Trelawny, increased substantially during the forty years since 1761. Many Scots came to live in these particular areas directly as a result of their countrymen's extensive transatlantic patronage network.[22]

Chapters 1 and 2 present a sample of 267 Scots in Jamaica over the entire period from 1740 to 1800, for whom biographical information has been obtained. Identifying the parishes in which they lived while on their Jamaica

---

[22]Like the map (1) produced from the Craskell and Simpson map (1763), Map 2 has taken into account the Jamaican Crop Accounts for the years 1778 and 1804. A list of plantations and estates, whose owners or managers were not known, was made from the Robertson map (CO 700/(Jamaica)/21–24, PRO, Kew) and then this list was compared against the crop accounts. If either a manager, attorney, or owner turned out to be a Scot, the property has been included in Map 2.

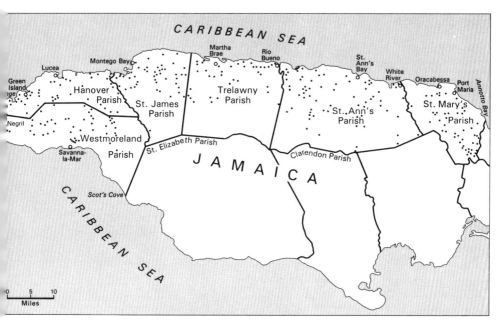

Map 2. Scottish residences in Jamaica, 1804

sojourns, where known, has provided Table 4.4. After eliminating the unknowns from the sample, the remaining data demonstrate a pattern similar to the one found in the 1754 landholders' list. The Scots in this sample clustered in the same parishes which independent sources have shown to have had a high number of Scottish residents.

Scottish residents in Jamaica chose to live in particular parishes, and within these parishes, in concentrated pockets. Pushing the surviving sources to the limits of their utility, I have attempted to illustrate the increasing Scottish concentration in these particular parishes and areas over time. There were, in the same style that Lorena Walsh described for the

Table 4.3. Scots v. non-Scots, 1804

Parish	Scots	Non-Scots	% Scottish
St. Ann's	69	153	31.1
St. Mary's	47	97	32.6
Hanover	46	118	28.0
St. James	44	116	27.5
Trelawny	49	89	35.5
Westmoreland	35	115	23.3
TOTALS	290	688	29.6 avg.

Source: James Robertson, "Map of Cornwall County, Jamaica," and "Map of Middlesex County," (London, 1804), Copy in Map Division, National Library of Scotland.

Table 4.4. Jamaican Scots' places of residence, 1740–1800

Parish	Percent
Total (n) 267	
Kingston	19.85
Other parishes	52.81
Unknown	27.34
Adjusted Total [267 minus 73 (unknown)] 194	
Kingston (53)	27.31
Other parishes (141)	72.68
Other parishes	
St. Mary	10.82
St. Ann	11.34
Trelawny	7.73
Hanover	9.30
St. James	9.80
Westmoreland	7.22
East Side parishes	3.61
St. Elizabeth	3.10
All others	9.80
Adjusted Total (194 minus 53: to remove Kingston from sample) 141	
St. Mary	14.89
St. Ann	15.60
Trelawny	10.64
Hanover	12.77
St. James	13.48
Westmoreland	9.93
East Side parishes	4.96
St. Elizabeth	4.25
All others	13.48

Source: Correspondence.

Chesapeake, neighborhoods—pockets of Scottish transients—which drew an increasing number of the country's youth to their little piece of the tropics.[23] An analysis of the patronage networks and interactions between the various correspondent Scots, as well as the mapping of some of these relationships will be carried out in the latter part of this chapter. With this

[23]Such neighborhoods can be much more easily demonstrated in eighteenth-century Jamaica, using Walsh's technique, than in her own region of the Chesapeake.

information, a clear idea of just how far, geographically and personally, one person's connections could stretch can be ascertained.

THE DATA FOR MARYLAND AND VIRGINIA

Providing a similar analysis of Scottish places of residence for the Chesapeake colonies has proven more difficult. County, or even colonywide, maps with the same detail as those for Jamaica simply do not exist for either the old colonies of Maryland and Virginia or the corresponding states after the American Revolution. The only comparable maps for the Chesapeake in this period are the Fry-Jefferson (1755/1775) and John Henry (1770) plans, both of Virginia, and the Dennis Griffith (1794) Maryland map.[24] Both of the Virginia maps are recognized to have errors and neither includes the names of all of the colonies' landowners; only those with the largest properties or those of any political note have been plotted. Similarly, the Maryland map was drawn well after the Scottish sojourners had left the colony. It too has only the very largest landowners on it.

Nor is there a complete run of powers of attorney or crop accounts for either of the Chesapeake colonies.[25] Such problems have been compounded by the great difficulty in trying to separate the Scottish transients in the area from the Scottish immigrants, highland or otherwise, and the rest of the creole population with Scottish ancestry.[26] The Fry-Jefferson and Henry maps, in particular, do however provide some indication of where those Scots who owned large properties tended to live. Both maps have been

[24]There is, as well, the recently released "Fairfax County, Virginia in 1760: An Interpretive Historical Map," prepared by Beth Mitchell (Fairfax, 1987). This well-done map has all of the county's landowners, their tenants, and property drawn in. (Available from the Fairfax County Publications Office and at the VHS, Map F232 F2 1987:1). The Fry-Jefferson map was first released in 1755 (after a 1751 survey) and was only slightly revised and reissued in 1775. The map has been published in many places, most recently in facsimile by the Virginia State Library in *A Description of the Country*, ed. E. M. Sanchez-Saavedra (Richmond, 1975). I have used this copy; it is dated 1775. The copy of the John Henry Map used here can be found in the Virginia Historical Society (Map F221/1770:2). It is available in facsimile from the University of Virginia Press, Charlottesville. The Griffith "Map of the State of Maryland from an Actual Survey of the Chesapeake and Delaware Bays" (20 June 1794) can be found at the Library of Congress, and as Map 752/1794, VSL.

[25]Both sets of records have been tremendously useful in identifying Scots and their places of residence in Jamaica. The irregular supply of records, especially for Virginia, has been a disappointment.

[26]Name analysis for the Chesapeake colonies is much more difficult than for Jamaica, because more people came to the colonies as immigrants. In Jamaica, few planned to stay permanently. For the Chesapeake, only those Scots who could be identified as Scots (while in Jamaica, because of low immigration and high mortality, Scottish names sufficed) have been included in this analysis.

analyzed for Scots. The Fry-Jefferson map shows 12 Scottish estates and 153 non-Scottish estates. There are 6 Scottish estates and 152 non-Scottish estates on the John Henry map. Scottish estates, on both maps, were less than 10 percent of the total number of properties.

Both the Fry-Jefferson and Henry maps reveal a dispersed settlement pattern, one very different from that in Jamaica. Scottish landowners, rather than being clustered in certain counties, tended to be strung along the northern reaches of the Potomac River and scattered across the rest of the colony. Nor do the maps reveal a very substantial increase in the number of Scottish landowners between 1755 and 1775. This distribution might, at first glance, appear highly unusual. It becomes far less mystifying with the realization that the two maps identify large landowners, who would certainly not have been a part of the tobacco transiency that formed the principal employment of the men in this study. The Scots owners of mapped properties were people who had built up enough capital to purchase and maintain property before the very large number of their temporary countrymen arrived. Migration from Scotland, at least of the sojourning traders and "professionals," began to increase dramatically around 1760 and continued to do so through the Revolution. These were the people who lived in towns, many of which acted as tobacco collection centers, as well as in the newer areas of settlement, like the colony's central piedmont and southside. They would certainly not have been included in such maps.

Despite easily available credit (from Scottish merchants) and high prices for tobacco, tidewater planters ran out of land after 1760. As important, acreage then under cultivation had begun to tire. The resulting pressure drove many into the piedmont and backcountry regions. Those who arrived from Scotland with no intention of staying went to where the tobacco was—the older tidewater areas and newer collection centers in the piedmont, which had been established to help the farmers get their crops more easily to market. Sojourners' experiences would certainly have been shaped by the declining prosperity in the older region, making the collection centers at and above the fall line much more important.

Those Scots who either came expecting to stay or who decided after they were in the colonies not to return to Britain also faced the tidewater's problems. In other words, people who purchased property met diminishing opportunities in these areas. Such an observation certainly helps to explain the lack of Scots on maps of the region. Those who came with the waves of immigration, especially after 1745, increasingly had to move to the piedmont and backcountry in order to find any land at all. They certainly would not have brought enough capital to buy what little remained in the tidewater.

Scottish residential preferences, then, were shaped by the Chesapeake economy. Committed to their older customers after 1760, the Scots main-

Table 4.5. Scots as percent of renters in Northern
Neck Counties

Year	County	% Scottish
1760	Northumberland	2.7
1768	Stafford	6.0
1773	Stafford	6.0
1761	Prince William	5.0
1773	Prince William	ca. 11.0
1777	Prince William	ca. 11.0
1764	Fairfax	ca. 7.0
1774	Fairfax	ca. 10.0
1772	Loudoun	4.7
1764	Frederick	7.8
1765	Richmond	4.4
1770	Richmond	4.4
1773	King George	5.3
1764	Culpeper	6.7
1773	Culpeper	7.2
1770	Fauquier	
1772	Berkeley	12.5
1777	Berkeley	10.9

Sources: BR 295 (8a–8b), 295 (11); BR 289 (4); BR
297 (3–4); BR 287 (2), 287 (5); BR 292 (3); BR 288
(1a–1b); BR 290 (3); BR 294 (7, 9, 10); BR 285; BR
293 (3); BR 284 (1–3); BR 229 (32); and in the Brock
Collection in the Huntington Library, San Marino,
California.

tained their stores in the tidewater. These were, in fact the ones which produced much of Glasgow's early tobacco wealth. Recognizing the change in the colonies' economy, they also opened new stores at the fall line, in order to gain the custom of the colonists who lived there. Among those colonists would have been many of their own emigrant countrymen.[27]

Examining surviving rent rolls from Virginia's northern neck (the peninsula between the Potomac and Rappahannock rivers) also demonstrates the general westward thrusts of Scottish emigrants. Counting the number of Scottish names, and comparing it to the total number of renters in each county, has provided Table 4.5. It reveals greater concentrations of Scots in the counties further inland. That concentration generally increased in the years before the American Revolution. Without correspondence, however, it is impossible to distinguish between sojourners and immigrants on these lists.

Because the Scottish sojourning involvement in the Chesapeake largely

[27]See Allan Kulikoff, *Tobacco and Slaves*, pp. 131–56.

Table 4.6. Chesapeake Scots' places of residence, 1740–1800

Place	Percent
Total (n = 139)	
Potomac River, Virginia	15.83
Potomac River, Maryland	12.23
Rappahannock River	20.14
York River	0.00
James River	13.67
Eastern Shore, Maryland	2.88
Western Shore, Maryland	3.60
Backcountry (Virginia)	3.60
Unknown	16.55
Norfolk/Southside, Virginia	11.51
Adjusted Total (n minus unknown = 116)	
Potomac River, Virginia	18.96
Potomac River, Maryland	14.66
Rappahannock River	24.14
York River	0.00
James River	16.38
Eastern Shore, Maryland	3.45
Western Shore, Maryland	4.31
Backcountry (Virginia)	4.31
Norfolk/Southside, Virginia	13.79

Source: Correspondence.

ended at the beginning of the American Revolution, and had more definite starting points than did its Jamaican counterpart, it has also been possible to identify the residences of Scots in the surviving correspondence and plot them onto a map. Table 4.6 portrays this information in numeric form. Map 3 (Addresses of Scottish correspondents, 1750–1783) geographically displays the results. The towns with sojourning Scottish correspondents living in them are indicated, with the number of correspondents actually there, over any part of the period, placed directly after the name of the town. This shows that the Scots about whose experiences something is known tended to live in certain places. These were, primarily, towns located along the Potomac, Rappahannock, and James rivers, where the Glasgow firms collected tobacco. Some towns and communities had a higher concentration of Scots than others; these were generally the places where more than one firm was represented or where one tobacco company had a particularly large store or warehouse, such as Port Tobacco, Baltimore, and Bladensburg in Maryland and Alexandria, Dumfries, Norfolk, Richmond, and Falmouth (among oth-

PENNSYLVANIA

MARYLAND

NEW JERSEY

Unspecified Maryland (1)
Mecklenburg (1)●

Baltimore (4)●

DELAWARE

Delaware Bay

Rock
Creek   Bladensburg●
(1)●   (4)
         ●   (1)●
              Annapolis●
Alexandria (10)
● Fauquier (5)   Piscataway●
Occoquan (2)●   ●(2)
Colchester (1)●   ● Port
Dumfries (13)●   ▷ Tobacco●
Culpeper (3)   (9)
●

VIRGINIA

Oxford
(3)

Falmouth (9)●   Leonardtown
Fredericksburg (2)●   ●(1)
Port Royal (2)●   Potomac
Westmoreland (1)●

Somerset
County
● (2)

Chesapeake Bay

Rappahannock R.

James River

York River
(6)

Richmond (6)●

New London (2)●

Osborne's (3)●   Williamsburg
Blandford (1)   (1)●
Petersburg (3)●   Cabin●
● Prince Edward (1) Point (1)

James R.
(4)

ATLANTIC OCEAN

Portsmouth (1)● ●Norfolk
                 (15)
●Halifax (1)   Nansemond (2)●

Map 3.   Addresses of Scottish correspondents, 1750–1790

ers) in Virginia. With the exception of Baltimore, all of these areas were important centers for tobacco collection and export.[28]

The discrepancies between Map 3 and the information from the Fry-Jefferson and Henry maps are easily explained. They consider different groups of people. The Scottish owners of large properties may or may not have started their careers as transients. In either case, they had acquired substantial property. Map 3 and Table 4.6, by contrast, are based upon the addresses of known Scottish sojourners—who did not, as a rule, own *any* property, let alone enough to warrant a place on John Henry's map. This is why, for example, no Scottish correspondents (as shown in Table 4.6 and Map 3) lived along York River, yet the Fry-Jefferson and Henry maps show a Scottish presence there. The Glasgow trade did not deal at all in this tobacco. It would have had no reason to station its employees there to collect tobacco, even though several Scots apparently held property there.[29]

[28]See Price, *France and the Chesapeake*, esp. v. 1, p. 667.

[29]The French did not like York River tobacco; hence, there was very little export market for it. Newspaper advertising showed virtually no Scottish ships trading between Glasgow and York River.

Both Map 3 and Table 4.6 are, of course, flawed in the same way as the sources; the information that they provide is not an independent measure of Scottish residential patterns in the same way that contemporary maps are. Such an observation doubly reinforces the notion that, at least in the Chesapeake, the Scottish transient involvement was limited largely to tobacco export and its associated mercantile activity along particular rivers. The absence of substantial records from a population in other occupations or places would, of course, leave us to paint such a monochromatic picture.[30]

The surviving correspondence and the resulting table and map closely correlate with the results of the analysis of stories and advertisements in the Glasgow newspapers. It is no coincidence that the areas which supported the highest number of Scottish transients, that is the Potomac, James, and Rappahannock rivers, were also the destinations that were most heavily advertised in Glasgow's press. The Scottish newspapers demonstrate that Scots were actively involved in these particular areas. They sought cargoes and passengers to go to the colonies. The link between Scotland and the Chesapeake was quite place specific.

Map 3 also strongly suggests that any intercommunity networks would be especially strong in the lower Chesapeake—the areas between the Potomac River and the mouth of the bay. These were, in fact, the region's major tobacco production centers. Here, communication was easy and the physical distances involved not very great. In this sense, at least, the Chesapeake and Jamaica resembled each other. Scottish sojourners would have had opportunities to move from one area of high Scottish concentration to another. That there were not many Scots in the grain producing regions to the north again serves as a confirmation to the argument made in the last chapter that grain was not particularly important to most Scottish traders and that their overwhelming dependence upon tobacco greatly contributed to their decline. As James Robinson instructed subordinate factors in 1774, "Confine your

---

[30]The one correspondent who might be able to provide another example lived in Annapolis. Dr. Alexander Hamilton was secretary of the city's Tuesday Club. Hamilton kept minute books which identified the members of the club present at most meetings between 1745 and 1755. Four of the eight initial members appear to have been Scottish. Of the next six members admitted, none had Scottish names. They did not, as far as it has been possible to determine, leave any independent records which could confirm my identification of them as Scots. If the club's members with Scottish names were, in fact, Scots (and not second or third generation Americans) then Hamilton's Tuesday Club records do demonstrate the presence of a small network of middling level people in Maryland's capital, both Scottish and non-Scottish. It will probably always remain unclear how they came to be in Annapolis, or whether they had come as emigrants or sojourners. See Records of the Tuesday Club, MS 854, Maryland Historical Society. Also see Breslaw, *Records of the Tuesday Club*, and Robert Micklus, *History of the Tuesday Club*.

Transactions to those who make Crops of Tobacco which is the only payment that can be depended on."[31]

INTERPERSONAL WEBS IN JAMAICA

Scrutinizing the sources used to create the biographies presented in Chapter 2, as well as examining additional manuscript records, makes it possible to identify many of the interpersonal relationships between individual sojourning Scots. It then becomes clear that random interactions did not often take place. The island's Caledonian residents had extensive dealings with each other, on both personal and professional levels. When a choice needed to be made, they almost invariably preferred their countrymen to other Jamaican residents. Even within this broad ethnic category, a hierarchy operated. Being Scottish was simply the lowest common denominator; once inside a particular network, however, all were not created equal.[32]

To be fair, the Scottish inhabitants of Jamaica did not shy away from interacting with others on the island; indeed they needed their custom. Though the Scots welcomed business from anyone in the colony, they behaved rather differently when it came time to allocate their own affairs. With remarkable consistency, they chose to patronize compatriots over others. The interactions they had with the community, thus, were largely one-directional.

A systematic analysis of the Jamaican Letters Testamentary series documents this claim. Anyone named in an individual's will to serve as an executor had to be officially appointed by governmental authorities in Spanish Town. Those who appeared in the capital and agreed to act according to the terms set forth in the will received official and legal permission to carry out their duties in a Letter Testamentary.[33] These documents name the testator, those whom he or she named to act on his or her behalf, and whoever actually received the appointment. Analysis of this data at twenty-year intervals during the period under study is presented in Table 4.7. As can be seen, Scottish executors serviced between 72 percent and 85 percent of the estates

---

[31]James Robinson to Robert Paton, 8 February 1773, TD 167/1/88, SRA.

[32]Bonacich claims in "Middlemen Minorities" that "Family, regional, dialect, sect, and ultimately ethnic ties are used for preferential economic treatment" (p. 586). For a useful theoretical discussion of the preeminence of kinship over other forms of patron-client interaction, see Eric Wolf, "Kinship, Friendship, and Patron-Client Relations in Complex Societies," esp. pp. 9–10 and 16–18.

[33]These letters are classified as 1B/11/18 in the Jamaica Archives. There is also a series of Letters Administrative, which appoint people to act for the estates of those who died intestate (1B/11/17).

Table 4.7. Jamaican Letters Testamentary

Year	Estates	Scots executors	Percent
	Scottish		
1744	18	13	72
1764	27	23	85
1784	33	28	85
1804	65	52	80
	Total		
1744	109	21	19.3
1764	139	35	25.2
1784	178	58	32.6
1804	229	84	36.7
	Non-Scottish		
1744	91	8	8.8
1764	112	12	10.7
1784	145	30	20.7
1804	164	34	19.5

Source: Letters Testamentary, 18/11/18/8, 19, 29, 20, 40, 41, Jamaica Archives, Spanish Town.

left by identifiable Scots. Jamaican Scots obviously chose each other to conclude their affairs. Administering an estate was difficult business, especially in a place with the payment problems which Jamaica had, and having a trustworthy representative thus became especially important.

Table 4.7 also records the figures on Scottish executors in the sample population. This analysis shows that the total number of Scottish administrators quadrupled between 1774 and 1804. Furthermore, when these figures are broken down into their component parts, Scottish executors handled only 8.8 percent of all non-Scottish estates in 1744. In both 1784 and 1804, they administered around 20 percent of all the island's non-Scottish estates. Such evidence demonstrates that Scots increasingly came to be trusted by their non-Scottish neighbors. As important, it reveals that they were not at all averse to handling non-Scottish business or interacting with island residents from "south of the border" especially when it came to money matters, which incidentally would have benefited their own coffers.[34]

To portray, in a more exact fashion and on a more personal level, the ways

[34]It has not been possible, because of time limitations, to analyze every year of these letters to determine the more subtle shifts. It has also not been possible to examine the Letters Administrative series, which probably provides a better measure of how Jamaican society perceived the Scots. Since the authorities appointed the executors for deceased without wills, it would be very interesting to see whether they named Scots to serve only for other Scots or whether they were used in non-Scottish cases as well.

in which the Scottish networks operated and the functions which they fulfilled, two representative examples will be used. Francis Grant, whose biographical sketch is presented in Chapter 2, had a house in Montego Bay and
resided in the northwest corner of the island. Dr. Alexander Johnston, who
has not yet been discussed in any detail, had eastern St. Ann's parish, along
the north coast, as his base of operations. All of the manuscript collections
and public record groups which I perused were examined for references to
each of these men. Every person who, in one way or another, had contact
with either Grant or Johnston was identified, along with the nature of the
interaction or connection and, where known, the correspondent's ethnicity
and place of residence. The resulting patterns could not be clearer. When
such contacts and correspondents are then located and plotted on a map,
communities or neighborhoods can be visualized.

Of those people who have been documented as having had contact, in
whatever form, with Francis Grant in the years between 1780 and 1796, 71
percent were Scottish.[35] This is an extraordinarily high number given that
the Scottish proportion of the island's white population was no higher than
about 30 percent for most of the period.[36] Such a finding cannot be explained on the basis of sample bias alone, because official records in Jamaica,
in addition to those that have survived in Britain, have been consulted here.
It has been possible to identify the places of residence of those with whom
Grant had interactions. In general, they lived in the same neighborhood as
he did.

Map 4 (The realm of Francis Grant) places the properties with which
Francis Grant had connections onto a map of the western part of the island.
Under each plantation or property is the name of the person with whom
Grant had contact. All are within about twenty miles of Grant's Montego Bay
house. When he chose to live away from home, he stayed most often at
Georgia Estate, in Trelawny parish, owned by his friend Charles Gordon.
Even here, at the map's eastern end, he remained within easy reach of most
of the properties where he knew someone or over which he had control. This
was his neighborhood.[37]

[35] Apart from the Powers [of Attorney] Series in the Jamaica Archives, there are significant
references to Francis Grant in the Gordon of Cairness papers (AUL), Stirling of Keir Papers
(SRA), Scrymgeour-Wedderburn Papers (privately owned, available through NRA(S)), the Seafield Muniments (or Grant of Grant, SRO), and Graham of Airth Papers (NLS).

[36] Richard Sheridan, *Sugar and Slavery*, reckons the Scottish proportion of the white population to be around 25 percent (pp. 369–70) in 1754. It is difficult to say how many whites were in
the island in any year, as the population changed so quickly, but analysis of probated estate
inventories in the Jamaica Archives suggests that by 1796, around 30 percent of the white
population was Scottish.

[37] The neighborhood can be defined as a circle from Montego Bay through western Trelawny and northern Westmoreland parishes. If Grant's house at Montego Bay is the center of

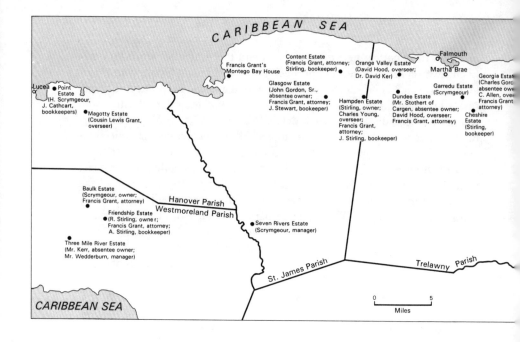

Map 4. The realm of Francis Grant

Just as it has been possible to identify Francis Grant's friends and acquaintances and determine where they lived, it has also been possible to determine the precise nature of his relationship with many of them. For some, he served as their "interest" or patron. He, and others like him, made the introductions into the island's society for incoming "men-on-the-make," controlled the early careers of aspiring young Scots, and used his positions of patronage to further their causes when he thought it necessary. In other words, he created a web or network, with himself at the center and all of his clients and contacts around him.[38] Grant obtained his authority from a primary patron, either the owner of a plantation, or someone else for whom he worked. When a primary patron sent people to Grant for assistance and

the circle, the neighborhood is within approximately a twenty mile radius. Jamaican travel was certainly slow, though it probably would have been possible to make the twenty-mile journey by horseback within a day. Long's *History of Jamaica,* v. 1, p. 465, remarks on the poor conditions of many Jamaican roads, making them impassable to carriages. On the new road between Montego Bay and Spanish Town, it was possible to traverse sixty of the ninety-six miles "over level grounds" on "a day's ride" (v. 2, p. 218). Scots were used to fairly arduous journeys. Henry Gray Graham, in *Social Life,* notes that Scottish travelers on horseback could travel approximately twenty-five to thirty miles per day (p. 41). In 1749, the first Glasgow-to-Edinburgh stage coach took twelve hours to travel the forty-six miles between the two cities. By 1788, the journey was half as long.

[38]For a discussion of webs and networks see Adrian C. Meyer, "The Significance of Quasi-Groups in the Study of Complex Societies." Grant's web was not at all unusual.

placement, Grant became the secondary patron for these people. They became dependent upon him for assistance and for carrying out the instructions of the primary patron. In such a manner, the Scots were able to perpetuate their system from one generation to the next.[39]

Patronage held everything together. The networks, on their most fundamental level, operated on Scottishness. Location within Scotland, after personal acquaintances, business links, and kinship (in ascending order of importance) increasingly differentiated the ranks of Scottish networks. As one Scot wrote from Jamaica,

> Mr. James Campbell was in this Island. . . . I have not heard form him since (altho I have wrote him) & I believe I may give up all expectation of his doing any thing for me as he has too much Bussiness to remember such as me (as I am not a Campbell) when out of sight. Mr. Maxwell . . . say'd he could be of little service to me, which I believe really to be the case, as he has a good many of his own poor Relations to provide for.[40]

Sojourners knew that "interest" or patronage held the crucial key to the island's society. Lewis Grant wrote from Jamaica that he had been "thrown abroad on the world on a few vague chances without either Trade or handicraft or any one friend to countenance or assist me in one of the most disagreeable spheres of life where scarce ought but Interest succeeds."[41] What people like Lewis Grant quickly learned was that the patronage system often placed one person's interest beneath that of others.

Because more and more Scots came to Jamaica over the course of this period, the ability to make distinctions between one's countrymen became crucial. Given one patron's limited opportunities to assist others, some sort of hierarchy which could differentiate between seemingly equally qualified individuals needed to be implemented.[42] Often, as has already been ob-

---

[39]Of course, the system operated within a particular generation as well. Francis Grant's brother John, the island's chief justice between 1774 and 1787, passed his contacts along to Francis who then used them to expand his own network. Francis was one of John's clients. There are several cases between 1780 and 1787 where John passed his power of attorney to his brother. See for example, John Grant to Francis Grant, 5 October 1782, Powers 84/166, or John to Francis, 19 March 1783, Powers 86/196, JA.

[40]Thomas Ruddach to Charles Steuart, 5 January 1777, MS 5030, p. 8, NLS.

[41]Lewis Grant to James Grant, 15 June 1774, GD 248/51/2/9, SRO.

[42]The patronage pecking order described above is typical of those Scottish professionals at home, "participating" in the Enlightenment. I strongly support Charles Camic's conclusion in *Experience and Enlightenment* that patronage extended beyond this small and elite group. For Francis Grant, the order went roughly as follows: after helping family members, Grant went on to his business contacts, influential people like the Stirlings and the Wedderburns. Following them, he assisted his neighbors from Scotland.

served, the resulting rules worked to the detriment of those arriving from Scotland. As Dr. Colin Maclarty wrote:

> I had conceived hopes of a settlement in the first Medical House in Kingston and some of my friends were endeav[ourin]g to accomplish it . . . but he [the practice owner] was under such previous engagements to a relation of his partners . . . that it put it entirely out of his power.[43]

Five years later, George Ross left one position in order to make way for someone with higher standing in the plantation manager's order. He wrote that "[a]bout three months ago I left Knolles & am still unemployed—altho am in hopes that William & K. Ross will soon have it in there power to provide for me & which they have promised."[44] The pecking order had already been put in operation and Maclarty, Ross, and others like them had to find suitable positions for themselves by using their patrons' "interest" where it had a higher place in the order than it did with the proprietor of the Kingston medical practice or the overseer of Knolles estate.

Seen from the other perspective, that of the patron or "interest," several cases have been found in Francis Grant's papers where he promised someone a position, only to find out that his own patron, the person for whom he worked, had someone else in mind, with more of a claim on his patronage than Grant's client. Fortunately for Grant, he had many contacts and was usually able to turn up equivalent positions.[45]

Sometimes, the clients had a difficult time accepting that their interest within a network stood below that of others. Harry Scrymgeour, who was one of Grant's clients and had lived in Hanover parish for sixteen years in 1789, complained to his brother Alexander Wedderburn (Wedderburn had assumed his wife's name when he married) in Scotland when he was passed over for an appointment as his cousin's attorney in favor of a nearer relation. "I ought not to have been fed with expectations and promises at the beginning which were carried all along through and then at the time when the opportunity offer'd of fulfilling them, to be at once disappointed."[46]

When the Wedderburns in the island tried to placate him by giving him someone else's estate executry, he complained that the deceased was an alcoholic and all he would get to do was sell slaves to pay debts. There was,

[43]Colin Maclarty to Betty Maclarty, 23 July 1787, John Cunninghame Letters, Acc. 7285, NLS.

[44]George to John Ross, 20 December 1792, GD 248/977/2, SRO.

[45]One example, which will be discussed in greater detail below, is the case of Charles Young, Charles Gordon's nephew (See Gordon of Cairness, MS 1160/6, AUL). Another example, also discussed below, is the case of John Stirling (Stirling of Keir, T-SK 11/3, SRA).

[46]Harry Scrymgeour to Alexander Wedderburn, 4 April 1789, Bundle 87/97/21 (2), Scrymgeour-Wedderburn papers, in private possession, access through NRA(S).

of course, little profit in that. The patronage, then, that Scrymgeour expected to receive from his cousin did not coincide with the patronage that his cousin could provide, given the limitations, however artificial and unofficial, imposed upon him by the etiquette of the pecking order. Harry Scrymgeour was not happy, especially since he had been placing friends of the Wedderburns in bookkeeping positions for as long as he could remember.[47]

If Maclarty, Ross, Scrymgeour, and others were losers, however temporarily, in the Scottish patronage networks because their contacts were not good enough, then there had to be winners. Returning to the career of Francis Grant provides an opportunity to examine some of their experiences. Himself a beneficiary of patronage, from his brother and many acquaintances, Grant was keen on helping whomever he could, especially when it might result in some personal benefit to himself. Providing patronage, as well as receiving it, was absolutely essential for those trying to gain their independence in Scotland, in Jamaica, or anywhere else. Charles Gordon, the owner of Georgia estate, wrote Francis Grant in January of 1788, after Grant's own tenure in the island had become quite lengthy:

> I am very often impositioned to introduce to you young men going to Jamaica which indeed I resent as much as possible as I know the trouble that such recommendations often give and that the services done in such cases are frequently very thanklessly requested but as such recommendations are often applyed for by friends, [whom] to refuse would be to disoblige, I hope you will forgive the trouble I am forced to give.[48]

Patronage spanned the Atlantic. The pecking order that operated in Scotland endured the ocean voyage along with the men going out to Jamaica. Gordon's view of his obligations was not the least bit unusual. In 1792, Mr. Stothert in Scotland wrote to one of his estate managers. His letter indicates the degree to which patronage then permeated both societies. Like Gordon, Stothert believed that to refuse to assist his kin, however distant, would throw the entire system open to question. And since his own position as patron (with power) was based upon having clients, he did not begrudge assisting those whom he could—even if it meant additional efforts.

> You will observe these Young men have no manner of claim on me, but the name, this One & his Father I never saw in my life, before last week. James intends being a planter . . . you will keep him at Dundee as Book Keeper, at the usual salary, if you are in no want, You must still give him employment till

---

[47]For an example of such a complaint, see Harry Scrymgeour to Alexander Wedderburn, 10 October 1784, Bundle 87/97/89/10, Scrymgeour-Wedderburn papers, NRA(S).

[48]Charles Gordon to Francis Grant, 25 January 1788, MS 1160/5/86, Gordon of Cairness, AUL.

you can get him agreeably provided, with some respectable Cousin that will pay some attention to his prudent behaviour.[49]

It was unusual for a primary patron to require his overseer (the secondary patron) to locate employment for his client on another estate if his own was unable to answer this demand upon it. If no opportunities arose immediately, the secondary patron would usually endeavour to locate some independently, by calling into play his own connections. This, in turn, served to enhance his standing with the primary patron. But he would not have been under obligation to do so, in the way which David Hood appears to have been to Stothert.

Having a position and "interest" was absolutely imperative for those on their way up in the world. The primary patron's connections did not cease with placement, nor were they transferred to the secondary patron. Often, the primary patron (e.g., Stothert or Gordon) would be called by both the secondary patron (e.g., Grant) and the client (e.g., Maclarty or Scrymgeour) when new positions were sought, when money was required, or when problems arose. As a result, letters from one patron to another were frequent. Alexander Clark wrote to William Graham in 1786 that

> All the young men that you recommended are doing well; James Graham has lately got a Charge in Hanover thro Mr. George McLauchlan's Interest. James Grame Garroch is in the employ of Mr. Wedderburne in St. James's. Mr. H. Hamilton is still at Hampden . . . Mr Robt Graeme from Garroch is in St. Mary's & promises to do well.[50]

Recounting the experiences of one person, as far as possible, can perhaps provide a better sense of how a patronage web operated in Jamaica. Charles Young, a nephew of Charles Gordon, knew that he would need assistance to procure a position (in order to earn his fortune) when he arrived in the island in 1792. He asked his uncle before he left and his uncle, much as he did not like recommendations, provided him with one to Francis Grant. After a seven-week passage, the adolescent Mr. Young made straight for Grant, to secure a position on his uncle's plantation. Unfortunately, there were no places available on Georgia at that particular time. On 18 February 1792, Francis Grant wrote to Charles Gordon that his nephew had "been arrived about ten days." Young had overcome his initial seasoning and was walking

[49]Mr. Stothert to David Hood, 18 February 1792, GD 241/189/1, SRO. Francis Grant was the attorney for Dundee estate while David Hood was the overseer. It is not clear whether "James" ever met Francis Grant.

[50]Alexander Clark to William Graham, 23 November 1786, MS 10925, p. 34, NLS. Note that not only are all the names mentioned here Scottish but also that all of these people are living in areas of high Scottish concentration.

in the piazza of Grant's Montego Bay house. Grant, for his part, believed (or at least claimed to believe) that Young would do well in the tropics. But he could provide no opening at Georgia without firing someone else, which he had not been instructed to do. "I propose," wrote Grant, "when he is perfectly recovered to place him on a pleasant healthy estate in St. James's, called Glasgow. It belongs to John Gordon Senr of Bristol [a transplanted Scottish merchant] whose Atty I have been for several years past. You may perhaps recollect our passing through it in going to see Walter Murray. It is adjoining . . . to Content."[51] All of the connections mentioned in this letter derive, as the lowest common denominator, from ethnicity.[52] Within this basic category, of course, there was another order at work.

Grant's intentions in this particular case went unfulfilled. On the 30th of March, about six weeks after Grant had initially written to Gordon, Charles Young wrote his uncle that "I am now settled here upon an Estate called Hampden in St. James's parish. It belongs to a Gentleman of the name of Stirling. It is a very agreeable and healthy plantation and we all board and lodge with the proprietor."[53] This particular proprietor was John Stirling, of the Stirling of Keir family (cousin to the John Stirling of Content plantation). Grant had effectively shepherded Young into another of his concerns.[54] John Stirling, still in his twenties, only a few years before had been in a similar situation. That is, he depended upon Grant for assistance and interest. The lawyers of Grant's network, however opaque, can be peeled away to reveal all of the connections and kinship relations between its various members.

Sometime before 1780, Sir Archibald Stirling of Keir had appointed Francis and John Grant to act as his attorneys, and named Francis Grant the estate manager, at a salary of £200 sterling per annum.[55] Grant had managed the property between 1783 and 1789, using the bookkeeping, overseeing, and other positions as berths for people like Young, whom he needed to assist. The property had been left to John Stirling, supervised by trustees, in

[51]Francis Grant to Charles Gordon, 18 February 1792, MS 1160/78/2, Gordon of Cairness, AUL.

[52]John Stirling has been identified as the owner of Content plantation, St. James, through Crop Accounts for 1778 and 1804. See 1B/11/4/8/190 and 1B/11/4/31/20, JA. It should also be noted here that in both of these years, the property's overseer was also Scottish. John Stirling later married the daughter of William Graham of Airth, whose correspondence appears above.

[53]Charles Young to Charles Gordon, 30 March 1792, MS 1160/6/80, Gordon of Cairness, AUL.

[54]Francis Grant had not been asked to do this by Charles Gordon. He used his own authority and initiative to cement his position with Gordon, from whom he also derived power and patronage.

[55]The exact power of attorney has not been found in the Jamaica Powers series, because the volumes before 1780 have not been examined. Nor is there a precise reference to this question in the Stirling of Keir Papers.

1783 by his uncle Archibald.[56] He arrived to take charge of it in 1789, at the age of twenty-three. He had never set foot on a Caribbean island, let alone a sugar plantation. Unfortunately for him, Francis Grant had not received precise instructions about what to do with John. He therefore hesitated giving him control of the estate.

Imagine John's frustration, as the young owner of a plantation, in a society where creating money in a hurry was a primary goal, as he was told that he could not immediately get to work. His reaction to his situation provides a crucial key into the ways in which patronage operated:

> [Mr Grant] mentioned . . . that it was hinted to him from home that I was to be some time in his Counting house; I told him that I never had the least intention to do so; because that I had learned enough of accounts elsewhere, in order to enable me to carry on the trivial business of an Estate. . . . He allowed, that I certainly was the proper person to take the management of this property, but that he expected previous notice of the change.[57]

Grant was bound by his orders; even if he wanted to help, for here he did have a position of power, he deemed it best not to act without the Stirlings' prior approbation.[58] Grant knew island society better than John Stirling anyway; young Stirling was forced to accept his patrons' (both primary and secondary) judgments. The Stirlings, who still held their position as trustees for John's estate, eventually insisted that young John receive some training at another of Grant's concerns before they would allow him to take control of Hampden the following year. Even then, Grant remained Hampden's attorney until 1794.[59] And, it appears that by using his authority (or his network) to secure Charles Young a place there, he maintained his positions of patronage.

Young's story demonstrates that the patronage networks spread across sizable regions of the island. Acquaintances constantly expanded their own connections by using whatever opportunities became available to them. In this particular case, Francis Grant was the person through whom connec-

[56]See the Last Will of Archibald Stirling, 25 August 1783, T-SK 15/23, SRA.

[57]John to William Stirling, 5 November 1789, T-SK 11/3/127/1, SRA.

[58]The Stirlings' operation of their sugar plantations is discussed in Chapter 2. It would have been pure idiocy to hand the charge of an entire estate to someone with absolutely no experience. Grant was right to insist upon instructions.

[59]The substitution took place when Grant prepared to leave the country. In his place, he appointed another Scot, Alexander McLeod (who also received a number of powers from Grant's brother John). See Francis Grant to Alexander McLeod, 12 August 1794, Powers 121/127-29, JA. John Stirling died of a fever on 24 March 1793 at Hampden estate. See William Fraser, *Stirlings of Keir* (Edinburgh, 1858), p. 77, and Francis Grant to William Stirling, 8 April 1793, T-SK 15/46/54, SRA.

tions were made. Young would have derived his network from Grant's, as well as from anyone else with whom he worked or lived. It has become possible to visualize such an expanding web.

When all of the people with whom Grant had connections are plotted and their relationships with him characterized, Chart 1 (Francis Grant's patronage web) results. Francis Grant has been placed at the center. Those Scots whom he assisted or for whom he acted directly are placed nearer the core and have heavy lines connecting them to Grant. Those whom Grant assisted as part of his responsibility to his own patrons are placed nearer the periphery and have solid lines drawn to both their primary patron and to Francis Grant. Finally, those Scots who became acquainted either as a result of knowing Francis Grant, or who otherwise met, have been connected to each other with a broken line. The nearer one got to the center of the web, the more influence he had with Grant, and the more he could expect to receive from him. The chart accurately portrays the extensive and tangled webs in which Scottish networks frequently resulted. While Grant's non-Scottish acquaintances have not been included here, it can be demonstrated that more than half of Grant's patrons, employers, and assistants came from Scotland.[60]

There were, of course, other Scottish patronage networks at work in eighteenth-century Jamaica. One of these, which substantiates the existence of the networks, but which operated in a different manner from Grant's, belonged to Dr. Alexander Johnston. His web is drawn by placing him at the center, but the nature of the connections was different.

Johnston's career and the paths which he used to advance it have been described in detail elsewhere.[61] Only the salient facts will be provided here. A physician from Aberdeen, Johnston moved to St. Ann's parish in 1763. He quickly infiltrated the parish's medical establishment and apprenticed himself to another Aberdeen practitioner, Dr. Alexander Fullerton. In a shrewd and calculating manner, which came to characterize Johnston's career, he attached himself to Fullerton for two years and then joined him in partnership. Both the exact terms of the agreement and the names of the patients

[60]The qualitative records were drawn from Scottish sources. They show 71 percent of the members of Grant's network to have been Scottish. To correct for such bias, I have surveyed the Jamaica Powers of Attorney series (and other official records) for Grant between 1780 and 1796. If those powers which are nothing but Grant's transferring his power to someone else (usually to Alexander McLeod of St. Catherine's parish, his brother John's friend) are discounted, there are forty-four cases where Grant is mentioned as one of the parties. Of these, twenty-five (or 57 percent) are transactions involving other Scots. Given that the number of Scots in the island was much less than this percentage, it certainly was no accident. Scots did not hesitate to accept business from anyone who offered it.

[61]See Karras, "The World of Alexander Johnston."

Chart 1. Francis Grant's patronage web

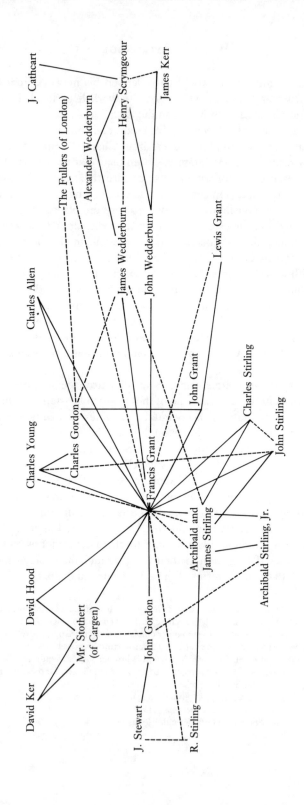

Johnston treated are known.[62] Analysis of his ledger reveals that as many as forty-two percent of the patients he treated had such Scottish names as Campbell, Ferguson, Leslie, Moffat, and Stirling. Johnston used his contacts, which he made through his ethnicity and his profession, to increase his own fortune, while doing as little as possible for others.

Johnston arrived knowing no one in the island, with the apparent exception of Dr. Fullerton. By the time of his death, he had an estate valued at near £20,000 and had served as a member of his parish's vestry.[63] The twenty-odd years it took him to achieve this level of wealth—albeit in Jamaica—strongly indicate that his networks constantly expanded. But they worked only in one direction. While Johnston occasionally, through his personal network, offered assistance to those in need who approached him, more often than not he declined to do so. Such tasks, he believed, slowed down his own ascent. Here he stood in marked contrast to Francis Grant, who prided himself on being able to use his patronage as successfully as he did. While Grant welcomed new Scots to the island, and did his utmost to serve them, Johnston viewed them as a tremendous imposition and did his utmost to avoid such connections.

He pleaded with his brother James in Aberdeenshire not to send him any more young men: "Do not be plaguing me with recommendations and people. Let them stay where they are."[64] The difference with Grant could not have been more apparent. The Scots' individual and collective success often depended upon patronage and by failing to act on anyone's behalf, Johnston made his fellow countrymen's success much more difficult to achieve. His selfishness and single-minded determination to earn as much as possible as quickly as possible show just how easy it was for the Jamaican environment to corrupt the etiquette, if not the thread, which held the Scottish webs together. Johnston broke an established chain, which, in fact (in the guise of Dr. Fullerton), had set him up in his very lucrative practice.

He has, nonetheless, left enough qualitative evidence for his acquaintances, patients, and friends to be listed in the same way and charted with the same technique employed for Francis Grant.[65] Map 5 (The realm of Alexander Johnston) portrays the St. Ann's parish resident's connections. Johnston's neighborhood, like Francis Grant's, extended about twenty miles from his house in the lush hills above Ocho Rios. Many Scots, as has been shown,

[62]See ibid., pp. 58–60.
[63]See ibid., pp. 73–75.
[64]A. Johnston to James Johnston, 21 August 1784, A. Johnston Papers, legal papers, HSP.
[65]Not all of Johnston's patients have been included—only those with large accounts who were regular customers after 1768. Many patients only saw the doctor once or twice, and so their relationship with him would not have been nearly as developed as those who saw him more regularly.

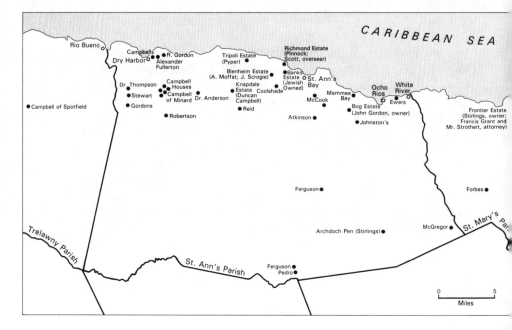

Map 5. The realm of Alexander Johnston

lived within this area. Like Grant, Johnston spent a considerable amount of time housesitting for people he knew. He often stayed at Blenheim estate when his Scottish friend Aaron Moffat was away on business.[66] When Johnston resided at Moffat's house, he was nearer the center of his parish, his social life, and his professional network.

Chart 2 (Alexander Johnston's patronage web) is a presentation of Johnston's network which, like Map 5, includes only the principle characters in his life. Johnston has been placed at the center. The chart then has contacts, acquaintances, and relations attached to it. The right side of the chart includes his principal patients and business contacts. Scots have had the letter (S) added after their names. They are connected to Johnston by a solid line. People Johnston knew through these contacts are connected to him by broken lines. Similarly, friends, neighbors, and relations appear on the chart's left side. They too are connected to Johnston with solid lines while those whom he only knew through other people have been connected to Johnston with broken lines. Such people (for example, the family of William Pyper) have been connected to their principal connection in the web by a solid line. Those individuals who filled more than one role have been placed nearer the center than those who did not.

[66]Moffat was the brother of the Countess of Elgin. His estate was situated beside that of another Scot, James Fraser. See James Fraser to Hector McDonald Buchanan, 10 September 1794, Robertson-McDonald Papers, MS 3945, f. 171, NLS.

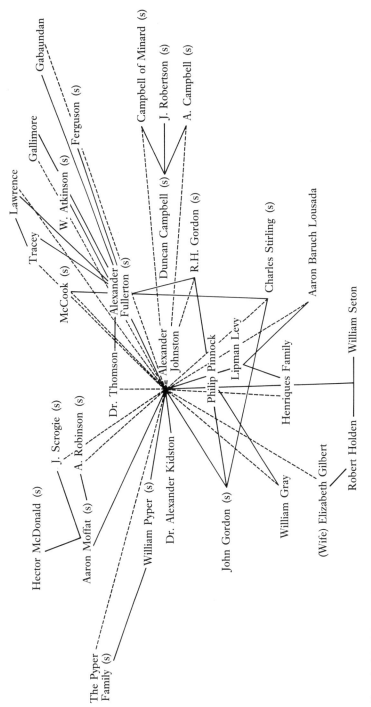

Chart 2. Alexander Johnston's patronage web

Patients and Business Contacts

Friends, Neighbors, Relations

It has been difficult to determine who knew whom on the web, apart from Johnston of course, so I have not put these connections onto the chart, as I did for Grant. Johnston's web differs from Grant's in that the secondary connections are fewer (represented by broken lines in Johnston's case, and those on the outermost fringes of Grant's web). Johnston also tended to keep the various component parts of his life much more separate from each other than did Grant. He did not like patronage, and his web indicates that he used it only when it was to his advantage. The lack of secondary connections indicates that patronage was basically a one-dimensional force.

Though Alexander Johnston claimed to disdain Scots, his principal network was populated primarily by them.[67] Here, it resembled Grant's. This indicates that Scottishness was the least common denominator for being a part of a web. Within that web, various distinctions could be made. Those who were nearer the center invariably tended to be family members and wealthy business acquaintances. Such people could often further Johnston's career, either through extending credit or making acquaintances of people who could. Johnston certainly did not pass his connections on to the next generation of incoming physicians.

To be fair to Johnston, who probably would not have chosen the web he had, it must be said that the English probably recognized him as a Scot from the very beginning. The northeast Scottish accent is like no other; one word would have made clear his origins.[68] He and others like him may have been forced to deal with other Scots because the English refused to accept them into their own communities and networks. Though there is no surviving documentation to support this assertion, there is nothing like an outside force to draw people together who otherwise have little in common. The group actually becomes what they are already perceived to be. Edna Bonacich, in "A Theory of Middlemen Minorities," explains:

> The host society can unite on one issue . . . the solidarity of the middleman community. . . . Middleman groups are charged with being clannish, alien, and unassimilable. They are seen as holding themselves aloof, believing they are superior to those around them . . . and insisting on remaining different.[69]

This perception, as Bonacich argues, both unites and isolates the minority group. People like Johnston who tried to avoid being a part of it were frequently held back for the simple reason that they were believed to be "clannish."

[67]See Karras, "The World of Alexander Johnston," p. 55.
[68]See *The North-East of Scotland: A Survey Prepared for the Aberdeen Meeting of the British Association for the Advancement of Science* (Aberdeen, 1963), pp. 197–98.
[69]Bonacich, "Middlemen Minorities," p. 591.

Nonetheless, Johnston's connections spanned the width and breadth of the parish, and spilled over into neighboring Trelawny and St. Mary's. It was in these parishes where Grant's and Johnston's networks (they were contemporaries for several years in the 1780s) had the opportunity to interact, allowing further tests of their scope and cohesion. Charles Stirling (of Ardoch) owned property in St. Ann's. Alexander Johnston served as his physician (and sometimes friend or acquaintance). The Stirlings of Keir, Charles's cousins, owned both the Frontier property in St. Mary's and Hampden in St. James's. Francis Grant acted as their attorney.[70] As far as it has been possible to determine, Grant and Johnston never met. But their personal networks did overlap beyond the simple connection. Charles Stirling, for example, dined at Content plantation in St. James's parish on 21 May 1785. Content was owned by John Stirling (of Kippendavie). Its plantation attorney was Francis Grant. James Graham, who attended the meal, wrote a letter indicating the date of the dinner engagement. He was also related to Ann Graham, one of Johnston's patients. Charles Stirling could easily, in the course of conversation, have mentioned his doctor to Francis Grant, or any one else who was present. Because James Graham had one of Johnston's patients amongst his kin, he too might have known him or known of him.[71] This rather convoluted series of connections indicates that many opportunities, as ordinary as a farewell dinner, existed for members of one Scottish network to learn about, if not interact with, those in another. Because James Graham did not report the contents of the dinner conversation, it will probably never be known whether or not either Francis Grant or Alexander Johnston was present or a topic for dinner table discussion.

In such a fashion, it became possible for Scots in one end of the island to move to the other, provided there was no one with a higher place in the pecking order waiting to displace them. In this country, mobility was high and change part of a normal existence. The island could be envisioned as a series of circles or webs overlapping from one end to the other. Those wishing to move would have used whatever connections they had, however simple, to propel themselves across one web's periphery and into another's core. A dinner invitation might have been all that was necessary to remind people of their mutual, though distant, relation-in-common.

The Scots who have been studied had absolutely no hesitation to leave one post in order to go to another. All they needed was a higher salary, a more illustrious group of patrons, or much greater independence—here defined as freedom from supervision. Such behavior was tolerated, antici-

---

[70]See Stirling to Grant, 17 May 1790, Powers 111/77, JA. It is possible that this simple tie would have brought the two into the same places at some point.

[71]The letter about the dinner was James to William Graham, 22 May 1785, MS 10925, p. 9, NLS. The Stirling and Graham relationships are detailed in Fraser, *Stirlings of Keir*, p. 108.

pated, and even favorably received. The quest for independence—here defined as fiscal well-being—took precedence over everything else. The networks that the Scots developed were designed to assist them; their success at providing opportunities for advancement in the end helps to explain why so few Scots left the colony as planned.

Sometimes changes on the road to advancement were not a matter of choice. Occasionally, the network system broke down because of internal feuding, squabbling at home, or other related incidents. Those on a web's periphery were usually the hardest hit. William Gordon, son of Sir Robert Gordon of Gordonstoun, had gone out to Jamaica sometime before 1760 as an overseer for Alexander Grant, a Kingston merchant turned planter. Apparently, young William Gordon fell out with his patron, Mr. Grant, because the latter believed him to be "a Spy upon his Actions by Sir Alexander [Grant of Dalvey, the London merchant and Alexander Grant's partner]. This consequently gave him an Aversion to William and made him resolve neither to treat him Civilly, nor Assist him but at last fell upon the Contrivance of getting him over to Mr. Sinclair." According to Gordon, the Grants, though once partners, now "had a most entire hatred for each other founded upon a full distrust of each others honesty so that a worse recommendation could not be framed for a Young fellow than from one to the other."[72] The well-oiled machine had failed to function. Fortunately for William Gordon, Mr. Sinclair bent over backward to assist him. Sinclair came from the same part of Scotland (the northeast) as the Gordon family did. He found Gordon short-term employment and began to encourage him to return to Britain for more education.[73] Sinclair argued that a British education (for Jamaica still did not have any educational institutions) would vastly increase the chances for profit.

Gordon went from one network centered on Alexander Grant into another centered on Sinclair. Each was run by and for Scottish sojourners. As a result, they became absolutely essential to the process of achieving success in Jamaica's tropical environment.

INTERPERSONAL WEBS ON THE CHESAPEAKE

The networks that existed in the Chesapeake operated very much upon the same principles as those just described in Jamaica. At their foundations

[72]Lewis Gordon to Sir Robert Gordon, 9 June 1760, La. MS. II 498, EUL. For a very detailed analysis of the Grant's dealings with each other, see David J. Hancock's dissertation "Citizen of the World: Commercial Success, Social Development, and the Experience of Eighteenth-Century British Merchants who Traded with America" (Harvard University, 1990).

[73]The connection was even more concrete than simple ethnicity. Archibald Sinclair was also the uncle of Jamaica's Mr. Kerr, a tenant of the Gordons. These are the sorts of connections used to differentiate between Scots.

lay one simple requirement: ethnicity. Building upon that, a hierarchy of region within Scotland, personal acquaintance, business acquaintance, and kinship differentiated among aspiring applicants. The systems operated on both sides of the Atlantic and were able to insure, after a fashion, that the Scots had, at the very least, an opportunity to fulfill their goals. Because of the heavy presence of merchants and factors among sojourning Scots in the Chesapeake, and the limited appearance of other middling professionals, these colonial networks were rather monolithic. Great patronage was to be had in the tobacco industry but there was little available elsewhere.

As in Jamaica, the size of a Scot's network varied in direct proportion to the amount of time lived in the colonies. That is, those in the Chesapeake began their residencies with extremely tight networks confined to very small local areas. These networks expanded with each additional year spent in the region. The first example, Alexander Wilson, had a brief career in Alexandria; his connections generally illustrate the networks found in the region among those who came to it when they were relatively young and inexperienced. Comparing such a case with those who had been in the Chesapeake longer makes it possible to see the fatal shortcomings of the Chesapeake operation.

Alexander Wilson's web reveals that his world was much smaller than those of Scots who lived in Jamaica, for two reasons. Wilson was in the Chesapeake less than three years. He, therefore, did not have ample time to form enough bonds to create a full-fledged network for himself. His lowly position, moreover, placed him in a very tightly controlled community, further limiting his opportunities to interact with those outside it. Wilson did not provide patronage; he received it.

The degree to which the tobacco companies superimposed rules on their employees was discussed in the last chapter. Wilson's colonial experiences further substantiate the claim that tobacco served as the primary focus of Scottish transients in the Chesapeake region. Just as the Glasgow firms restricted their employees' behavior within business hours, so too did they regulate leisure activities. Wilson's acquaintances were either fellow Glassford and Henderson employees, or low-level employees of other tobacco firms conducting business in Alexandria, or other neighbors or friends from home. As such, his network was localized and small.

Wilson's network, apart from his employers, consisted nearly entirely of those in situations similar to his own. His opportunities to advance himself outside of the tobacco economy were, as a result, extremely limited.[74]

---

[74]He did know his employers' chief factors, Alexander Henderson and Henry Riddell. This seems to have been a fairly typical experience. New arrivals would often stay for some time with the firm's chief representative who would then assign them to a particular store. The connections and interactions, except in times of promotion or demotion, did not usually proceed beyond this stage.

For his part, Wilson recognized that he lived in a restricted world. In one of his many letters home during 1769, he identified his friends, all of whom were Scottish sojourners employed in tobacco.

> With regard to my companions I have only 3, one of which is a lad about 17 years of age who lives in a Store about a stone cast from ours. The second and oldest is a lad about 18 years of age and lives in a store contiguous to ours. The 3d & last is a young man who comes somewhere from about Glasgow and lives in the Store with myself.[75]

Devoting much of their attention to business, many apprentices and factors had little opportunity to interact with others, Scottish or otherwise, in the colony. During his tenure in the Chesapeake, Wilson continued to write to his parents that he was meeting many "Scotts."[76] Friendships outside of well-defined Scottish networks took a clear second place to business and the pursuit of independence. James Bartlett, a tobacco factor for Cunninghame and Company wrote that, "There are many honest good & industrious men in this County whose custom is valuable and their friendship worth cultivating."[77] Surely Bartlett expressed a perception common among Scottish sojourners and their masters alike. Friendships should only be formed if they were advantageous to the firm's business (and thus, many tobacco transients erroneously believed, to themselves). Thomas MacMurdo, similarly, learned the right things to do in order to hold on to business. "As for the planter[s]," he wrote, "I am a great deal better reconciled to them and I have learned the way to sooth their rough genious a little."[78] The Scots in the region dealt with the rest of the community only in very specific ways, which they believed would maximize their own benefits. Such behavior created a perception of clannishness which, when coupled with their domination of the tobacco trade, contributed to their increasing dislike by the rest of the population as the Revolution drew nearer.

Alexander Wilson returned to Scotland after only a short time. It is questionable whether his network would have expanded very much had he stayed, especially with the Revolution on the horizon. Others involved in the tobacco economy, like James Robinson, had more friends and business acquaintances. He had, of course, been in the colony for a longer period of time and had a higher position within his firm than did Wilson. Like

---

[75]Alexander Wilson to his parents, 17 December 1769, f. 11, Letterbook, TD 1/1070, SRA. The three lads were later identified as Anthony Ramsay, George Reid, and Robert Park—all from around Glasgow.

[76]See, for example, Alexander Wilson to his parents, 20 November 1770, Letterbook, f. 17, SRA. Wilson's letterbook mentions very few people indeed who were not Scottish.

[77]James Bartlett to James Robinson, 18 July 1774, GD 247/59/Q, SRO.

[78]Thomas MacMurdo to his Father, 25 April 1785, ACC 7199/4/1, NLS.

Wilson's, however, at both the core and the periphery of Robinson's web were fellow Scots. Nearly all of them, in one way or another, were involved in the tobacco business.[79]

Generally, as in Jamaica, Scottish networks in the Chesapeake primarily involved ethnocentric interactions and were very localized by community and neighborhood. A much more diffuse network can be discovered by examining the related Steuart and Parker Collections of manuscripts. Norfolk merchant James Parker really stands at the center of both sets of records. In this particular example, the pecking order described for Jamaica and suggested by Wilson's early experiences sometimes became irrelevant or outmoded as business acquaintances developed into kinship relations. The result was a confused entanglement in which those offering patronage often had to differentiate between various kin when it came time for a decision. Choices, as a result, became increasingly difficult.

James Parker was born at Port Glasgow in 1729; he went to Virginia sometime around 1745, probably as an employee (in similar circumstances to Alexander Wilson) of the tobacco firm, Spiers & Company.[80] In 1758, he became William Aitchison's partner in a new firm (Aitchison was also a Scot) and in 1760, he married Margaret Ellegood. William Aitchison married her sister, Rebecca Ellegood. The women were American born. But they counted another well-known Scots merchant (and later, Loyalist), Neil Jamieson among their cousins.[81]

It is extremely unusual for sojourners to marry members of the host society. Scots after 1760 almost universally avoided it, but those who had made their fortunes earlier (and who acted as models for the newer transients) behaved rather differently.[82] The reasons for doing so usually involved money in one way or another. A year before Parker's marriage, his friend Alexander Molleson wrote to him:

> Why don't you Marry a Rich old Widow and Get Ritch all at once & come home to us. But I believe Jamaica the properest place for that purpose. If you

---

[79]Again, the problem of biased sources must enter the discussion. Most of the sources upon which this argument is based were found in Scottish archives. Some, however, like the Glassford and Jamieson papers are still in American archives, though they largely concern loyalists and tobacco merchants. I am not concerned with Scottish immigrants. Because of the permanent nature of their residence, they might very well have been integrated more with their neighbors.

[80]See the accession analysis, 920 Par I, LRO, and Hast, *Loyalism in Revolutionary Virginia* (Ann Arbor, Mich., 1982), p. 10.

[81]Neil Jamieson's wife, Fernelia, was first cousin to Parker's wife. See Hast, *Loyalism*, p. 82.

[82]Thomas Devine, in *Tobacco Lords*, discusses marriage between members of the Glasgow tobacco families (pp. 10–12) but does not say anything about the number of factors who married American wives and later became either tobacco lords or immigrants.

thought we might both succeed [at finding rich women to marry] I would go there a fortune hunting along with you.[83]

Molleson's letter reveals that Parker went to the Chesapeake, first and foremost, to become wealthy. The standard way for Glaswegians to earn fortunes, by attention to business, could be bypassed simply by marrying a wealthy widow. And Jamaica seemed to be a better place to do this.[84] The new couple could then retire to Scotland and live off the wife's money. As a result, the sojourn would be completed much faster than it would have otherwise. As it turned out, Parker had managed to marry well.[85] His connections, already quite dense, became even thicker.

Parker had been concerned in another Chesapeake trading business, Steuart and Parker, before his involvement with William Aitchison. Charles Steuart, Parker's partner in that firm, brought his family into the already tangled web. His daughter Jeannie was effectively raised by the Parkers; they considered her as their own kin. Other members of Charles Steuart's extended family, who lived in Orkney, were sent, through these connections, to both Virginia and Jamaica (as well as to Tobago and Grenada). This particular series of relationships had indeed become an entangled web, even before it ever began to deal with other business connections.[86]

The Parker and Steuart letter collections contain many references to Scots in the Chesapeake. There were not, however, very many connections between them and members of the Virginia gentry, or any other Virginians for that matter. Though these people were the Scots' customers, their absence from the bodies of surviving correspondence strongly suggests that few dealings between the groups took place outside of the stores.[87] Those

[83]Alexander Molleson to James Parker, 3 November 1759, 920 Par I, 1/1, LRO.

[84]Molleson probably based his remark on more than a popular assumption. Archibald Grant of Monymusk, an M.P. from the northeast of Scotland, had been to Jamaica in the late 1740s and married his third wife, Elizabeth Callendar, a wealthy Jamaican widow, in 1751. She brought him an estate worth £15,000 sterling as well as several Jamaican properties. (See "Marriage Settlement," 13 August 1751, GD 345/1445, SRO.) Archibald's son by his second wife and Elizabeth's daughter by her first husband also married, ensuring that the family fortune would stay in one place. Richard Oswald, the Scottish merchant in London, who certainly was known in Glasgow, married Mary Ramsay, a Jamaican heiress. She brought substantial property to her husband.

[85]The Ellegoods were a respected and substantial loyalist family. See Hast, *Loyalism,* p. 82, for a description of the interrelationships between family members.

[86]Steuart had been sent to Virginia as an employee of a Glasgow tobacco merchant in 1741. He made his fortune there. A very good biographical sketch of Steuart and his career can be found in MS 5041, pp. 262–64, NLS.

[87]I have not been able to locate a series of public records for Virginia and Maryland comparable to those for Jamaica's *Letters Testamentary* and as easy to use. As a result, it is difficult to provide concrete analysis about the degree to which interactions between Scots and non-Scots took place. Ledgers and account books often list all of the customers that a particular

interactions between James Parker, Charles Steuart, and the non-Scottish population about which evidence does remain indicates that there were few feelings of good will from one side to the other. Early in 1769, Parker reported that some of the Glasgow factors wanted more New England rum and that unless they could procure it from Parker and Aitchison, "They will be obliged to deal with some of our [non-Scottish] Neighbours whom they absolutely abhor & detest."[88] Such problems, on both sides, increased markedly as the Revolution approached. Distrust reached epidemic proportions. On 3 November 1774, Edmund Randolph wrote James Parker a terse letter indicating that he had assumed Thomas Jefferson's business. Parker, obviously miffed, annotated the letter "a Scoundrel from the beginning."[89]

The reasons that things had progressed to such a state can, in part, be traced to the Scots' own behavior. Like many other Chesapeake houses, the Parkers and Aitchisons dealt extensively with other Scots.[90] Creating interpersonal interactions, not destroying them, was their specialty. Charles Steuart, who became a Superintendent of Customs for North America [in 1756?], also had many of his countrymen among his primary patrons. He, in turn, often used his positions of patronage to assist fellow sojourners from home.[91] After the mid 1760s, Steuart spent most of his time in Britain acting in the government's service. He could therefore provide even more links and more opportunities to those in America. The story of the interrelationships between members of this vast network forms the subject for the rest of this section. To the uninitiated, Edmund Randolph for example, Scottish clannishness created problems for the planters. For the Scots, this clannishness simply made good business sense.

Business contacts became kin who had more business contacts who also became kin. This particular Scottish network constantly expanded. It was much broader than Wilson's or any other tobacco factor's, and because of the kin relationships, much larger than those in Jamaica in terms of its geographic area, which stretched from New York, at the height of the Revolution, and North Carolina to Scotland and even the west Midlands in England.[92]

---

merchant had, but there is little evidence contained in them to indicate a relationship on anything more than a purely commercial level. Scots, of course, had absolutely no hesitation about having non-Scottish customers; the question is whether there is some way to determine the extent to which the Scots preferred to deal with each other.

[88]James Parker to Charles Steuart, 5 July 1769, MS 5025, p. 140, NLS. There was clearly a very strong preference, among Scots, for dealing with each other rather than with the locals.

[89]Edmund Randolph to James Parker, 2 November 1774, 920 Par I 9/1, LRO

[90]For an excellent and thorough account of the firm, the interpersonal relationships, and the related families, see Hast, *Loyalism*, pp. 10–11.

[91]For an example, see Charles Steuart to James Parker, 31 October 1772, 920 Par I 27/46, LRO.

[92]Another of the Ellegood sisters (Ann Elmslie) married a Liverpool merchant and returned to live with him in the west Midlands in 1768. During and after the war, she was often called

These were highly articulate and mobile Scots whose determination to succeed kept them loyal to the crown and ultimately prevented the very success
which they had long worked to achieve.

In Virginia, most lived from the James River south, and were clustered
around Norfolk and its environs. The geographical breadth represented in
the web did not insure its occupational heterogeneity. With only one or two
exceptions, all of the networks' members were merchants or factors, involved
in one way or another with tobacco. Most had some kinship ties to at least
one other person in the web, though frequently to more. The one or two
non-merchants who did appear, along with all of the women, had no business dealings with the traders. They found their way into this network
because they were relations, either by blood or by marriage, who managed to
use their connections with the Scottish merchants to their own advantage.[93]

Occasionally, such bonds broke down. George MacMurdo, who was not
part of this particular network but a member of a similar one, wrote to his
mother in 1772, when his kinship ties had failed him. "You talk to me of
being happy in a number of relations; what are my relations to me unless
they act as such? If they were friends, something might be said for them, but
at present, they are no more to me than as many Jackasses."[94]

If James Parker stood at the center of the web, his wife merits her place
immediately beside him. Margaret Parker represents the means through
which many connections were made. The women in this family brought a
considerable amount of capital and, just as important, business acquaintances to their husbands. In addition, the women here were extremely well-
spoken, strong characters (as the records prove); they often served as sources
of the information that was passed between the men on the network's different spokes.[95]

Family and business had become so entwined that those on the periphery
did not just communicate with the center; they interacted with others on the

---

upon to take care of the Parker or Aitchison children when they were on their holidays from
school in Scotland. It was often a cause for her husband's complaint. See, for example, her letter
to Parker, 9 January 1789, 920 Par I 28/8, LRO.

[93]For example, Dr. John Cringan, a Scottish physician, came to Virginia after the Revolution
ended (for want of opportunity at home) and lived in the area above the falls of the James. He
married Jeannie Steuart and received a substantial dowry from the match. This placed him very
near the center of the web, even though he was not a merchant, because Jeannie had been raised
by the Parkers. Cringan and Miss Steuart had met while she was visiting relatives and business
associates in the area where Cringan lived. See for example, Margaret Parker to Charles
Steuart, 15 December 1786, 920 Par I 33/9, LRO.

[94]George MacMurdo to his Mother, 25 October 1772, Acc. 7199/4/1, NLS.

[95]It would appear that since the true kinship lay with Margaret Parker, Rebecca Aitchison,
and Ann Elmslie, their closeness as sisters was absolutely essential in ensuring the smooth
operation of the family networks. Their husbands turned these family advices into business
transactions.

periphery as well. This would have seemed to be the perfect way to achieve success for those who participated in the network. Unfortunately, the unpopular position which many of these people adopted during the war, combined with perceived clannishness (which, at least here, was not far off the mark) and the real Chesapeake Scottish tendency to invest all of their capital and energy into the tobacco economy insured that they had little upon which to fall back when the time came in 1776.

To demonstrate the operation of the network from start to finish, the present discussion will focus upon the family's children, their education, and their entrance into their respective professions. The ways in which simple decisions were made and followed through is indeed highly reminiscent of the experience described for the Caribbean. That is, the children of this very well-connected web were educated in Scotland (as were their fathers), had a profession decided for them, and were then reintroduced to the colonies (or to the United States). Their paths, along every step, were determined and supervised by the networks from which the parent or relation came.

In 1771, Charles Steuart sent his young Orkney-bred nephew, Thomas Ruddach, to Port Royal, Virginia. There he would learn how to be a merchant in the tobacco business. Steuart thought the Orkney Islands, in the northernmost reaches of Scotland's territorial waters, no place for an ambitious young man to learn a trade. He believed it to be a backward region and one where opportunity was in short supply. "It was his misfortune indeed," lamented Steuart, "to be kept so long in his own country (I mean only the Orkneys—no national reflection) where I fancy they have very indifferent schools."[96] Because the family was not particularly well-off, the colonies were then considered the fastest way available to make a fortune. Things had changed precious little from the last generation when Steuart found himself in the same position, and was sent to Virginia. Though he offhandedly acknowledged the high quality of Scotland's schools, he did not believe that they could solve the problems of all those who wanted to improve their wealth and status. Steuart, like most Scots who did not come from Glasgow, preferred the West Indies as a starting point for those seeking increased fortunes abroad. But because he had better connections in North America, especially Virginia, where things seemed to be booming in 1771, he sent Thomas Ruddach there, to acquire an "independent living."[97] William Aitchison had, the year before, advised him to do so, indicating that he would lend his patronage where he could:

[96]See Charles Steuart to James Parker, 28 June 1771, 920 Par I 27/41. Steuart should have known; he also came from Orkney. He was educated in Kirkwall and later in Edinburgh. See MS 5041, p. 267, NLS.

[97]In 1771, the tobacco boom was still going strong. The Credit Crisis came in 1772. See, for example, Price, *Capital and Credit*, p. 162, and Kulikoff, *Tobacco and Slaves*, pp. 123–31.

I should prefer some of the Glasgow Companys [for Thomas Ruddach's place], their Business is now much more general then used to be[.] 2 or 3 Years will qualifie a Young man very well to do for himself. At some time should you choose to send him out unprovided, you know you are entitled to everything JP or myself can for him & you may rely upon it.[98]

Aitchison and Parker's assistance came in handy. Steuart's connections with a Mr. Ingram in Glasgow, over whose patronage others had a greater claim, could only procure Thomas Ruddach an apprentice position with Alexander Ritchie on the Rappahannock River—provided he was willing to serve for five years.[99] The terms were unacceptable to Steuart who sent his nephew to Virginia with a request that he work for Alexander Diack, one of Parker and Steuart's former Norfolk store assistants, who now maintained a business of his own. Diack could not offer Ruddach employment himself but found him a position with the Glasgow firm of Bogles and Scott, working under a Mr. Gilchrist, in Port Royal. Steuart intended his nephew to serve Gilchrist four years "until he comes of age." He did, however, also insist that Ruddach be given leave to change positions should a better one offer.[100]

Bogles and Scott ceased trading sometime in 1772, leaving Ruddach unemployed. When the Port Royal store broke up, Mr. Gilchrist sent Ruddach back to Parker, who now offered him a position in one of his own stores.[101] Parker's patronage proved unnecessary this time. Steuart had seen that trouble was brewing in Virginia and that there was no end in sight. When Bogles and Scott failed, he went into action. Charles Steuart had long had a nagging feeling that the West Indies were a better place to make a fortune anyway.[102] He was not alone. Henry Moncreiff, whose brother Archibald worked for Spiers & Company (a Glasgow house) in Maryland, wrote his brother that he was not altogether happy. This apparently made him to decide to send a younger brother to Jamaica instead.

I am far from being Satisfy'd to the state of your Connections in the Company. . . . It is not the want of money that Led me to advise you not to enter into deep Connections with the Company. . . . [Your younger brother]

[98]William Aitchison to Charles Steuart, 6 April 1771, MS 5026, p. 259, NLS.

[99]Salary began at five pounds and increased five pounds per year. There was no guarantee of promotion, and Ruddach would not have been able to leave his position for another one. See James Ingram to Charles Steuart, MS 5026, p. 263, NLS.

[100]See Charles Steuart to James Parker, 28 June 1771, 920 Par I 27/41, NLS. Such an agreement between a clerk and an employer was uncommon, a tribute to the power of Steuart's name and the importance of his connections.

[101]See Thomas Ruddach to Charles Steuart, 19 September 1772, MS 5027, p. 212, NLS, and Ruddach to Steuart, 10 February 1773, MS 5028, p. 27, NLS.

[102]Remember that Steuart was not from Glasgow and was thus able to conceive of places other than the Chesapeake for acquiring independence! See Charles Steuart to James Parker, 28 June 1771, 920 Par I 27/41, LRO.

Willie . . . will never succeed in any library live. I have therefore made what Interest I cou'd & have got him fixed to go to Jamaica . . . the Prospect before him there is a very good one.[103]

At the end of October 1772, Steuart wrote Parker to inform him of the decision at which he had finally arrived. Once again, Steuart turned to his network of business acquaintances to achieve the desired result.

I was at a loss how to dispose of Tommy Ruddach. I had written about him to Patrick Maxwell [a Scott] at Grenada, an old Virginia Acquaintance; who came home last month, and told me if I would have him brought up a West Indian planter, he would recommend him to a Cousin of his, a Mr Balfour [also a Scot], who he thinks is one of the best in Those Islands. . . . I gladly accepted his offer.[104]

Parker had concluded that "upon the whole, these Islands seem to afford the best prospect for lads of small expectations."[105] For his part, Thomas Ruddach, happy to have been given a chance to leave Orkney and search for a fortune, appeared indifferent and offered to do whatever his uncle Charles asked of him. While he really liked Virginia, and had obviously become part of the Parker network there, he knew the etiquette of the patronage game. Even though he had been offered an appealing position with a Virginia Scottish firm to establish and operate a West Indian business for them, he solicited his uncle's advice. "Please let me know your thoughts of the above, as I will be regulated entirely by your opinion." He knew enough not to anger someone who had his interests in mind.[106]

So it was that Ruddach left Virginia, fortuitously before the war, to embark on a new career in Tobago, one of the Caribbean islands ceded to the British in 1763. After a brief attempt to learn the planting business, Thomas Ruddach returned to his training as a merchant.[107] His younger brother Charles had already been found a place in a Scots network in Jamaica. Charles's patron, Malcolm Laing, a Kingston merchant and planter, placed him on one of his properties in the island's east end.[108]

---

[103]Henry Moncreiff to Archibald Moncreiff, 6 September 1774, File 13, Moncreiff of Tullibole Papers, privately owned, NRA(S). Willie never made it big in Jamaica. He came back two years after going out, a victim of poor health. His older brother waited until he had recovered and then procured him a place in the East Indies, where he made a very substantial sum.

[104]Charles Steuart to James Parker, 31 October 1772, 920 Par I 27/46, LRO.

[105]Ibid.

[106]See Thomas Ruddach to Charles Steuart, 10 February 1773, Steuart Papers, MS 5028, p. 27, NLS.

[107]See Thomas Ruddach to Charles Steuart, 25 July 1775, MS 5029, p. 83, NLS.

[108]See Malcolm Laing to Charles Steuart, 11 September 1775, MS 5029, p. 99, NLS. Charles Ruddach moved plantations several times, because of the difficulties he experienced

Charles Steuart was not the only one in this particular network to believe in the value of formal schooling in Scotland followed by vocational or professional training in the colonies. Like many of his countrymen in the Caribbean, James Parker insisted that his children receive a proper Scottish education. Of course, the pressures placed upon the family by the Revolution made removal from the colony a particularly expedient idea.

In 1775, with trouble for Scottish merchants a well-established reality, James Parker sent his eldest son Patrick (Pate) to be educated in Edinburgh, with James Macknight, a cousin of his who happened to run a school. Pate had been placed in good hands. Macknight wrote Parker that Pate "shall be taken Care of in all points by me as if he were my Own Son."[109] Pate's schooling progressed at a good speed for the next several years, despite Macknight's observation that the young Parker had been cursed with a lazy tendency. "If he does not make progress in learning, I assure you it is not owing to want of care either in his masters or in me. At present," he wrote, "he stands the Eleventh from the head of the class which I think a great deal considering that there are near Eighty Boys in the class with him."[110] Parker's son was clearly clever and Macknight believed he would have been much nearer the top of the class if he was not so slothful.

Father had already begun to think of his son's future. He would need a career, which would allow him to create wealth fairly quickly, because his father's success, so tightly tied to Virginia and its tobacco economy, seemed to be drying out and gradually shrinking with each new day of hostilities between the British and the Americans. Macknight solicited Parker's advice on the subject:

> You very properly desire him to think of some business: But it ought not to be left altogether to himself to make the choice; because he shews no inclination to one business more than another and therefore if you prefer any business, Let me know and I will converse with him upon it, & write you how he relishes it. The sooner he fixes on a business, it will be so much the better, because I would direct his Education so as to fit him for it.[111]

Pate had not yet made up his mind. So Macknight, in an effort to stimulate his awareness and help him make a decision, sent him to Edinburgh University from 1779 to 1780.[112] Either Pate or his father, it is unclear which,

with absentee owners. Each time Laing found him a new place. His career can be precisely followed in the Steuart Letters. See especially Charles Ruddach to Charles Steuart, 9 April 1778, MS 5030, p. 247, and 21 October 1778, MS 5031, p. 84, NLS.

[109]J. Macknight to J. Parker, 25 May 1775, 920 Par I 39/1, LRO.

[110]J. Macknight to J. Parker, 29 April 1778, 920 Par I 39/2, LRO.

[111]Ibid.

[112]There is no Patrick Parker in the Edinburgh University Matriculation Roll until 1784 (EUL), well after Pate was there. It is likely that he simply attended classes at the university without formally enrolling.

decided in that year that Pate would enter a mercantile career, making further formal university education unnecessary. In 1782, while serving an apprentice appointment in a Glasgow counting house belonging to another of his father's friends, Mr. McCormick, Pate wrote to his father, now imprisoned in France, "I think it is now full time for my doing something for myself, for as the Scotch people say, I will 'have the world for the winning.'"[113] He returned to Virginia the following year, 1783, long enough to help his mother settle her affairs and accompany her to England in 1784, where his father and siblings then lived. The whole family was once again together, albeit in Britain, for a few months that year.

Young Pate would be the first to go, in order that he might venture back to the Chesapeake. He did not seem to be aware that, as a Scot, he would not be particularly welcome. He must have counted on his mother's American birth, and her quiet residence in the country during the war, to help him overcome his father's vehement and vocal loyalism. Of course, he had another reason for leaving his family to return to the United States. While in Virginia to collect his mother, Pate had become attracted to his cousin, the daughter of his mother's sister. In 1785, Pate again went to Virginia, over his father's fierce objections, to become a merchant. James Parker, by this point, hated the Americans and everything about the country. The last thing he wanted was to see his son living there, practicing the same business, associating with the same people. The bulk of Parker's network had disappeared with the war, either back to Scotland or to points tropical, but some people in it remained. Among them were several Norfolk and Princess Anne residents. While they did not like dealing with Scotsmen, they informed Pate that "as long as I sell as Cheap as other People, I shall have all of their Custom, for my mothers sake."[114] Here, family, on the maternal side, was enough to secure at least the promise of business. In the end, it was not enough.

Four years later, in 1789, James Parker's younger son, Charles Steuart Parker, who also had been educated in Scotland, left for a career as a merchant in Grenada. (The island was acquired by the British in 1763 and already had a number of Scots living in it.)[115] Such a profession was by no means James Parker's first choice for this son. He had always intended that

<hr/>

[113]Pate Parker to James Parker, 5 July 1782, 920 Par I 40/5, LRO. James Parker was imprisoned by the French, after the ship in which he was traveling to Britain wrecked. See "The Memorial of James Parker, to the American Loyalist Commissioners," 920 Par I 19/5, LRO, for complete details of Parker's wartime experiences.

[114]Pate Parker to James Parker, 10 July 1786, 920 Par I 40/35, LRO. Pate accepted this promise at its face value. He would find out the hard way that his father's associations were much more important. The Virginians drove Pate into a bottomless pit of debt.

[115]Glasgow's emphasis was beginning to shift to the West Indies, and, after Jamaica, Grenada was one of the most popular areas. See the discussion in Chapter 1, the records of Alexander Houston and Company (NLS), and Ferguson, *Scotland: 1689 to the Present* (Edinburgh, 1968), pp. 182–84.

Charles "should study either Law or Physic if his genius was equal to it."[116] But because Parker could no longer afford such education he had him bred, like his brother, a merchant. Using his connections from Virginia, James Parker asked James Campbell, a former Virginia Scot who went to Grenada during the Revolution, to procure his son a place.[117]

Both Pate Parker's career in Virginia and Charles Steuart Parker's career in Grenada are well documented. Each used a network, composed predominantly of Scots, which had been acquired through their father's connections and networks in Virginia, to obtain the positions necessary to begin their quests for independence. The networks and webs which the Scots developed spanned more than the Atlantic Ocean, they spanned different generations. It is ironic, then, to note that the principal connection, James Parker, withdrew his support from his eldest son.

James Parker was extremely unhappy with Pate's decision to go to Virginia, as well as his decision to marry his cousin, so much so that the two very nearly became completely estranged:

> As you have taken this Desperate resolve If Instantaneous ruin ensue, with your eyes wide open, why consult me after announcing your will. In short you very well know that it was only in obedience to your amiable mothers request that I consented to your going there at all, I soon saw ruin coming upon you & wished to draw you out of it by all means in my power.[118]

Virginians were, he went on to say, "the most unprincipalled villains on earth." The elder Parker, in a bid to get his son out of Virginia, had used what little was left of his patronage to arrange places for Pate in both the Caribbean (with his brother) and South Carolina. Pate refused to comply, breaking down the network. The destruction was nearly complete. From this point on, Pate never believed he could please his father who for his part, never believed a word that his son wrote to him, whether about his family or (especially) his business. He had after all gone to the country that James Parker considered to have been the cause of his ruination and the devastation of all he had worked so hard to acquire for his family.[119]

[116]James Macknight to James Parker, 25 November 1784, 920 Par I 39/10, LRO.

[117]For a description of the Scotsmen with whom Charles Steuart Parker became associated (and James Campbell's inability to get him into either Munro's or Thornton, Baillie, and Campbell's houses because these Scots had their own nephews for whom to find places), see Charles Steuart Parker to Pate Parker, 3 December 1789, 920 Par I 46/1, LRO. For a description of Charles Steuart Parker's career, which paralleled many of his counterparts in Jamaica, see Letters from Charles Steuart Parker, 1778–1800, 920 Par III.

[118]James Parker to Patrick Parker, 20 October 1787, 920 Par I 41, LRO.

[119]Details of the feud between Pate and his father can be found in Sections 40 and 41 of the Parker Family Letters I, LRO. Parker made many dockets on the letters he received from his

CONCLUSIONS AND COMPARISONS

The stories, maps, and charts presented in this chapter provide focal points for comparing Scottish sojourner networks in the Chesapeake and Jamaica. Both colonies had areas of high Scottish concentration: in Jamaica, these were primarily the six parishes at the island's north and west; in the Chesapeake, Scots transients lived predominantly in the tobacco-gathering towns along the James, Rappahannock, and Potomac rivers. The areas in Jamaica with large numbers of Scots continued to draw new recruits from Scotland, in increasing numbers, as the second half of the eighteenth century progressed; indeed, they continued to do so well into the nineteenth century. Things in the Chesapeake were quite different. The areas with high Scots concentrations did not attract many Scots beginning their quests for independence after the American Revolution. Nor did any other part of the states of Virginia and Maryland. Those who arrived tended very much, like Pate Parker, to have had prerevolutionary connections. Until 1776, however, Glaswegians continued to flock to the Chesapeake in search of fortunes.

Some differences between Scottish networks in the two areas did exist. In the first place, Scots in Jamaica were a much more occupationally diverse group than their countrymen to the north. Their networks tended to reflect this. With Francis Grant as an illustration, it is apparent that many of his Scottish clients and patrons were apprentices and absentees which, given his occupation as estate manager and attorney, was to be expected. It is also clear that among the people with whom he had extensive interaction were a judge (his brother, the island's chief justice), several merchants, and some doctors. They lived, for the most part, within a twenty-mile radius of his house at Montego Bay. Several of the people within his network, his brother for example, resided in more distant parts of the island. Those people who lived farther away had, of course, fewer interactions with Grant than those that lived in his neighborhood. But they often served as a safety net. If part of his network was unable to provide the patronage he needed or wanted, Grant had others upon whom he could call. In such a fashion, Scots in Jamaica moved easily from one place to another. If the patron looked hard enough, some connection, perhaps an event like Charles Stirling's dinner at Content

---

son: "Profession of affection, but in words only" (40/126), "P. Parker complaining for want of goods was *plainly* not fit for a *mercht*" (40/101). Father never forgave son for dishonoring his requests not to return to Virginia as a merchant and not to marry his cousin. Pate, while he knew the reasons for his father's wishes, attempted to succeed at his business to compensate and show his father that Virginia could be a place to make a fortune. His business was poor (probably because of his association with the remnants of the old Scots network) and he died in 1795 very much in debt. James Parker appears to have been vindicated. On the letter Pate wrote from his death bed, Parker scrawled "P. Parker. Self Reflections when too late" (40/152).

plantation in St. James parish, could always be found. These relationships made Scots networks in one end of the island accessible to those on the other side of it.

The network of Alexander Johnston, who avoided using his patronage authority to assist his countrymen, reveals both similarities and differences to Grant. While Johnston's primary web was comprised of people within twenty miles of his house, he did know people, both Scottish and not Scottish, in other parts of the island and could have called on them if he needed. Occupationally, they were every bit as diverse as Grant's acquaintances. Ethnically, however, they were more diverse. Grant had an extremely strong tendency to associate exclusively with his countrymen. Indeed around 70 percent of Grant's interactions could be so characterized. The nature of Johnston's profession really precluded this. He had to treat as many people as possible to reap maximum financial awards. Even so, as much as 42 percent of his business was with other Scots. The difference to Grant, however, was one of degree, not one of kind.

By contrast, the Chesapeake networks, because of the overwhelming importance of the tobacco industry to Scottish sojourners, were far more circumscribed. Of course, Alexander Wilson's network was quite small and localized. He had just begun his Chesapeake career and his experiences were fairly typical. Often, young lads would enter the colonies knowing only a few other souls: friends who had already come over, the chief factor for the company that employed them, and their immediate neighbors in the town in which they lived. The longer they remained in the colonies, the larger their networks became. Nearly everyone in the web was a Scot involved in the tobacco business. There were few, if any, opportunities to diversify without completely forgetting one's connections.

Interestingly enough, some of the larger Scottish Chesapeake networks, as exemplified by Parker-Steuart, had substantial geographical breadth, though the occupational diversity again appears to have been almost entirely lacking. Examination of this particular network revealed that despite connections in several colonies, there was no safety net for anyone once the Revolution came, especially after loyalties had been declared and oaths sworn. Business relationships had become kinship ties and, as a result, were elevated in status and importance within the network. Even so, this extended family had no safeguard from the consequences of allegiance to the British side. Bigger was not necessarily better.

Scots communities and networks did not exist in a vacuum. Even though there were certain areas of Scottish concentration in the colonies, which have been described in this chapter, it would be a fallacy to argue that the Scots kept entirely to themselves. Simple demographics would have prevented complete segregation, however self-imposed. In terms of their business relationships, however, they were less flexible. They accepted business from others but did not often assign their own affairs outside of the networks described in this chapter.

The Scots sojourners in Jamaica lived comfortably amongst fellow colonists. They certainly preferred to interact with each other, as both their correspondence and the Letters Testamentary reveal, but they also knew that independence could be achieved with much greater speed if they accepted custom and assistance from others in the island. So it was with the Scots in Virginia for a while. Their innovative system of trading tobacco became extremely popular. As a result, these sojourners allowed themselves friendships with their neighbors, because they thought it good for their business. In the final analysis, however, transient Scots were not perceived to be industrious or attentive to business but rather connivers, plotting the destruction of liberty and economically maneuvering the planters into a terrible position. As the Revolution approached, many Scots did not hesitate to demonstrate their hitherto hidden contempt for their neighbors and customers. Business had turned troublesome, so there was now no reason even to appear sympathetic. As James Bartlett wrote his supervisor:

> The differences 'twixt Britain & her Collonies allarming as they indeed are, appear in a much worse light to the ignorant & illiterate than to those of Sense and education hence it is that the many worthless Beings I have to deal with, and who look upon it as meritorious to defraud a merchant rejoice at our distress.[120]

The outcome of Scottish sojourns in Jamaica and the Chesapeake are the subject of the next, and final chapter. Questions of success and failure, in the context of changing political and economic environments, will be considered at greater length there, as will the thorny question of Scottish involvement in the American Revolution.

[120]James Bartlett to James Robinson, 28 November 1774, GD 247/59/Q, SRO. The reasons for the anti-Scottish feeling in the colony came directly out of the domination of the tobacco trade.

5

THE PARADOX OF SUCCESS:
LUCRATIVE CAREERS
AND FAILED GOALS

James McLeod, a young tobacco factor in Virginia, explained his motivations for undertaking a transatlantic crossing. He clearly expressed not only the reasons for Scots to sojourn but also the results which they expected.

> Could I live decently by my industry at home I most certainly would chuse it, but as I have never found that to be the Case, you will excuse me if I think it would be more agreable to me to live at a distance from my former acquaintances till such time as I can get something to enable me to live on a good footing with them. I must also confess that I am quite tired of living in a state of dependence.[1]

Travelers to either Jamaica or the Chesapeake believed that their new homes were only to be endured for as long as it took to (a) earn enough money to (b) go back to Scotland with "a comfortable independence." But in both places they were destined for disappointment. To understand why, one must consider their ambitions and their behavior and at the same time measure the results of their labors.

Despite a common aim, the two groups are differentiated by their experiences and outcomes in the new world. Those who went to Jamaica were more occupationally diverse than their countrymen in the Chesapeake. And they did not hesitate to change their situations if a better one arose. That option was simply unavailable to most Scottish visitors in Virginia and Maryland. Jamaica's high rate of absenteeism allowed the Scots a degree of personal freedom and control that was virtually inconceivable to most employees of tobacco firms in the Chesapeake. Sojourners in the Caribbean formed ethnically based webs to assist them on their quests for fortunes. So did

[1]James McLeod to Donald McLeod, 7 September 1776, MS 19297, NLS.

those on the mainland, but their networks were inextricably linked to tobacco.

For the denouement of this tale, we must learn whether or not Scottish transients in Jamaica and the Chesapeake were successful. Two complementary approaches to this question can be employed. The first gauges individual financial prosperity. Through the survival of several important groups of public record, it has been possible to determine precisely how much some Scots were actually worth (or at least claimed to be worth) at particular moments in time.[2] Each of these measures is based upon notions of relative wealth in the society from which it came. Such records allow us to determine with some precision whether the Scots acquired more or less than their non-Scottish neighbors in the colonies. A second comparison invited by surviving records is between the Scots' achievement in the colonies and their position if they had remained at home. Despite the sojourner's profession of love for Scotland, not all middling and "merchandising" Scots, as James McLeod pointed out, were able to earn a suitable living there. If the colonial residence increased a person's standard of living, surely it must be viewed as a success.

A second approach is to ask whether sojourners achieved their own goals. If they did, then their colonial stay should rightfully be considered to have been worthwhile. If, however, they did not realize their own aims, the sojourn must ultimately be considered a failure. In other words, if the sojourner either failed to return home or did not have enough capital to acquire the sought-after independence in Scotland, he definitely would have considered his experiences in the colonies to have yielded an unacceptable outcome.

This definition of success and failure might not be a particularly useful notion for a twentieth-century historian evaluating the relative prosperity of different societies. But to eighteenth-century Scots, the goal of returning home was all-important and often all-consuming. In light of their experiences, we might be able to conclude that their goal was unrealistic or impractical. Nonetheless, it shaped their behavior, and it is the scale they used to measure their own achievements and shortcomings.

Many Scots in Jamaica never returned to Scotland because, they claimed, they had not accumulated enough in the colony to sustain them adequately at

[2]Inventories of probated Jamaican estates are catalogued 1B/11/3, in the Jamaica Archives. An alphabetical index, arranged chronologically, is available. Evidence and claims filed before the several commissions dealing with American Loyalists can be found largely in record groups T 79, AO 12, and AO 13 at the PRO, Kew. Transcripts of the Loyalist material are located in the United States, as part of the Manuscript Department at the New York Public Library. Slave Registration Returns are also located at the PRO, in T 71. By sampling these sources for different years, it is possible to arrive at estimates, in pounds, shillings, and pence, of the financial benefits the Scots gained from their colonial residences.

home. Although a particular writer may have complained of not being able to fulfill his plan, a probate inventory or deed could reveal the true extent of his capital accumulation. Similar comparisons can be made in the Chesapeake. Needless to say, the differences between claims and reality could be substantial. By simultaneously evaluating the degree to which the Scots fulfilled their own two-part plan and measuring objectively their financial position, we can develop a clearer understanding of the results achieved by Scottish transients in these two plantation societies.[3]

The second problem to be addressed in this chapter is peculiar to the Chesapeake. In Virginia and Maryland, the Scots remained loyal to Great Britain before and during the American War of Independence. The reasons many Scots chose the king's side are examined here, especially in light of what they hoped to gain from tying both their fates and their fortunes to the expanding British Empire. With hindsight, their decision would later serve them well; from their perspective in 1776, it failed them miserably. Most Scottish sojourners in the Chesapeake colonies did not even come close to achieving their financial aims.

Pondering the position of Chesapeake Scots during the American War of Independence and comparing the situation of their Jamaican countrymen at that time has made one conclusion obvious. Though Scottish transients in both Jamaica and the Chesapeake often met with what they considered to be unsatisfactory results, things were much worse for those in Virginia and Maryland than for their countrymen in the Caribbean.

TROUBLE IN THE TROPICS

Scots in Jamaica rarely achieved both parts of their expressed goal. As a result, many sojourners considered themselves to have been less than successful and characterized their island experiences as negative. When measured against other groups, they accomplished much more than they cared to admit; they did at least as well as, and often better than, their neighbors. The number of Scots who lived in the island increased, as did their measurable assets, over the course of the period from 1740 to 1800. With growing frequency, they earned enough money to purchase significant amounts of property, land as well as slaves, in Jamaica.

---

[3]To my mind, the single best discussion of definitions and the relative and varying degrees of wealth can be found in Alice Hanson Jones, *Wealth of a Nation to Be* (New York, 1980). With probated estate inventories as her principal source, she examines per-capita wealth in the three mainland regions of the colonies. A good historiographical overview of this field can be found in John J. McCusker and Russell Menard, *The Economy of British North America, 1607–1789* (Chapel Hill, N.C., 1986), pp. 258–76; a chapter entitled "Wealth and Welfare" includes the British Caribbean colonies and the somewhat limited literature on them.

The Jamaican economy underwent constant and profound expansion throughout the period. Even so, as Seymour Drescher has noted, it came nowhere near to approaching its limits.

> The largest frontier was still where it had been throughout the eighteenth century, in Jamaica. In the 1770s [Island historian Edward] Long estimated Jamaica's still undeveloped acreage at over 1.9 million acres, excluding provision grounds. The Jamaicans themselves claimed that at least half the commercially arable land on the island was patented and still undeveloped in 1789.[4]

So much uncleared and uncultivated land did not indicate stagnation. In 1768, 651 sugar estates operated in Jamaica. By 1786, just eighteen years later, the island supported 1061, which represented an increase of 63 percent. This larger number of properties did much toward raising the output of staple crop. Jamaica's sugar crop stood at 35,943 hogsheads in 1770. Twenty years later, in 1790, production had reached 55,600 hogsheads, and ten years after that it had grown to 70,100. In just three decades, the island's sugar crop had doubled. Dynamic development continued into the new century. In 1805, 99,600 hogsheads of sugar were produced in the island (a 30 percent increase in only five years).[5]

In order to bring about the increases in output, the island's residents, both black and white, brought more and more of Jamaica's uncultivated land into monoculture production. As a result, they did not grow nearly enough of their own food stuffs; they could not subsist without importing. Nor did they have any real manufacturing industry with which to produce consumer goods.[6] Obviously, food and goods had to come from Britain and its other colonial possessions. As might be imagined after considering the impressive production statistics, and the crop's market value, the West Indian colonies were tremendously important to the empire's economy. Both Jamaican imports from and exports to the United Kingdom increased significantly from the 1770s onward. But the sharpest gains took place after 1785, as the society entered a period of prolonged growth. Throughout the years of this study, the British West Indies clearly were the most important of Britain's non-European trading partners and Jamaica was first among the islands.[7]

---

[4]Drescher, *Econocide*, p. 64.

[5]These figures come from Noel Deerr, *The History of Sugar* (London, 1949–50), v. 1, pp. 176, 198–99.

[6]The thoroughly depressing subject of the West Indies' failure to produce enough provisions for the slave population during the American Revolution, and Britain's reaction to it, is discussed in Richard Sheridan, "The Crisis of Slave Subsistence in the British West Indies during and after the American Revolution," *WMQ* 33 (1976): 615–41.

[7]See Drescher, *Econocide*, pp. 16–24. British trade statistics that support this argument can be found in B. R. Mitchell, *British Historical Statistics*, esp. pp. 492–97.

This expansion could not have been easily achieved without a significant increase in the colony's population, both black and white. While the proportion between the two groups (just under 10:1) did not change drastically, the absolute numbers did. In 1768, around 167,000 blacks and 17,000 whites populated the island. By 1787, the figures had grown to (approximately) 237,000 blacks and 23,800 whites. Four years later, available information puts the figures at 250,000 and 30,000 respectively. In less than twenty-five years, the white population had increased by 76 percent. Many whites hunting for ways to improve their fortunes realized that as the number of blacks in Jamaica increased, the number of positions for whites would also rise. The Scots, with a variety of skills and training, took advantage of the situation.[8]

The Chesapeake was different. Maryland's white population grew by 45 percent and Virginia's by 59 percent in the two decades between 1760 and 1780. Perhaps even more significantly, the Chesapeake's white population was more than twenty times larger than that in the island during the 1780s. And despite an increasing black presence, the black-to-white ratio never exceeded 1:2 in Maryland and 1:1.3 in Virginia.[9] The greater number of whites in the region left fewer opportunities for an ambitious group of transients than were to be found in Jamaica. These societies could fill most openings from within their own expanding ranks. As a result, the Scottish presence there was limited and fairly confined to tobacco trading. While many in Jamaica came remarkably close to fulfilling their ambitions, those in the Chesapeake did not. Such a claim is relatively easy to demonstrate.

A full series of probated estate inventories for the island can be found in the Jamaica Archives. (This particular set of the island's records is nearly complete from 1674 through the nineteenth century.) By tabulating the reported values of Jamaica estates probated between 1740 and 1800, it is possible to determine just how financially "successful" the Scots really were. I have selected four years in which to carry out this procedure. Each was chosen with the idea that it be spaced far enough apart from the others to demonstrate any large trends and changes which took place during the period. The starting point (1742) was picked to correspond roughly with the beginning of this study and the other three sample years were then chosen at regular eighteen-year intervals.

For each year, the value of every probated estate has been recorded and the Scottish ones, where possible, identified.[10] This four-year sample,

[8]The Jamaica population statistics come from Brathwaite, *Creole Society*, p. 152.

[9]Population statistics come from *British Historical Statistics*, p. 756. Of course, there would have been pockets in the colony where the number of blacks exceeded the number of whites. Both colonies came closest to numerical racial parity in 1750.

[10]I have again used surname analysis and, as always, omitted any names that could have been either Scottish or English.

Table 5.1.   Scottish estate inventories in Jamaica (rounded to nearest pound)

	1742	1760	1778	1796
Total number of estates	176	148	237	317
Total Scottish estates	33	33	46	93
Total non-Scottish estates	143	115	191	224
Scottish estates as % of total	18.7	22.3	19.4	29.3
Total estate value	£315,353.	£311,476.	£774,929.	£1,466,092.
Total Scottish estate value	£45,846.	£67,656.	£154,507.	£431,169.
Total non-Scottish value	£269,507.	£243,820.	£620,422.	£1,034,923.
Scottish Share of Total value	14.5%	21.7%	19.9%	29.4%
Average estate value	£1792.	£2105.	£3284.	£4669.
Average % increase		17.5%	56.0%	42.2%
Average Scottish estate	£1389.	£2050.	£3359.	£4641.
Average Scottish increase		47.6%	63.8%	38.2%
Average non-Scottish estate	£1897.	£2120.	£3248.	£4620.

Source: Estate Inventories, 1B/11/3/22–23 (1742), 1B/11/3/39–40 (1760), 1B/11/3/59–60 (1778), and 1B/11/3/84-85, Jamaica Archives, Spanish Town.

though limited, provides an important indicator of the rising fortunes of Scots in Jamaica (Table 5.1).

The value of Jamaica's Scottish estates took off after 1742 and continued to surge ahead, at least through 1796 and very probably after it. The average Scottish head of household's estate (£1389) in 1742 was worth significantly less than the average non-Scottish estate (£1897). The gap between the two cohorts narrowed in 1760. And by 1778, the mean Scottish estate (£3359) had become slightly bigger than the mean non-Scottish estate (£3248).

Colonywide estate values from 1742 to 1796 increased 259 percent, an impressive gain by any standard. This figure can be further broken down; non-Scottish inventories expanded by 243 percent during the period. Scottish inventories, however, grew by a whopping 334 percent, a much stronger and more substantial increment. Because the Scots were a minority group within a larger population, the faster growth of Scottish estates as compared to their neighbors is immediately noticeable.[11] Richard Sheridan, in his essay, "Domestic Economy," has shown that wealth per free white person, between 1770 and 1775, amounted to around £1200 sterling. According to the information provided by the estate inventories, the Scots left estates that

[11]The inventories must be used with caution. Not everyone who died in the island had their estates probated (or recorded) and many people who lived in Britain owned property in the island (even if they had never been there) and had an inventory entered into the public record. More often than not, land was excluded from the inventory; the value of the land would have added significantly to the estate.

averaged above this per-capita estimate. Although there are methodological problems in comparing individuals with households, the average household size would have had to be at least three people in order for the Scots to have been less well-off than average.[12]

Not only did estate values increase, but more and more Scots went to Jamaica in order to capitalize on opportunities there. The Scottish proportion of inventoried estates grew from just under 20 percent in 1742 to nearly 30 percent in 1796. Most of this growth took place in the years between 1778 and 1796. The increased Scottish presence found in the island's parishes and the rise in advertisements in the Scottish press after the American War leave no doubt that Jamaica's importance to Scotland, as both a trading partner and a market for its exported native sons, continued to grow. Clearly and unreservedly, when compared to others the Scots in Jamaica did extremely well over the long run. They were, in fact, much more successful than they cared to confess, probably because to have done so would have meant admitting that they had given up their original intention to go home as quickly as possible. Sojourners, in theory, should not have left £2000 estates in a society in which they had no stake.

Jamaica's Scots left estates that were valued in direct proportion to their number in the population. In other words, in 1796, Scots comprised 29.3 percent of the probates and possessed 29.4 percent of the value of all the inventories. In 1778, the figures were 19.4 percent and 19.9 percent respectively. In a society that was known for an uneven distribution of wealth, one ethnic group was able to achieve a nearly balanced population-to-wealth ratio.[13] As important, Scottish estate values did not vary as widely as those of the colony as a whole. The gap between the wealthiest and the poorest Scot was not as large as it was for other whites in the island.[14] This convergence can probably be explained by considering the Scottish preference for certain (middle-class) occupations.

[12]Sheridan, "Domestic Economy" in *Colonial British America*, ed. Jack P. Greene and J. R. Pole (Baltimore, 1984), p. 49. The figure of £1196 sterling is presented in McCusker and Menard, *Economy*, table 3.3, p. 61. For some interesting and alternative figures, see Sheridan, *Sugar and Slavery*, p. 230. The two figures are not an exact comparison. The estate inventories are a measure of head of household's wealth and the other is a measure of property held by each free white person. It is difficult to provide a more exact comparison because accurate population figures for Jamaica are not easily available, nor has any systematic demographic analysis of Jamaican families yet been carried out for the eighteenth century.

[13]It should be noted here that for the year 1778, the largest estate, that of Sir Simon Clarke, was removed from the sample. His estate, valued at £269,592.6, would have been 25.9 percent of the total of £1,044,521.18. Similarly, for 1796, three estates, each amounting to over 10 percent of the total were removed from the calculation. The figures are given in currency (divide by 1.4 to arrive at the sterling value).

[14]As an example, in 1796 the gap between the richest (£35,813) and poorest (£85) Scottish estates was £35,728. Among non-Scottish residents of that island, that gap was £132,417.

By 1817, the Scots had continued to improve their acquisitive performance. Analysis of the slave registration returns for the six sample parishes that were discussed in the last chapter (Hanover, St. Ann, St. James, St. Mary, Trelawny, and Westmoreland), along with three other parishes for comparison (Portland, St. George, and St. Thomas-in-the-East) reveals the continuation of the trends described here (Table 5.2).[15] Scots amounted to between 12 percent and 29 percent of the total number of white slaveholders in each of the parishes but they held significantly more than 12 percent to 29 percent of the slaves. In other words, the average Scot possessed more slaves than the average white. The gap between rich and poor became even more pronounced. And the Scots positively improved their standing.

The data culled from the 1817 slave registration returns also demonstrate that Scots had now spread themselves throughout the island. St. Thomas in the East parish had a higher Scottish concentration than Trelawny parish. (Though Trelawny's Scots, among the island's most established, had the highest numbers of slaves per Scot.) Similarly, small numbers of Scots, more affluent than their non-Scottish neighbors, resided in Portland and St. George's parishes. It therefore seems to me that the transient population had expanded its networks from its bases on either end of the island.[16]

Adding up the figures for the six sample parishes in 1817 shows that Scots came to 23.5 percent of the sample, but they held 32.4 percent of all slaves. Such results speak clearly. A smaller number of people possessed a greater amount of "property." This goes a long way toward explaining the Scottish tendency to extend their sojourns. More time in Jamaica effectively meant more property there and, as they erroneously believed, enough property guaranteed a successful Scottish independence. They had done rather well for themselves in the Caribbean; their wealth could be easily seen and sized up. In Scotland it would not have been quite so easy to observe, thus the temptation to stay.

The probate records and registration returns have provided at least two tangible measures of the increasing success in acquiring property encoun-

---

[15]The Slave Registration Returns (T 71, PRO) were the products of a parliamentary act. Britain abolished the slave trade in 1807 and in 1834–38 ended the institution entirely. In order to insure that property owners were doing what they could to raise the birth rate and decrease the death rate of their slaves, yearly records of the numbers, names, and conditions of the slaves owned by each individual were kept. The first in the series, in 1817, are considered here.

[16]Barry Higman has argued that Portland and St. George had the greatest natural disadvantages for climate and transport, while St. Thomas in the East was a very productive sugar-growing region. It is therefore no surprise that it resembles the other parishes with significant Scottish populations in the island's west. See Higman, *Slave Population and Economy*, pp. 20 and 64, for a discussion of the other parishes' decline in the early nineteenth century. For a contemporary eighteenth-century description of the parishes see Original Correspondence with the Board of Trade, CO 137/28/184–5, PRO, Kew.

Table 5.2. Slave registration returns, 1817

	St. Ann	St. James	Westmoreland	Trelawny	Hanover	St. Mary	St. George	Portland	St. Thomas in the East
Total number of slaveholders	961	331	643	836	710	706	477	309	699
Number of Scots	185	63	157	96	205	220	78	47	178
Number of non-Scots	776	268	486	740	505	486	399	262	421
% Scottish	19.25	19.03	24.42	11.49	28.89	31.17	16.36	15.21	25.47
Total number of slaves	24,846	9,234	21,500	28,635	24,170	26,946	13,609	8,131	26,401
Number of slaves owned by Scots	7,056	2,882	7,250	8,206	9,670	8,787	3,390	2,125	10,862
Number owned by non-Scots	17,790	6,352	14,250	20,429	14,500	18,159	10,219	6,006	15,539
% Scottish-owned	28.4	31.2	33.7	28.7	40.0	32.6	24.9	26.1	41.2
Slaves per white slaveholder	25.86	27.89	33.4	34.25	34.04	38.17	28.53	26.31	37.77
Slaves per Scot	38.14	45.75	46.18	85.48	47.17	39.94	43.47	45.21	61.02
Slaves per non-Scot	22.92	23.70	29.32	27.61	28.71	37.36	25.61	22.92	36.91

Sources: St. Ann's Parish, T71/43; St. James Parish, T71/201; Westmoreland Parish, T71/178; Trelawny Parish, T71/224; Hanover Parish, T71/190; St. Mary's Parish, T71/33; St. George's Parish, T71/158; Portland Parish, T71/151; St. Thomas in the East Parish, T71/145.

tered by those who went to Jamaica. They are consistent with each other, as well as with the larger growth in the island. It is, of course, quite another problem to determine how much, if any, of the value of a Jamaican estate could actually be extracted from the island and put toward the goal of independence. It is abundantly clear that Jamaican wealth was difficult to transport.

Throughout the period, slaves constituted the most valuable component of most people's estate inventories. Such property did not translate very well at all to Scotland, which did not permit this system of human bondage within its own boundaries.[17] Land, the other primary source of wealth (which usually was *not* included in the probate materials), simply could not be moved from one place to another. Therefore, to have been successful in Jamaica, as the probate inventories and slave registration returns indicate that Scots often were, also delayed the return home. The nature of most Jamaican assets precluded their transportation to Scotland. Retaining island property thus became a fairly attractive possibility, when compared to possible losses upon liquidation.[18]

Faced with these choices, Jamaican property owners had to decide what to do with their estates. Perhaps there was some point above which an owner believed an estate could provide a proper Scottish independence and below which it required more investment. To determine whether or not such distinctions existed, it is first necessary to look at relative costs throughout the period. Given that the average Scottish probate, in 1778, left a Jamaican estate valued at £3358 (Jamaican currency or £2398 sterling), the question of just how much it was worth and how much it could procure in the (albeit unlikely) event that it could be entirely liquidated must be addressed. To be sure, it was not a great sum which would open vast new levels of the social hierarchy.[19]

One English historian has shown that small squires, whose status was very probably the equivalent of that to which the Scots aspired, had revenue of between £450 and £800 per annum, which translates roughly to an estate

[17]A useful historiographical discussion can be found in James Henretta, "Wealth and Social Structure," in Greene and Pole, eds., *Colonial British America*, pp. 262–89.

[18]Richard Pares in *Merchants and Planters* (Cambridge, 1970) and *A West India Fortune* described this choice. Pares accepted the notion, which many planters had, that they were being robbed by their managers. Even so, many believed that the losses they would have incurred in trying to sell the estate in a buyer's market would have been greater than allowing the attorney to continue to cheat. Another useful, and important discussion of this point can be found in Bryan Edwards, *A History, Civil and Commercial, of the British West Indies*, 5th edition (London, 1819), v. 2, pp. 300–308.

[19]Alice Hanson Jones, in *Wealth of a Nation*, pp. 258–93, attempts to answer similar questions about relative wealth in the colonies compared to England and other places. It is also important to remember that the actual value of the estate would have been greater than that derived from analysis of the probate records, which ordinarily did not include any land.

valued between £9000 and £16,000.[20] As the century progressed, however, there is evidence of small squires complaining that £500 per annum was no longer enough upon which to live as a gentleman.[21] Certainly, Scotland was a much poorer society than England; estates were worth less and money would buy more north of the River Tweed.

Sir John Sinclair defined middling estates in Scotland as producing between £500 and £2000 Scots (about £275 to £1100 sterling) annual income in 1760. Their values, arrived at by multiplying annual income by twenty, would have been between £5500 and £22,000 sterling. By 1814, moderate properties had risen to produce between £1000 and £3000 (sterling) in rent each year.[22] It is quite unlikely then that the transients would have been able to buy sufficient Scottish property to ensure their independence with the proceeds of their estates. In other words, a Jamaican estate worth £2400 sterling (in liquid form) could procure an estate in Scotland with revenue of only £120 per annum. This income was certainly less than what the Scots believed was required to be independent and less than English gentlemen earned. As Scotland's economy expanded further, and began to industrialize, property prices, rents, food prices, and wages all increased, further decreasing the purchasing power of an estate of £2400.[23]

Continuing to look at contemporary sources makes clearer the relative costs of living in Jamaica and in Scotland. The *Statistical Account of Scotland*, published in 1791, provides some useful details about life in each of Scotland's parishes.[24] By presenting figures for rental charges per acre, in some parishes, as well as the total amount which tenants of a particular parish paid in rent, it provides some sense of how much it cost to live in Scotland. These figures ultimately suggest that by 1790, if not before, Jamaican property could have been considered a much more easily obtainable, and more lucrative, investment than Scottish estates. For sojourners, owning property at home became an increasingly elusive goal.

[20]Dorothy Marshall, *English People in the Eighteenth Century* (London, 1956), p. 42. Here I use the convention of valuing an estate at twenty times its annual rental.

[21]W. H. Lecky, *A History of England in the Eighteenth Century* (London, 1887), v. 6, p. 171.

[22]T. C. Smout, *History*, has provided these figures (pp. 286–87). Their values would have ranged from £20,000 to £60,000.

[23]Devine, *The Tobacco Lords*, notes that the big tobacco magnates, those who controlled the houses, bought Scottish estates valued at well over £20,000. Their annual income derived from the property would therefore have been around £1000. Devine has also noted that many lived above their means (pp. 18–33). Henry Hamilton, in *An Economic History of Scotland*, describes a 50 percent increase in the price of food between 1750 and 1791 and a rise in wages to between 2.5 and 3 times their old levels (pp. 377–80).

[24]The country's ministers submitted reports to Sir John Sinclair who collated and published them in an extremely important multivolume work. As a result, a good deal of information, though not often in easily comparable form, about details of house rental prices, acreage costs, farm rentals, and the price of provisions is available for most of the country.

Land in Kilwinning Parish, Ayrshire, rented for three shillings per acre in 1742. By 1792, it rented for eighteen shillings.[25] In 1791, farms in Strathdon, the westernmost parish of Aberdeenshire, rented for between five and twenty pounds per year. In Dunblane parish, central Perthshire, farm rentals began at five shillings per acre and went up to fifteen shillings. With these prices, a fifty-acre farm could cost anywhere from £12.10 to £37.10 per year—just to rent.[26] Glasgow ground rents were even higher, a direct result of the wealth circulating from the tobacco trade. In the Gorbals district, across the River Clyde from the city, rents ranged from between £3 to £5 per acre annually.[27] Because a Scot with a Jamaican estate worth £2400 would have been hard pressed to find more than £120 per year on which to live, he could not have afforded to buy enough property to satisfy his expectations. Renting was a viable alternative, though it would have meant that the spending power of annual income would decrease even more. To be able to rent a fifty-acre farm in Perthshire and live on one hundred pounds per year was not the reason people ventured to Jamaica. Every bit as importantly, sojourners who leased a farm would remain in a dependent condition.

As a result, Scottish transients faced a stark choice. They could either rent land at £2 per acre in Scotland or buy it, on easy credit terms, at £7 per acre in Jamaica.[28] With several years' additional attention, many thought, Jamaican property would provide enough to purchase that oft-dreamed about Scottish estate. Therefore, staying in Jamaica to work for the difference became less obnoxious to them.

Dr. James Currie provided a contemporary estimate of how much it took to secure the sojourn's purpose. His threshold is substantially higher than what Scottish estates in Jamaica were worth, even as late as 1796. "£4000 Sterling," he wrote, "will make a bachelor independent."[29] He is referring to a property which yielded about £200 every year. Currie's figure seems a bit on the low side, given the increasing prices of property purchases and rentals in Scotland.[30] If £4000, however, really was the pivotal amount which was

[25]The *Statistical Account*'s Kilwinning information is discussed in Graham, *Social Life*, v. 1, p. 211.

[26]For Dunblane, see Sir John Sinclair, *The Statistical Account of Scotland* (Edinburgh, 1791), v. 7, p. 323; Strathdon can be found in v. 13, p. 171.

[27]Sinclair, *Statistical Account*, v. 5, p. 540.

[28]Here I use Bryan Edwards's figures in *The History of the British West Indies*, v. 2, pp. 287–308. Edwards breaks down the cost of running a sugar plantation in an effort to show what the returns on investments were. The figure of £7 I employ here is the rough equivalent of his £10 currency per acre charge.

[29]James Currie to Dr. James Currie, 1 July 1787, printed in *Memoirs of James Currie, M.D.*, v. 2, p. 5.

[30]A Scot with income of £200 per annum would have spent half of his income to rent a house in Edinburgh. If he decided to go the "country" route, he would not have been able to buy very much land at all.

absolutely essential to achieve independence then, the average Scot had not yet achieved it (£4000 sterling equaled £5600 currency) at the time of his or her death. Holding to their aim of returning home independent, they were certainly correct still to be living in Jamaica. As James McLeod had indicated, there was little point in going back without that for which they strove. This realization surely contributed to mounting feelings of frustration and helplessness. As a result, despite their skill at acquiring substantial property in the island, many Scottish sojourners had extremely negative experiences in the Caribbean. They did not often become absentees.

While it is true that a substantial number of West Indian absentees lived quite well in England, fewer Scots appear to have done the same, for several reasons. First, the Scottish transatlantic movement really did not get underway until after 1740, when many of the largest sugar estates had already become absentee-owned. Fewer fully-operating properties were available. Second, a number of absentee estates became so as a result of marriage. Jamaican heiresses returned to England and married there, passing their properties to their husbands. Third, many Scots simply did not know when they had had enough. Their desire for independence in Scotland became so clouded with what they had been able to achieve in the colony that they consistently upped the ante required to go home. More in Jamaica, they thought, guaranteed more in Scotland. Though £2400 sterling might have been an average estate, there were many Scots in the island with far greater ones. Obviously the allure of high living and easy wealth had seduced them.[31]

The careers of the sojourning Scottish professionals described in earlier chapters fell into a pattern, and can be used to support this general argument. Nearly all of them had demonstrably successful professional business ventures. Robert Stirling, the Kingston merchant turned sugar planter, ran an extremely profitable trading business. So did Alexander Grant of Auchinoney, Sir Alexander Grant of Dalvey's cousin. Alexander Johnston, the St. Ann's parish physician, established a very lucrative (at least in the books) medical practice for himself. The island's chief justice, John Grant, one of a very few Scots in the island who had been trained in the English bar, was a highly successful lawyer. His brother Francis was a well-known and well-respected attorney. Such a list could go on almost indefinitely. In the first stage of their quest for independence, as the inventories demonstrate, the Scots seemed to be doing splendidly. They succeeded at using their training, wits, education, and networks to reap financial rewards.

[31]For example, in 1778 George Gilchrist's property was valued at £7700 (1B/11/3/60, JA), and in 1796 William McMurdo, a Kingston merchant, left property valued over £35,000 (1B/11/3/84).

"View of Loch Awe," drawn by Robert Johnston while he was visiting Scotland, 31 October 1813. Powel Collection, R. Johnston, Drawings, The Historical Society of Pennsylvania.

"The unfavourable Situation in which West India concerns generally is now," wrote James Fraser in 1808,

> and has been so long placed, had greatly disappointed me in my fond expectation of The result of many years labour and Industry enabling me to leave this Country with an opulent fortune to spend a few years of the latter period of my life in my native Climate.[32]

While the Scots were quick to blame other people and the environment for their own disappointments, it is easy to see in retrospect that their troubles were caused by their own constantly-increasing goals and the way in which they chose to implement them. In part, these requirements were based upon the rising cost of acquiring independence in Scotland. The Scots themselves were also changed by continued financial success in Jamai-

---

[32]James Fraser to Hector McDonald, 12 June 1808, GD 47/651/2, SRO. Fraser, of course, spoke after this period, when the slave trade had been abolished. But he had been in the island for many years before slave imports became illegal. His remarks can be seen as representative of a significant number of people who found themselves in similar situations before 1807. They perceived the West Indies to be their problem. In reality, their success in the islands prevented them from realizing their own ambitions. In short, they allowed themselves to be corrupted.

ca. Their ability to make money in the island encouraged them to want even more. And the more they gained, the harder it became for them to leave without significant losses. In the words of one of them, "I am grown almost tired of the Drudgery of my Profession and should now be glad to be creeping towards Independancy with less Labour."[33]

From this point forward, their careers and experiences can be placed into two categories. Those in the first, represented here by Robert Stirling, Alexander Johnston, and Alexander Grant, along with most others in the sample, did not translate their island profits into their own desires for a Scottish independence. The culprit preventing the completion of their goal was property. Owning an estate in the colony, especially one that produced revenue and allowed its owner leisure, became very important. It provided a short-term solution to the Scots' larger problems. Until they could return home, they would have some visible symbol of their success, a sort of instant gratification.[34] So, many of them bought. And bought again.

They severely overestimated the possibilities for profit. Making money from a plantation required investing money in it. Often the investment yielded a poor return. Bryan Edwards captured the problems which those who purchased property frequently faced:

> It is not wonderful that the profits [from a sugar estate] should frequently dwindle to nothing; or rather that a sugar estate, with all its boasted advantages, should sometimes prove a mill-stone about the neck of its unfortunate proprietor, which is dragging him to destruction.[35]

Edwards did his best to convince his readers that sugar planters, despite reputations to the contrary, did not often make enough money. He argued that their estates generally generated a much smaller profit as a percentage of capital invested than did English farms. Nor was he alone in his warnings. Just as planters regularly underestimated the relative costs of owning a plantation, they repeatedly overestimated productivity levels. As Robert Hamilton remarked of his family's property in St. Mary's:

> Pemberton Valley often dissappoints us, and I must Say it is one Estate that has hitherto been most ungrateful considering what has been laid out upon it,

[33]Dr. Macglashan to Roger Hope Elletson, 23 December 1765, ST 14, v. 1, HL.

[34]Though the Jamaica Deeds series is virtually complete for the island's entire history, it has proved impossible (with limited time and resources) to check the history of the property transactions of every individual in the sample. The problem of property has certainly been raised enough times in existing correspondence to provide the basis for the argument presented here. The exact details and the degree to which the problem was either widespread or localized can be determined with further study of these deeds, located in the Island Record Office, Spanish Town.

[35]Edwards, *History*, v. 2, p. 300.

however I am hopefull it will now begin to raise business, tho, by the by it is what I cannot perswade my Sister In Law to believe, for which indeed I cannot much blame her, as she has been Soe often dissaopinted in the expectations she has had reason to entertain of it.[36]

Hamilton privately gave instructions for Pemberton Valley to be surveyed in the unlikely event that the family should decide to rent or even sell it. In the end, because enough British security could not be acquired, the family kept this estate well into the nineteenth century. It eventually generated profits, but they were sporadic and not to be depended upon. Even so, to have sold would have meant a much greater loss.[37]

Sir Archibald Stirling of Keir, three decades later, took great pains to correct his cousin Patrick Stirling when the latter wrote looking for money to invest in his Jamaican property. Sir Archibald, through his frustrations with his brother Robert over the past several decades, knew that spending more money did not guarantee that expectations could be met. Jamaica was "a distant Country where appearances are so exceedingly deceitful or rather bewitching that the best inform'd of you all are not proof against the infatuation."[38]

He refused his cousin's request. He did not wish to invest more in a country that was prone to natural disasters. Hurricanes, drought, and slave revolts were only a few of the possibilities.[39] Usually, either because overly ambitious productivity levels had been established or because of one of these natural or slave-induced disasters, the one year a property-owning Scot anticipated before he could return home to independence became two, which became ten, which became an eternity.[40]

James Fraser's experiences provide a perfect example. He had acquired "Capital" worth "upwards of £50,000." The problem was that it was in the form of property in St. Ann's parish. Fraser found that he did not have enough income to support his return home in a comfortable style. In Jamaica, he could "do little more than pay of Contingencies." In an effort "to aid and assist" his goals (or in other words, make more money), he accepted a

[36]Robert Hamilton to Dr. William Aikenhead, 16 October 1747, Hamilton of Rozelle, v. 5, p. 73, GUA. Such complaints were frequent and are certainly, at least in part, caused by unrealistic expectations on the parts of owners and managers.

[37]Another sugar estate that generally failed to meet its owners expectations was the Hope estate in St. Andrew's, Jamaica. The correspondence between its owners, Roger Hope Elletson (and later his heirs) can be found in the Stowe Collection, HL.

[38]Archibald to Patrick Stirling, 16 July 1774, Stirlings of Keir, T-SK 15/11/114, SRA.

[39]According to Edward Brathwaite, between 1770 and 1820 Jamaica experienced seventeen earthquakes, ten hurricanes (most between 1780 and 1800), four droughts, and nine great fires (Creole Society, pp. 4–5).

[40]For Archibald Stirling's critique of his brother's opulent lifestyle, see Chapter 2. The letter can be found in the Stirling of Keir Papers, T-SK 15/11/1, SRA.

sheriff's position in Surrey County (the eastern third of Jamaica, including St. Thomas in the East, St. David's, Portland, and St. George's parishes). Of course, he was able to do so by using "the Interest I hold." In Fraser's view, the problem with this position was its distance from his home in St. Ann's. As a result, he often was forced to leave the estate under his overseers' control—a course not known for its efficacy.[41] He became frustrated because he earned money as sheriff, but quite possibly lost money by having to depend upon his employees to run his plantation. While it is certain that he reaped financial rewards, he did not believe that they were enough to compensate him adequately. "My official Situation tho considerably productive, is attended with great expence yet still under present circumstances. . . . it will not avail me in the object I hold in view."[42]

One way of hastening the speed with which fortunes were acquired was to do what Fraser did—take on an extra office. Preferably, it would be nearer to home. Another way, which was certainly more popular, was to finance the cost of living and the cost of expanding property with credit. It was extremely plentiful, but it too had its drawbacks, especially for those trying to make a quick getaway.

As Harry Scrymgeour wrote his brother in 1785, of one of his countrymen who had succeeded at business as a merchant and purchased property with the proceeds:

> You would hear . . . of the deplorable state in which Mr. Kerr has left his affairs, which shows you the frequent instability of people's fortunes in this Country, at least of those who aspire to embrace the soil. There has already appeared £53,000 Stg. Debts."[43]

Scrymgeour noticed, as did only a few of the others, the direct correlation between property and the risk of debt. Yet he was not above falling victim to its allure; he acquired an estate sometime between 1785 and 1790 and quickly became an absentee. He found himself forced back to Jamaica to

[41]In Fraser's case, his £50,000 estate would have been worth about £37,500 sterling, and would have generated an annual income of £1786—surely more than enough to live independently in Scotland. Fraser's problem was first, that his estate could not be easily liquidated (the old problems of land, slaves, and a credit shortage) and second, that he had probably gotten used to a particular standard of living. To have left, selling out at whatever price he could get, would have meant a cut in it. Therefore, he had to balance again his acquisitions in Jamaica and his hope of returning home.

[42]James Fraser to Hector McDonald, 12 June 1808, GD 47/651/2, SRO. Despite Fraser's remonstrances, it is certain that Fraser would not have taken any position that did not result in some financial benefit.

[43]Harry Scrymgeour to Alexander Wedderburn, 27 July 1785, Earl of Dundee, 87/97/89/13, NRA(S).

assume control of his property. In his case the fears that prevented many Scots from returning home came to fruition. His summons was explicit:

> There is no doubt you should return to Jamaica and lose no time; You find your present fortune not equal to a comfortable settlement here. . . . The man appointed to manage Mount Pleasant in your absence, is not doing well, and indulging in strong liquors, for this reason you should return soon.[44]

Even those who had managed to become absentees had precarious fates. But the alternatives were worse. Many believed that more money would be lost by trying to sell or rent a property than by maintaining it.

Mr. Cargen, who had succeeded at becoming an absentee, wrote to his overseer from his house in Edinburgh, in 1792, about some houses he owned in Montego Bay. He claimed that it was cheaper to keep them uninhabited than it was to sell them in Jamaica's market: "I would have often sold them separately . . . provided I would have given a length of time for the payment but rather than give an extraordinary delay, I thought it as proper to keep them on, though to a great loss."[45]

Cargen, like many other Scots, wanted to liquidate his property in the island but the expenses of so doing, he decided, did not make it particularly practical. And he, of course, had somehow managed to extract himself from the island, though others were much less fortunate.

The experiences of a few Jamaican Scots, such as Francis Grant and his brother Chief Justice John Grant, show that it was possible for Scottish sojourners, or any others for that matter, to become absentees. These people took their money out of the country as quickly as they earned it and immediately invested it in British securities and properties.[46] Such people could, after purchasing Scottish property and insuring that it met their needs, take whatever money they had left, and reinvest it in a Jamaican plantation. They accepted whatever income came to them from it, if anything came at all, as a supplement to their aim rather than a substitute for it. This method guaranteed a lucrative income from Jamaica in good years, but it did not mean a terrific hardship to them in bad ones.

[44]James Wedderburn, Inveresk, to Harry Scrymgeour, 2 November 1790, Earl of Dundee, 87/97/101/1, NRA(S). Notice the theme of the irresponsible manager here.

[45]Mr. Cargen to David Hood, 18 February 1792, GD 214/189/1, SRO.

[46]Francis Grant, on 2 August 1791, wrote Charles Gordon that he had money in England for which he had no use (MS 1160/6/73, AUL). William Fraser, in the *Chiefs of Grant*, v. 1, p. 528, notes that Francis Grant held substantial Jamaican property. He did not, so far as it can be determined from the deeds and Powers of Attorney in Jamaica, purchase an estate while he was in the island. For his part, John Grant had his Scottish friends purchase an estate (Kilgraston) for him in Perthshire, with the proceeds of the money he had been able to extract from Jamaica (see, for example, John Grant to Charles Gordon, 28 November 1785, MS 1160/6/39, AUL). The trick was, as John Grant well knew, to get money out of the country.

Of course, their Jamaican estates were also subject to the same adverse conditions—credit problems, slave rebellions, droughts, and hurricanes—that affected the estates whose owners still resided in Jamaica. The simple difference was that the people who invested their money in Jamaican property *after* they had left the island were able to live in Britain; they had established other sources of income. For them, an irregular year or two was certainly unfortunate, though not disastrous. In the end, British creditors knew that their returned clients had acquired a British property and could hold that as security against any loans made to improve West Indian lands. To those who mattered in Britain, then, owning a Jamaican property was not in itself enough to impress. A Scot must also have been able to achieve a British property with the proceeds of his Caribbean career. The crucial step, then, which few Scots seemed to have known about or, if they did know, were able to act upon, was to get their money, which had been earned and recorded in the books in Jamaica, collected and changed into British currency as quickly as possible. It could then be immediately removed from the country. As Robert Hamilton remarked, even if he did not achieve it, "I am determin'd to remit my Effects to Britain in the most expeditious and best manner I can."[47] Keeping it in Caribbean soil and slaves or on paper only spelled financial difficulty and failure.[48]

Therefore, Jamaican Scots generally failed to realize both parts of their own goal in coming to the Caribbean. Despite meeting with a good deal of success in their professional pursuits, the majority of them were simply not able to return to their native country with what was deemed enough capital to enjoy an independent living. Those who did so proved exceptions to the rule; they succeeded only because they invested their money first in Britain, rather than in Jamaican properties. In this crucial respect (for it is the measure by which the Scots judged themselves), and in this respect only, the Scottish sojourning experience ended in failure, despite all of its great financial benefits.

Crisis in the Chesapeake

At roughly the same time that Scots in Jamaica capitalized on a pronounced period of economic expansion, their countrymen in the Chesapeake saw their domination of the tobacco trade rapidly falling away from them. A number of important factors contributed to this decline. First, like Jamaica,

[47]Robert Hamilton to George Arnold, 29 June 1736, Hamilton of Rozelle Papers, v. 2, p. 8, GUA.

[48]Alexander Johnston, an otherwise successful physician, invested his earnings in the land, all the while planning to return home when the property reached an acceptable level of productivity. His property was valued at over £10,000, but it was in Jamaica, making it difficult for him to extract enough money from it on which to live in Britain. He never returned.

the Chesapeake economy continued to develop and evolve until the American Revolution. But, unlike Jamaica, it began to produce other staple crops, such as grain, in increasing quantities. And as tobacco became less important, however slightly, to the Chesapeake economy so too did the part played by Scottish factors and merchants.

To be sure, the tobacco moguls in Glasgow continued to dominate their business and extract substantial profits from the region at least until the early 1770s. After 1772, a credit cutback in Britain led to a similar one in Virginia and Maryland. As tobacco factors began to call in their many debts, they became easy prey for those who sought to demonstrate Britain's ill intentions toward the colonies. The Scottish success at cornering the market rested upon the store system and easy extension of credit. When credit became less readily available to many planters, Scottish operatives in the Chesapeake became extremely unpopular and were often distrusted, cheated, abused, and even assaulted.

It is certainly ironic that the Scots who suffered the most in the colonies were only carrying out the orders of their Glasgow employers. There can be no doubt that this obedience made the sojourners' plight worse. Rather than choosing the side of collective independence for which many colonists fought, the Chesapeake Scots elected to maintain their own course of action. They sought individual independence through individual enterprise. Because most of them were traders and understood British mercantile policy, they strongly believed that their own success was clearly tied to Britain's imperial economy. And it was this economy's shortcomings against which many Americans were fighting.[49]

The story really begins in 1765, as Parliament passed the Stamp Act. It was designed to raise revenue to pay for the recently ended, and very expensive, French and Indian War. The tax was intended to charge directly those who most benefited from the British victory. Interestingly enough, it had few American supporters. Virtually everyone in the colonies believed, for one reason or another, that it was a bad policy.[50] As Mary Beth Norton has argued, "To the colonists of 1765, independence was not at issue, nor, for that matter, were there many Americans who did not favor some sort of imperial reform. The Stamp Act aroused nearly universal opposition in the colonies."[51]

[49]See William Brock, *Scotus Americanus*, p. 130. This spirit of individual enterprise is discussed by Weber in *The Protestant Ethic and the Spirit of Capitalism*, trans. Talcott Parsons (New York, 1958).

[50]A useful study of the Stamp Act and the American reaction to it is Edmund Morgan, *The Stamp Act Crisis* (New York, 1962).

[51]Mary Beth Norton, *The British-Americans: The Loyalist Exiles in England, 1774–1789* (Boston, 1972), p. 3. Norton, of course, uses the term "independence" in the collective American sense. The Scots attached a completely different meaning to the word, as should by now be clear.

Like their neighbors, the Scots in the colonies (as well as a number in Britain) joined loud and persistent appeals to the British government to get rid of the unpopular, and unfair, measure. Scottish profits would have significantly decreased if they had to pay the tax. Parliament, in rare capitulation, bowed to the nearly universal pressure against it, and repealed the act in the following year. But the British government still needed to raise revenue. As a result, Parliament enacted new imposts, the Townshend Duties, in 1767. Westminster had learned not to try to impose direct and internal taxes, like the Stamp Act; this time the taxes were indirect and external. They were levys against imported glass, paint, paper, and tea before such goods could enter America. The colonial response was, of course, to boycott these products. Nonimportation agreements sprung up across the colonies. The Scots, whose business largely depended upon importing enough goods to satisfy the planters and cover the costs of tobacco purchases, also opposed these new taxes.[52] They readily signed nonimportation pacts; there is, however, some question about whether or not they strictly observed them. They may have violated the pacts because their customers had requested prohibited products, and they saw a chance to make a profit. In any event, active opposition to the duties led to their repeal in 1770. The tax on tea, however, remained in place. Parliament did so not out of a desire to raise revenue, but rather to ensure the continued existence of British East India Company business ventures. The company did, after all, have a monopoly on imported tea.

After the initial success of these nonimportation agreements, however, things began to change. More often than not, Scottish sojourner and American colonist found themselves on opposite sides. The Chesapeake's tobacco economy, like the sugar economy in Jamaica, had been fueled largely through an enormous extension of British credit, much of it from Glasgow. In June of 1772, several of the big London financial houses collapsed. When those houses began to protest bills of exchange and return them, a panic mentality set in. Every firm was owed money but few colonists could pay. As a result, the Scots hesitated to extend any new credit.[53] Richard Sheridan described the resulting dilemma which faced many, if not all, Scottish merchants:

> With the stoppage of credit, the firm's ability to survive was placed largely beyond its control. On the one hand, it needed to collect debts owing in Virginia in order to pay its creditors who were chiefly London tradesmen. On

[52]The Scottish store system provided goods to the planters in return for their tobacco. If the cost of goods became more expensive, profits for the Scots would have diminished or prices to the planters would have increased, or both.

[53]See Price, *Capital and Credit*, pp. 131–37 for a discussion of the crisis as it affected Chesapeake houses.

the other hand, its customers—the tobacco wholesalers and retailers—might refuse payment or have their estate tied up in bankruptcy proceedings. One weak link in this chain might bring down houses that were reputedly on a strong foundation.[54]

In order to avert damage to themselves during the credit crisis, the Scottish merchant houses instructed their employees to take actions that did much to change the average resident of the Chesapeake's perception of his Scottish creditors. For many years, the Scots made goods readily available to the planters of Virginia and Maryland. In return for tobacco, they offered easy credit terms. Suddenly in 1772, for reasons which were not really important to many planters, the means they had long used to maintain their increasingly affluent way of life was threatened. Latent xenophobia, which had been subdued while the Scots provided goods and worked to repeal unpopular taxes several years before, soon rose to the surface.

The Scots in the colony expressed their concern. John Robinson, the Cunninghame Company's chief factor wrote:

> The melancholy account of the Bankruptcys and unsettled Situation of the Trading people in Britain is moving, and gives great concern to every body here; the sudden transition from affluence to want must have had a mournfull effect on the unhappy sufferers.[55]

The Scots took action to prevent further damage at home, which mightily irritated the planters. Credit had not only been tightened but the Scots began to collect old debts, using local courts to obtain judgments against their debtors whenever necessary. The planters had borrowed beyond their means and this shut-off of credit led to conflict between planters and merchants.[56] Money became very scarce. "The times here are so dull," wrote James McLeod in 1773, "that I never saw the Country so poor before[. T]here is scarce anything at all down here now, As for money there is no such thing to be gott. Bills were sold last Court at 35 which were commonly sold at 15 per Ct."[57] In the eyes of the planters, their problems were caused by Scots, unsympathetic foreign creditors who kept largely to themselves while nurturing malignant intentions. The planters (correctly) believed that any money the Scots could collect would soon leave the colonies, effectively denying them the way of life to which they had become accustomed. Chesapeake residents did not see that the Scots in their midst were simply

[54]Sheridan, "The British Credit Crisis of 1772 and the American Colonies," *JEH* 20 (1960): 177.

[55]James Robinson to Cunninghame Company, 22 August 1772, TD 167/2, p. 11, SRA.

[56]Kulikoff, *Tobacco and Slaves*, p. 129.

[57]James McLeod to Donald McLeod, 24 August 1773, MS 19297, f. 2, NLS.

trying to achieve the same "independent" existence for which the planters strove. They neither understood nor cared that the Scots in the colonies were simply doing what Glasgow told them to do. What mattered most was that they were being forced to pay money, which they did not have, to foreigners.[58]

Richard Sheridan has analyzed the number and size of debts owed to both Scottish and English merchants in 1776. He conclusively shows that more people were indebted to Scots than to the English. Virginians, in Sheridan's sample, owed English merchants a total of eighty-two debts. Nearly three times as many people (208) had used the Glasgow houses as creditors. The nature of the obligations differed. Of the 82 debts owed to English merchants, one-third of these were for sums between £100 and £299. Sixteen percent were for sums between £300 and £499, while 11 percent fell into the highest range, between £1000 and £1999. Though the Scottish houses had more debtors, each one generally owed less. Of the 208 obligations, 78 percent were between £100 and £299. Thirty-two (15 percent) amounted to somewhere in a range between £300 and £499. There were no debts due in the highest groups, which began at £700. Because, as Sheridan has effectively shown, the debts owed to Scots were smaller than those owed to the English, the people who owed the Scots would have been much more affected by having to pay them than those who were indebted for larger sums.[59] They were small and middling level planters, by and large, who depended upon extensive credit in order to improve their estates. Such people did not hesitate to go where they could get the best terms; many of them contracted obligations with more than one firm. As these companies began to call in their debts, the planters felt pressured and resentful. Such hostility was easily directed toward their Scottish creditors. And then, increasing revolutionary rhetoric channeled the negative feelings toward the British state. As a result, Scottish quests for independence in the colonies became, in the planter's mind, active hostility to colonial quests for collective independence.

Because they were moneylenders, foreign ones at that, the Scots in the Chesapeake during the 1770s found themselves in a truly unenviable position. Demands for payment from Glasgow increasingly conflicted with the colonists' refusals to pay. They were assaulted from all sides. In the words of Edna Bonacich, "Middleman minorities are noteworthy for the acute hostility they have faced. . . . Conflict between the middleman and the host society arises over economic matters and solidarity."[60] But the credit crisis was not all that angered the planters.

[58]See Kulikoff, *Tobacco and Slaves*, p. 130.
[59]See Sheridan, "Credit Crisis," pp. 180–85. In effect, he believes that small planters were indebted to Scots and larger ones to English merchants.
[60]Bonacich, "Middleman Minorities," p. 589.

Scottish livelihood, in Glasgow and the Chesapeake, did after all, depend upon importation. That boycotts were the chief means to protest Parliamentary policy proved extremely inopportune for the Scots. By 1773, still worried about contracting credit, they stopped supporting nonimportation, which often did not affect themselves or the price of tobacco. They viewed any new struggles, like resisting the Coercive Acts, as problems peculiar to New England. The Boston Tea Party, considered not only lawlessness but also a waste of perfectly good tea, did much to raise the concern of Scots in the Chesapeake about their futures. As Henry Moncreiff in Scotland wrote his brother Archibald, a Maryland merchant, "I am Sorry to see by the Papers, that you People of Maryland have meddled So much in the Boston affair. I hope you will not suffer by it, tho' I am afraid it will affect you."[61]

As tensions in the Chesapeake rose, actions of the local courts were disrupted by mobs. The unassuming Scots, who were being pushed toward loyalism, were changed into actively hostile figures. The colonists owed them money, but they were now being prevented from collecting it.[62] Increasingly, they saw lawless disorder rising around them and they began to fear for their property as well as their persons. A contemporary account expressed their apprehension:

> Everything is in the greatest confusion. . . . A Scotsman is in danger of his life (at least being tarred and feathered) if he says a word that does not please them. . . . They have a set of people chosen for every county whom they call committee men; Those have the charge of rummaging all ships, stores, merchants books, &c, whenever they please. What glorious work this is! and really the free spirit of American liberty, to set people to search merchants books, that cannot perhaps write their names.[63]

Scots left the colonies after 1774 in increasing numbers. They had realized that there was little chance in the present American climate for them to achieve their aims. Others stayed, believing the hostilities would be short-lived and easily suppressed. When they found out, in 1776, just how wrong they were, they had to make a crucial choice. Most quit the colonies. A few joined the American militias, deciding that more opportunities existed for them in Virginia than in Scotland, at least with what they had already achieved. Others moved to the back country, in a final effort to remain neutral.

It is in this historical context that the central question must be considered. Did Scottish sojourners in the Chesapeake succeed or fail? Obviously, many

[61]Henry Moncreiff to Archibald Moncreiff, 6 September 1774, File 13, Moncreiff of Tullibole, privately owned, NRA(S).

[62]See Brock, *Scotus Americanus*, p. 128.

[63]Extract of a letter from a "Gentleman in Virginia" to his correspondent in Glasgow, dated 22 November 1774, *Caledonian Mercury*, 14 January 1775.

Scots made their way home in the years around the Revolution. But whether they did so with independence in hand remains to be determined. As Sheridan's prewar debt figures indicate, many Scottish houses at the time of the revolution were owed a great deal of money by tobacco planters. The firms' operatives, who actually lived in the new world, were in a completely different situation. They did not, as a rule, directly share in their employers' fiscal success.

According to Jackson Turner Main, a bachelor could have survived in the Chesapeake on around twenty-five pounds per year.[64] But this amount was really the minimum and did not make for a particularly enjoyable existence. The tobacco employees in the region were paid anywhere from five pounds per year (in which case room and board would be provided) for those just beginning their training to around a hundred pounds per year for chief factors who had been in the colonies for long periods of time. It should be easy to see that the universal plan to procure a Scottish independence cost substantially more than a Virginia salary provided. There would have been very little room for sojourners either to put money away or to enjoy life. This contrasts quite noticeably with Jamaica. Bookkeepers and estate attorneys there often started at a hundred pounds sterling per year and increased their salaries from that amount over time.[65]

To compensate for low wages, those in Virginia and Maryland often turned to extracurricular activities. Many expected a certain standard of living, which their salaries and positions would not allow. In the words of one factor, "all I expect to make by them [the extra goods] is onely what will help bear my expences here which otherwise would exceed my abilitys."[66]

In some sense, acquiring an external trade also provided a measure of individual independence in its traditional definition. To maintain a business free from Glasgow's intervention was a far more appealing prospect to a young merchant or factor than to toil long days for someone else's gain. Far more than those who worked alone or for absentees in Jamaica, the Chesapeake Scots were dependent upon the instructions and orders of others, whether inside or outside the colonies. As a result, they often had little room to devise creative ways of earning money. The companies knew that

[64]Jackson Turner Main, *The Social Structure of Revolutionary America* (Princeton, N.J., 1985), pp. 115–16.

[65]The main source of income to the Chesapeake Scots, salary, was paid in sterling, usually as a credit in the employer's books. They could draw against this amount for cash. If they did not use it, then the largest part of their income was safely placed in Britain. It only remained for the sojourner to return home with enough credits in the books. The Jamaicans had to get their money off the Jamaican books, out of property, and into Scottish coffers. So, while opportunities for earning money were better in Jamaica, shrewdness was important, if one had any hope of extracting money from the island.

[66]James McLeod to Donald McLeod, 13 February 1774, MS 19297, f. 5, NLS.

these restrictions were troublesome. And, as a reward, the longer one person stayed with a particular firm, the greater the latitude offered to create an external trade.[67]

Even so, most of these sojourning Scots, despite having sought and gained permission from their employers to operate their own businesses, still did not meet their own aim of returning home with enough money to maintain a comfortable independence. Like Jamaicans, they failed to achieve both parts of their plan. They returned to Scotland in the years before and during the American Revolution, with little or no savings to show for all their efforts and a bitter attitude toward America and its inhabitants. They had succeeded, like those in Jamaica, in accumulating paper debts and money in their employers' books. Individually, they had not done particularly well at all.

Perhaps just as important as their inadequate income and the Chesapeake planters' increasing hostility toward them were the weaknesses of their connections. The Scots in Virginia and Maryland did not have patronage webs strong enough to help them in this time of crisis. As the last chapter observed, a distinction existed between Scottish networks in Jamaica and those in the Chesapeake. Occupational diversity, essential to the vitality and utility of any patronage web, was easily observable in Jamaica. In the Chesapeake, however, it was completely lacking. If the principal industry around which the webs were based was shut down or disrupted, as happened to the tobacco factors, there was virtually nothing in the networks themselves to serve as a substitute. Had more Scots decided to weather the American Revolution, the result would have been a large number of unemployed workers. Lucrative positions were hard enough to come by within a Scottish network. Outside of them, the chances would have been quite small indeed.

The Scots in the Chesapeake could not count on customer support, nor were they well situated to help themselves. The provincial legislatures (and the elites they represented) were hardly more sympathetic.[68] Delegates and burgesses saw a group of traders to whom many people in the colony, probably including themselves, owed money, and who violated trade embargoes by sending capital to Britain. The actions of the legislature effectively and

---

[67]There is, however, at least one case of a firm actually forbidding it. William McLeod, James's brother, wrote that factors who worked for Spiers, French, and Company "are now altogether deprived of [their private trades] under the penalty of £500 Sterling." He went on to caution that the "above circumstances you may keep to yourself as I imagine the Company would not choose it should be publicly known." William to Donald Macleod, 2 June 1772, MS 19297, f. 25, NLS. Whether his experience was at all common has been impossible to determine; few records openly address the subject.

[68]Wallace Brown in *The King's Friends: The Composition and Motives of the American Loyalist Claimants* (Providence, 1965) considers Maryland's and Virginia's treatment of the loyalists to have been among the most moderate of the colonies. For a concurring perspective, see Robert M. Calhoon, *The Loyalists in Revolutionary America, 1760–1781* (New York, 1965), pp. 458–72.

finally put the Scots in opposition to the American cause. Hostilities on both sides increased, though there was still substantial ambivalence and resistance to the patriot cause among many colonial residents.[69] By openly making life difficult for creditors, or even punishing them, revolutionaries would have increased popular support for their cause. This course had the added advantage that the debts in question could not be collected. Money and property, legislators believed, could stay in the hands of those who needed it most.[70]

Virginia enacted stringent measures. In August of 1775, the Virginia convention had recommended that British natives who were not active enemies to the American cause be treated with leniency. They would be allowed to live, as best they could, and would not be required to fight the British. In December, this order was rescinded. Certainly, Governor Dunmore's raids on Norfolk from his ship in the bay and the assistance the Scots offered him were, at least in part, to blame. Now, every freeman in the colony, regardless of birthplace, would be forced to fight or leave the country. In some places, such as Norfolk, this resolution had little effect. Many Scots had already left and continued to do so. Those few who were intent on staying were generally left alone. Stronger action was needed. In December 1776, the General Assembly expelled all those born in any part of Britain who either worked for or were partners in any British merchant house. They were given forty days to leave the state.[71]

The growing anti-Scottish feeling, which culminated in these measures, resulted in substantial reverse migrations. Alexander Wilson, who now lived in Glasgow, remarked that he had

> seen within the course of this 12 months past most part of the folks (Scotch people I mean) that I was acquainted with there have come Home. . . . Were you at the Cross [in Glasgow] now you would see nobody almost but provincials (The name they go under here). Ships used to come in sometime ago with Dozens of Factors and Assistants at a time. The Town is very full of them at present.[72]

[69]Richard Beeman, in *The Evolution of the Southern Backcountry* (Philadelphia, 1984), pp. 129, 133, has remarked that Lunenberg County's residents were largely uninterested in the revolution before 1775 or 1776. Once involved, they became remarkably attached to the "patriot's" cause, because they expected some form of compensation, financial or otherwise.

[70]See Brock, *Scotus Americanus*, pp. 130–31.

[71]An excellent discussion of these events, particularly as they related to Norfolk (where many of Virginia's Loyalists lived), can be found in Hast, *Loyalism*, pp. 84–85. For details of the actions of the Virginia Convention, see the *Journal of the Convention*, 11 August 1775 (pp. 24–25) and December 1775 (p. 70), Rare Book 133063-9, HL.

[72]Alexander Wilson to Sandy Miller, 25 November 1775, Alexander Wilson letterbook, TD 1/1070, SRA.

The situation across the Potomac was not drastically different. Alexander Hamilton, a Maryland factor, noted that things in 1775 were rapidly deteriorating. "Our provincial Convention is now sitting," he explained,

> and unless the moderate part get the ascendancy I am greatly affraid I shall be obliged to pay you a visit [in Scotland] as well as many others. The most unexceptionable conduct will not screen any Man. . . . In times of Anarchy and Confusion, People's principles as well as Estates grow worse, However I am determined to stick by them until I am drove off.[73]

Such attitudes were common. The notion of giving up a fortune hunt—especially an incomplete one—was not terribly appealing. Yet, Hamilton soon found himself packing his bags. Thinking the war would be short, he went to live in the backwoods of Virginia for the duration.[74]

Other Scots, like Neil Jamieson, went to live in New York, the loyalist capital.[75] Some, like Thomas Ruddach, struck out for the West Indies.[76] Even more occupied themselves in the best way they knew how in Glasgow. Alexander Wilson, the Alexandria apprentice, became a bookseller. Others entered counting houses or worked as retailers. Many spent a good part of their days discussing the problems in the Chesapeake. As one somewhat disgusted correspondent remarked: "The Men folks in this Town [Glasgow] are so taken up [with] the quarrels between the Mother Country and the Colonies that they can think or talk of nothing else."[77]

For the Glasgow tobacco lords, however, life went on as usual. Their employees might have suffered, but they at least still tried to enjoy the wealth they had created before the troubles broke out. "You could wish perhaps to hear something of your old Friends that are settled in this place," wrote one merchant to another,

> some of them are the better for this unfortunate war, but by far the greater part much hurt by it. Your old friends Messrs Spiers & Cunningham ride about in their Chariots & will keep Company with none but Nobility. Indeed even some of those of the poorest sort [of merchant] are rather below their notice.[78]

With the signing of the peace treaty in 1783, the tobacco transients were often sent scurrying back to Maryland and Virginia to collect their em-

[73]Alexander Hamilton to James Brown and Co., 2 August 1775, Letterbook, on microfilm, EUL [Mic. M. 23].
[74]See Alexander Hamilton to John Anderson, 18 October 1784, EUL.
[75]The best source for Scottish activity in New York is the Jamieson Papers, LC.
[76]For another example, see the Bogle Papers, 1773–1778, Mitchell Library, Glasgow.
[77]Henrietta Dunlop to [James Dunlop], 18 August 1775, Dunlop Papers, Box 1, LC.
[78]Alexander McCaul to James Parker, 15 July 1782, 920 Par I 17/2, LRO.

ployers' debts. Many did not seem altogether happy about this mission, remembering their treatment before the war, but viewed it as their obligation. James Dunlop Senior, who had moved to the Virginia backcountry when hostilities erupted, expressed his discomfort with the idea of debt collection:

> I am Really uneasy abt the Business Messrs Ritchie intend to employ you in att Dumfries. From my own experience I can assure it will be a disagreeable business. You may settle the Orders and gett Bonds but as to the Collection . . . Depend on it you cannot doe it yourself. Reside in Dumfries or goe to Court. Your life would not be safe.[79]

One reason that young Dunlop's life might not have been safe was that the Governor had proclaimed in July of 1783 that no person could return to Virginia who had left it after 1775.[80] Adele Hast has argued that those Scots who had left the colony, either for New York or Scotland, before the war were certainly made to feel unwelcome in Norfolk. Those who had simply moved to the backcountry were looked upon much more kindly.[81]

Despite such hostility, historians have shown that significant efforts were made to resume the Glasgow-Chesapeake trade.[82] But by the early 1790s, after encountering difficulty in collecting their debts and continued hostility to their presence in the states, the Scots returned home and turned their attentions toward other areas, especially the West Indies.

It is not likely that the Scots in the Chesapeake fared any better after the war than they did before it. Surviving correspondence certainly suggests that they did not find the former colonies any more appealing than they previously had. Thomas MacMurdo wrote to his father in 1786, "Oh! Puppa could you behold the State of this boasted land of liberty at present you would exclaim what a Mutation. Their taxes are exorbitant, the provisions raised[,] 100% custom duties."[83]

That MacMurdo disliked the postwar environment should not come as a surprise. Returning Scots were not made to feel welcome by citizens of Virginia and Maryland and their job, collecting debts, did not exactly win them many friends. They were repeatedly frustrated.[84] It is difficult, as a

[79]James Dunlop Sr. to James Dunlop Jr., 5 March 1784, Dunlop Papers, Box 2, LC.

[80]See Dunlop, Sr., to Dunlop, Jr., 12 July 1783, Dunlop Papers, Box 1, LC.

[81]Hast, *Loyalism*, p. 134.

[82]See, for example, Devine, *Tobacco Lords*, pp. 161–68.

[83]Thomas MacMurdo to George MacMurdo, 27 April 1786, Acc 7199/4/1, NLS.

[84]This issue would prove to be the stickiest in settling the American Revolution for good. The 1783 Treaty of Peace provided for the collection of just debts due to the British. Many people refused to pay what they owed. In 1794, the Jay Treaty established a bilateral commission to arbitrate the claims. By 1802, after yet another failure, a new treaty provided for the Ameri-

result, to imagine that many of them would have achieved very much toward their own independence. When they returned to Glasgow, without either their employers' debts or great rewards for their efforts, this particular chapter of Scottish-American history drew to a close. For individuals, its legacy could not be measured in pounds or property acquired, but rather in loyalism and losses.

SCOTTISH LOYALISTS: ONE EXPLANATION

Historians Mary Beth Norton and Adele Hast have argued that the relevant question about the behavior of the Scots or of any other group during the Revolution should not be "why loyalism?" but rather "why not?"[85] American historians have not often considered that the war's final outcome has dictated the questions we have asked. Because the "patriots" or "rebels" actually emerged victorious, their positions have come to be accepted as both widespread and logical. But the losers also had logical perspectives. It is important to remember that many people in the colonies before 1776 did not want change. They had no ideological commitment one way or another; they simply wanted what was best for their own pockets.

From Scottish point of view, loyalism was not an aberration. The last section showed how Scottish factors and tobacco merchants were pushed, by political and economic events, into the loyalist camp and out of the colonies. But it is by no means a complete picture. For many in the Chesapeake, loyalism also held a positive attraction. Sojourning Scots were drawn to it for both economic and psychological reasons. In the words of Adele Hast:

> With few exceptions, the Scots . . . [in Norfolk] were loyalists. While political views and economic interests were factors in their loyalism, the hostility and prejudice they had always encountered were undoubtedly strong elements in adherence to the British cause.[86]

The Scottish response to the unfolding political drama in Britain's mainland colonies has been the subject of some very fine scholarship.[87] Nonethe-

---

can government to pay the British government £600,000 in full settlement of all claims, for His Majesty's government to distribute. By 1811, the debts were finally paid, though not the total amount owed. Of course, most of the original claimants had long been in their graves. See John Bassett Moore, *International Adjudications Ancient and Modern*, 3d series (New York, 1931), v. 3, esp, pp. 1–17; for a table of debts due and their owners, pp. 419–22, and a list of those who applied for relief from the bilateral commission, pp. 334–45.

[85]See Hast, *Loyalism*, pp. 6–7. This position had previously been asserted by Norton in *The British-Americans*, p. 8.

[86]Hast, *Loyalism*, p. 74.

[87]Such work has focussed on the relationship between Scottish intellectuals—the en-

less, as Hast has pointed out, significant questions still remain about why the Scots as a group remained loyal during the events surrounding the Revolution. There has not yet been concerted historical effort to discover the reasons for "North Britons," in places as disparate as Virginia and Massachusetts, "rallying 'round the Union Jack" rather than joining the provincial armies.[88] In this section, the link between Scottish ethnicity and the Chesapeake loyalists will be further examined with the hopes that it can, at least, be used to suggest some possible nonideological explanations for the Scottish response to the American War for Independence.

Two crucial questions are central to this analysis. First, what were the Scots' economic interests and how would they have been best served? Second, were there any factors, common to this particular ethnic group as it existed in Virginia and Maryland, that acted as a psychological bond, both among group members and with the British Empire itself? By considering these two problems, it is possible to understand better why many, if not most, Scots insisted on giving His Majesty's government full support and cooperation.

The first problem has already been at least partially addressed in the last section. Every historian who has studied Scots in the Chesapeake has come to the same conclusion: economic self-interest dictated behavior against the American cause. The tobacco economy and all of its material benefits depended upon British laws and support. Given the sojourners' customary reliance upon tobacco, they would have been foolish to throw away their livelihood. As William Brock has argued:

> Fifty years of enterprise and effort were placed in jeopardy [by rebellion]. The loyalism of Scots in America was not perverse allegiance to an alien King, but a determination to preserve national interests that had been so greatly advanced under the descendants of James VI and I.[89]

There was, as well, an important psychological link between Scots sojourners in the colonies and the United Kingdom. Transient Scots in the

---

lighteners—and political rhetoric and ideology emanating from America, and also on the identification of many American loyalists as Scots' born. For a very good example of the former, see Andrew Hook, *Scotland and America: A Study of Cultural Relations* (Glasgow, 1975), esp. chap. 3; also Dalphy Fagerstrom, "Scottish Opinion and the American Revolution," *WMQ* 11 (1954): 252–75. The most detailed example of the latter type of work can be found in William Brock, *Scotus Americanus*, chaps. 7 and 8, Other scholars, most notably Hast, have touched on the demographic profile of loyalists in particular places, including the Scots (*Loyalism*, pp. 171–77).

[88]Wallace Brown in *The King's Friends* discussed the character of the loyalist claims in each of the states, but did not make any generalizations. Mary Beth Norton in *The British Americans* discusses loyalists from all the colonies who went to England (not to Scotland). William Nelson in *The American Tory* (Oxford, 1961) does try to paint a general picture of loyalists in the colonies. Scots illustrate his view that foreigners were distrusted.

[89]Brock, *Scotus Americanus*, p. 127.

Chesapeake, as well as being members of a middleman group, were also members of an ethnic and cultural minority. Who would protect them from the Anglo-American majority? Only the British, they believed, had enough power to do so. This reasoning would also help to explain why so many German emigrants found themselves joining the loyalist cause. European minorities in pre-Revolutionary America enjoyed nearly the same rights as other citizens. Removing the source of that protection, which was British authority in their eyes, proved an intimidating and daunting prospect for them. Most had fled from persecution, or at least inferior conditions, and had no desire to endure it again. American claims of the benefits of independence were unconvincing.

Those in the colonies had to endure increasing aggression. John Campbell, a Maryland factor, wrote, "We fear Scotch Factors are looked upon herein general with a very jealous Eye & Enemies to the Country; & Indeed by their [the rebels] Conduct they would endeavour to render us so, however we may be otherwise inclined."[90] Incidents against Scots in the Chesapeake continued to increase. As Campbell wrote two years later, from the safety of Glasgow:

> You had great reason to fear my incurring the displeasure of the present Despotic Rulers in America. It was with the utmost difficulty I obtained permission to leave the country. . . . My situation whilst in America especially for the last 6 or 7 months was truly disagreeable—deprived in every sense of the smallest freedom of action or even sentiments, amidst a constant howling for liberty & execration of arbitrary measures.[91]

The Scots faced a simple dilemma. They could give up what they had hoped to achieve (whether land or trade) under the British government's protection, and become Americans, with uncertain prospects for employment. American aggression toward foreigners, especially those who lent money and extended credit, did not encourage them to make this choice. Alternatively, they could vote for the status quo.

Many Chesapeake Scottish sojourners seriously underestimated the length of time the war would take. They did not have a real appreciation of the depth of the colonists' determination to drive out the British. This misunderstanding was perhaps in some part a result of their isolation in fairly close-knit communities. Positive interactions with non-Scots became less frequent. Scots believed that the Americans, who were never to be taken seriously, could easily be suppressed and vanquished. After all, many knew from Culloden how the Hanoverians dealt with rebellion. "Do they think that Britain is to protect their ships and men in time of war for nothing,"

[90]John Campbell to DW, 11 January 1774, GD 136/416/2, SRO.
[91]John Campbell to Will Sinclair, 28 August 1776, GD 136/416/4, SRO.

asked Alexander Wilson incredulously, "I'm much mistaken if they don't pay dearly. . . . they had better behave themselves in time . . . for if they don't they'll perhaps get their ears sing'd."[92] When the hostilities escalated, the Scots were caught off guard. "The Confusions on your side of the Water have gone a much greater length than we expected," wrote Henry Ritchie as early as 1775.[93] By the time the war had entered its fourth year, James Parker was not alone in believing that it would soon end: "The Rebellion I think cannot exist another Year if we do nothing more than prevent their trade, they are all now Quarelling amongst themselves."[94]

By 1783, when the peace treaty was signed, many Scots believed that their country had been given a bad deal. As Henry Moncreiff quipped with some annoyance, "The Peace we have got is a Stupid one for Britain."[95] His country, especially Scotland, would suffer by it. About the only positive thing it provided was the legal right of British merchants to collect their just debts. But, more important, many Scots did not trust Americans to provide good government. Their experiences before the war continued to affect their assessment. As Glasgow merchant James Ritchie wrote:

> Britain by this peace will be degraded, humiliated, and weakened. Our En-
> emies particularly France and Holland will gain what she loses [here he almost
> certainly meant the tobacco trade], but I am greatly deceived if America will be
> a more free, happy, or richer Country than she would have been if she had
> remained connected with Britain.[96]

In short, they remained bitter about their American experiences and the losses they endured in the Chesapeake. But they had few regrets, for there was a silver lining in this cloud of defeat. By remaining demonstrably loyal, the Scots were able to pursue, in other British colonies, the same aims that had taken them to Maryland and Virginia. Grenada, St. Vincent's, India, and of course Jamaica all underwent profound expansion during the early 1800s. The Scots were there, as if to lead the way. They lost control of one of their most lucrative colonial markets (which did much to engender the vitality of the nineteenth-century Scottish economy) but were able to preserve their places in future British colonial development, which lasted well into the twentieth century. For the generation of 1776, the economic results were immediately horrific—at least for those in the American colonies—but for their posterity the gamble with loyalism paid off again and again.

[92]Alexander Wilson to William Shaw, 1 March 1774, TD 1/1070, SRA.
[93]Henry Ritchie to James Dunlop, 31 August 1775, Box 1, Dunlop Papers, LC.
[94]James Parker to Charles Steuart, 9 January 1779, 920 Par I 13/1, LRO.
[95]Henry Moncreiff to Archibald Moncreiff, 18 February 1783, Moncreiff of Tullibole; private possession, NRA(S).
[96]James Ritchie to James Dunlop, 28 November 1782, Dunlop Papers, Box 1, LC.

Though many Scots had gone back to Scotland, they did so without enough to procure an estate there. To determine just how much they had managed to achieve in the colonies, the Loyalist Temporary Support and Compensation Claims can be utilized. These documents have been preserved in the Public Record Office in London and are available, in transcript form, from the Manuscript Division of the New York Public Library.[97] By analyzing them in much the same way as I did the Jamaican estate inventories, I have been able to measure Scottish success (or, more properly, disappointment) in the Chesapeake, and make a comparison with other groups of claimants. But it must be remembered that the people who filed Loyalist Claims were not included in the correspondence sample.[98]

Few of the tobacco transients claimed compensation. The reasons should be perfectly clear. Those who worked in such capacities did not earn enough to have acquired property in the colony. As a result, they would have lost only their income. While they could have filed a temporary support claim, it is much more likely that they found alternative employment once they returned to Glasgow. Further examination of these claims makes it quite apparent that the Scots, unlike their Jamaican counterparts, did not do as well as their non-Scottish neighbors (Table 5.3). They lost less property, which in all probability meant that they had owned less, and they received a smaller percentage of what they had requested from the commission than others did.[99]

Sixty (28 percent) of the 213 Chesapeake claimants were Scottish. When the awards authorized by the commission are added together, and those of the Scots tabulated separately from the others, it is clear that the Scots received an amount directly proportional to their representation in the claims. That is, the 28 percent of the claimants in Maryland and Virginia who were Scots received 31 percent of the total award.[100] Only 38 percent of

[97]The principal record groups at Kew are T 79, AO 12, and AO 13. All of these collections have some form of index. The research for this section was actually carried out using transcripts of these record groups in the New York Public Library; I cite the New York volumes throughout this discussion. Appropriate references to the PRO series, where known, are also included. But because the British record groups have been renumbered since the NYPL transcripts were made in the early years of the century, it has proved rather complicated to match some of these volumes to their PRO counterparts.

[98]The 213 loyalist temporary support claims examined here contain only four members of the sample presented in Chapter 1. Three were involved with tobacco (two were father and son); the fourth was Dr. John Ravenscroft's widow, introduced in Chapter 3.

[99]Claims for temporary support amounted to a very small portion of the total claims for Loyalist compensation. In effect, anyone who lost an income as a direct result of their loyalism could apply for a pension. While a figure is not available for the final total of temporary support compensation awarded, the Virginia and Maryland cases do not comprise a large percentage. Many more people from New York, Pennsylvania, and the Carolinas made claims.

[100]It should be noted here that the Scots in these records have been precisely (in almost all cases) identified as such in the claims.

Table 5.3. Chesapeake temporary support claims

	Maryland	Virginia	Total
Total number of claims	80	133	213
Number of Scottish claims	11	49	60
Scots as % of claimants	14	37	28
Commissioners allowed, annum, in sterling	£3541.0	£6418.0	£9959.0
Commissioners allowed, lump sum payments, sterling	£283.5	£636.0	£919.5
Scots received, per annum, sterling	£680.0	£2385.0	£3065.0
Scots received, lump sums, sterling	£0	£70.0	£70.0
Scots receive X% of allowance by commissioners, per annum	19.2	37.2	30.8
Scots receive X% of lump sum granted by commissioners	0.00	11.0	7.6

Source: American Loyalist Series Transcripts, Vols. 4–8, "Examinations and Decisions of Fresh Claims for Temporary Support, December 1782–1790" (AD 12/99–102, PRO), New York Public Library.

the Chesapeake claims were filed by former residents of Maryland. Of these, 14 percent were Scottish, and they received 19 percent of the total granted by the commission. The rest of the claims came from Virginia. Of these, 37 percent were Scots and they received 37 percent of the colony's awards. It therefore seems reasonable to assume that the Scottish population of Virginia was significantly larger than that of Maryland.

Unfortunately, the claims for temporary support reveal more about the way the commission operated than they do about Scottish abilities to succeed. Individuals filed their claims and the sitting commissioners evaluated them according to some very stringent guidelines. In general, they did not accept claims from people who had another source of income, however deserving they might otherwise appear. This might explain why Maryland Scots received more in temporary support than those in Virginia; they simply had no other source of income. Nor did the commissioners seek, in these or any other compensatory claims, to reward people financially for their loyalism. They granted sums sufficient only to insure that the claimant's accustomed way of living would not be drastically altered—for better or for worse—as a result of allegiance to the king. Thus Captain Jonathan Martin, who had actively fought for the British, was denied assistance because "He was a farmer. . . . The War has made him a Gentleman."[101] Others who

[101]Loyalist Transcripts, v. 7, p. 294, NYPL. There is substantial evidence that many Scots actually joined British forces. See, for example, Brock, *Scotus Americanus*, pp. 71–73, 145. Mobilization took place both at home and in America and many families in Scotland had sons

were undeserving still had to be paid, based upon the guidelines. I. F. D. Smyth's was "a case in which we mean to recommend an allowance to a very undeserving Man whose former Allowance we have not only superseded but whom we have reported to the Treasury of having been guilty . . . of wilful and corrupt Perjury."[102]

Some, like the German brothers George and Adam Grave, successfully demonstrated a need for support and also tried to gain the commission's sympathy, which was easier to come by. Financial reward was nearly impossible. "No man," the commissioners remarked, "can have a stronger claim upon the Bounty of Government than these."[103] The Graves brothers had faced torture and death at the Americans' hands, so they claimed; they received the meager sum of thirty pounds for their trouble. At the same time, men with more genteel occupations, like Barrister George Chalmers, who owned property in Britain, received the hefty sum of one hundred pounds per annum.[104] The commission's members, and the government which instructed them, missed a perfect opportunity to make rewards for services rendered and move away from their traditional and restrictive class values. In this instance, the Scots did no better and no worse than anyone else in the colonies.

Another indication of the degree of Scottish success can be found in the Compensation Claims for lost property. The commission's own reports provide an excellent guide to the restrictions under which it operated and the ways in which the claims were analyzed and finally decided.[105] The most important of these restrictions, especially to Scottish merchants and their employees, automatically disallowed all claims for British debts owed before the war.[106]

Table 5.4 records the Loyalist Commission's own data about the number

---

going off to fight the war. An army officer's commission was much sought after in Scotland. As ever, commissions were awarded through patronage. See, for example, George Dunlop to James Dunlop, 25 April 1782, Dunlop Papers, Box 1, LC.

[102]LT, v. 7, p. 26, NYPL.

[103]LT, v. 5, pp. 327–28, NYPL.

[104]It was this low only because Chalmers had already begun to develop other sources of income in Britain. LT, v. 2, p. 176, NYPL.

[105]See LT, "Index of American Claims," v. 11, pp. 7–62, NYPL. The reports and the procedures the commissioners used are there transcribed. For a good secondary source discussion, see Moore, *International Adjudications*, v. 3, pp. 1–431. It is clear that the commission(s) scrupulously adhered to parliamentary instructions. Basically, each claim was dissected into its component parts and then categorized according to rules determined by Parliament. Certain categories were disallowed. Corroborating evidence, in the form of oral testimony, as well as official papers had to be offered to substantiate every claim. Witnesses were often discredited, thus eliminating the chance for compensation.

[106]Because the peace treaty allowed for debts to be actively collected the commissioners were not allowed to use government money to reimburse creditors.

Table 5.4. Chesapeake Loyalist compensation claims

	Maryland	Virginia	Total
Total number of claims	73	147	220
Total number of Scots claims	20	71	91
Total number of non-Scots claims	53	76	129
Scots as % of claimants	27	48	41
Total value of claims	£433,526	£785,528	£1,219,054
Total value claimed by Scots	£94,972	£363,387	£458,359
Total value claimed by non-Scots	£338,554	£422,141	£760,696
Scots claim as % of total claim	22	46	38
Average claim	£5,938	£5,343	£5,541
Avg. Scots claim	£4,748	£5,118	£5,037
Avg. non-Scottish claim	£6,387	£5,554	£5,896
Total awarded by Commission	£129,214	£196,110	£325,332
Total awarded to non-Scots	£106,998	£117,139	£224,137
Total awarded to Scots	£22,216	£78,979	£101,195
Scots award as % of total award	17	40	31
Scots award as % of Scots claim	23	22	22
Total awarded as % of total claim	37	25	27
Average award	£1,770	£1,334	£1,478
Average non-Scottish award	£2,018	£1,541	£1,737
Average Scottish award	£1,110	£1,112	£1,112

Note: The Claim of Henry Harford has not been included in the Maryland Claims, for reasons discussed in the text.

of claims for compensation and the amount awarded. The method of analysis used is identical to that used for the Temporary Support Claims.[107] By identifying the number of Scots filing in each colony and comparing that number to the total number of people "seeking the bounty of government," one can easily observe that Scots comprised around 40 percent of all claimants and claimed about 38 percent of the total amount requested for Maryland and Virginia combined. They made up nearly half of those from Virginia requesting money and filed to receive nearly half of the total requested amount. The sums in Maryland were similarly proportional. Such a finding would be consistent with the temporary support measures described above. As a group, the Scots claimed a share of the total which was proportional to their representation among the claimants.

Comparing the sizes of the claims actually reveals something quite different. The average Scot in Maryland requested around £4748, and in Virginia

[107]In this case, the excessive claim of Henry Harford for Maryland (£477,850, or 110 percent of all the other claims combined) has been omitted from the calculations, as have his awards, which totaled £210,000, or 162 percent of all the other claims combined. The commission's priorities are quite clear. Calhoon, *Loyalists in Revolutionary America*, p. 501, observes that the loyalist commission in general benefited the wealthier loyalists.

sought £5118. In both colonies combined, the average (Scottish) claim was £5036. Interestingly enough, in both Virginia and Maryland, the average Scot's claim was smaller than that of his or her non-Scottish neighbor. Those who were not Scottish requested the commission to pay them, on average, £6387 in Maryland, £5554 in Virginia, and £5896 in the two combined. In other words, the Scots had acquired less property than other loyalists. And, Scots in Maryland had done less well than their countrymen across the Potomac. The sizes of the claims, over £5000, seem quite substantial, though it is certain that many, if not all, were inflated. The commission had no way to verify an amount because missing property could not be produced as evidence. Therefore, they awarded much less than what was requested. But this aspect is not the worst of the picture for the Scots.

By looking at the table, the reader can easily see that the Scots actually received just over 22 percent of the amount for which they had asked in both colonies. In Maryland, the figure was 23 percent and in Virginia 22 percent. Their neighbors fared significantly better. The average non-Scottish award was 32 percent of the average non-Scottish claim in Maryland, 28 percent in Virginia, and 30 percent in the two combined. This important discrepancy can be explained in a number of ways. It is possible that Scottish claims contained greater amounts of confiscated and lost property in the prohibited categories (such as debts), or that the sums reported were more visibly inflated than their neighbors'. It can also indicate a discrimination on the part of the commission itself, perhaps not particularly likely. Finally, it could simply recognize the fact that Scottish property was just worth less than non-Scottish property.[108]

In terms of what the commission actually allocated, *in toto*, Scots fared a bit better. In Maryland, they received 17 percent of all awards (omitting Henry Harford's), in Virginia, 40 percent and 31 percent for the colonies combined. But, when their representation in the claims is considered, the discrepancy is quite stark. They were still losers. In Maryland, 27 percent of the claimants were Scottish, yet they received only 17 percent of the awards. In Virginia, 48 percent of the claimants were Scottish. They received less, 40 percent, than that percent of the total awarded. In both colonies, though especially in Maryland, the Scots did not do particularly well with the Loyalist Commission in their efforts to recover property. Their neighbors had clearly done better.

Where the Jamaican estate inventories showed that Scottish estates increased at a faster pace than non-Scottish ones and that they were comparable in value, the Loyalist claims for Maryland and Virginia show that the

[108]For all the colonies, claimants received 37 percent of the requested amounts. Therefore, the Scots in Maryland and Virginia not only did worse within their own colonies, but also did not fare well compared to loyalists in other places.

average Scot claimed less than his non-Scottish neighbor and was awarded even less.

What has also become abundantly clear, however, is that the British government made no effort to reward the Scots for their loyalism. By not doing so, it actually discriminated against the Scots, who were, for all intents and purposes, nouveaux riches. Their wealth lay in debts; debts were disallowed. The government did not consider anything but traditional measures of status, that is, land and other confiscated property. The status quo was thus maintained. As a group, Scots in the Chesapeake remained loyal to their king and country. Because of this loyalty, whatever advances they had made, whether small or large, were lost to them as soon as they made their position known. It is a little ironic that the government they readily supported really failed to compensate them adequately for the losses they incurred. This ensured their positions as losers in the Chesapeake.

The losses can not only be quantified to demonstrate a collective loss; they can also be used to show how loyalism affected individual colonists. Daniel Fraser, a Scot who ran a trading business on the Virginia rivers, and who left with the expelled factors, received more than 50 percent of his request for compensation. The commissioners noted that "by following the Business with Industry he has acquired a Property and was in a good way of making a sufficiency to support him comfortably in his old age."[109] Fraser was a typical Scot—working toward individual independence. He claimed £685.11 (much more than the average white per-capita wealth of around £132) and received £353 as a settlement.[110]

Alexander Stenhouse, a Scottish physician, went to the colonies in 1756. In 1764, he settled in Baltimore city, where he practiced medicine until he left the colony in 1776 because, he stated, of his loyalty. He claimed to have about £2000 sterling due him in debts. His income, as he reported it to the Commissioners was around £700 sterling per annum in the years before 1770, and even higher between that time and the Revolution. Sadly, as the commissioners remarked, "the part he took in the Troubles occasioned it to decrease."[111] He also said that he owned both a house and a lot in Baltimore. According to the tabular statement, he filed a claim for only £1250

---

[109]LT, v. 59, pp. 5–11, NYPL.

[110]The amount of the claim can be found in ibid., p. 11, and the settlement of the claim in LT, v. 11. For the £132 figure, see McCusker and Menard, *Economy,* Table 3.3, p. 61. Alice Hanson Jones has defined the wealthiest category as greater than £400 sterling. Here is clearly such a claim, yet the commission denied it, keeping Mr. Fraser in the middle bracket (£100–£399). It must also be remembered that this figure is for both the upper and lower southern colonies combined. (The upper south would have had a smaller amount than the lower south.) If Fraser had a family, he would have been pushed further into the middle range.

[111]LT, v. 35, pp. 93–94, NYPL.

sterling which was entirely disallowed. As far as can be determined, he received nothing for his loyalism.[112]

Not all Scottish sojourners left the colonies. Some stayed, but they were also losers. While they might have been able to save any property they had acquired, they had to give up the plan to return home. James Dunlop and Henry Ritchie, for example, left the tobacco-producing areas of Virginia to buy up tobacco in New York and Philadelphia, where restrictions were fewer. They still had enough leeway in these colonies to operate their businesses, despite problems with international trade.

Yet becoming an American seems to have been about the only way for a Scot to have succeeded financially in the Chesapeake. Few chose this alternative, because it did not seem at the time to be a particularly wise thing to do. The British, after all, would soon regain control and punish the rebels. One who chose to stay, merchant John Hook, had what could be considered a fairly typical experience. In June of 1775, Charles Lynch, Hook's zealous neighbor in Bedford County, accused him of "aiding the British and criticizing liberty." Hook, summoned to appear before the Committee of Safety, refuted Lynch's charge by saying that he disapproved only of the Bostonians destroying good tea. But he did not profess revolutionary ideals. He went on to assure the committee:

> I wish the liberty and Prosperity of this Country as sincerely as any of them possibly can. So I hope, a difference in oppinion as to the mode of attaining the same, will not be judged sufficient grounds for declaring one of such sentiments an enemy of American liberty.[113]

The committee, apparently did not believe Hook, perhaps because he confessed to making many of the inflammatory remarks of which he had been accused (though he claimed ignorance), and it may well have had him imprisoned. Perhaps, like many others, they did not trust the Scots to support the revolt. In any event, Hook was released from prison (whatever the charges) on 19 January 1777; he renounced his British citizenship and swore an oath to the American cause on 10 October, certainly hoping that he would finally be left alone.[114] By staying in the colony and pledging allegiance to the Revolution, Hook was able to ensure that his acquired property and wealth would not be forever lost. As such, he is one of a very small number of Scots who had gone out as sojourners (and about whom anything is known) who remained in the Chesapeake during the war. And his experiences were

[112]LT, v. 11, NYPL.

[113]Answer of John Hook to the charges of Charles Lynch, June 1775, MS 22174-C, VSL.

[114]See the Release from Gaol, 19 January 1777, MS 22174-j, and the Oath of Allegiance, 10 October 1777, MS 22174-k, VSL.

far from happy ones. The growing and often vehement anti-Scottishness was enough to drive even the hardiest out of the main areas of settlement, if not out of the colony itself.

The experiences of Hook and the Loyalists reveal that the Scots lost no matter what they did. Either they went home at the beginning of the war and failed to realize their stated ambitions, in terms of independence, or they went home thinking that they had made a good living in the Chesapeake and that by remaining loyal to Britain they would receive what was legitimately due them. The Loyalist Compensation Series demonstrates that those who took this path never received the full value of their claims. In the final analysis, only those who stayed in the colonies were able to hold on to their fortunes, but to do so they had to remain in the colonies, thus giving up the other half of the original two-part ambition which caused them to leave Scotland in the first place.[115] In this they resembled the Jamaicans. The paradox was unyielding.

[115]Here, several careers demonstrate the transition from transient to emigrant. John Hook and merchant William Allason are indicative of this type of metamorphosis. See the Hook Papers and the Allason Papers (Acc. 13), both at the VSL.

AFTERWORD:
THE SCOTS AND CHANGING
NOTIONS OF INDEPENDENCE

Voltaire once described history as a pack of tricks that the present plays on the past. He failed to mention that the people of the past have their own dissembling tricks. The most troublesome for historians is the tendency to change without notice the meaning of words.

Joyce Appleby, *Capitalism and a New Social Order*

Historians like to understand the meanings of terms with some degree of precision. Ideas—liberty, equality, freedom—have, unfortunately for us, meant different things to different people at different times. To complicate matters even further, "the variations are not merely diachronic (changing usages over time), but also synchronic (divergent applications of the term occurring simultaneously)."[1]

Michael Kammen has suggested that "liberty" had different meanings in the late eighteenth century. These multiple definitions have formed the core of many scholarly studies. But if liberty had multiple meanings, so too did "independence." Yet, the idea and meaning of this term has undergone far less scholarly scrutiny than has that of liberty.[2] In 1776, the mainland colo-

---

[1]Michael Kammen, *Spheres of Liberty: Changing Perceptions of American Liberty* (Madison, Wis., 1986), p. 17.

[2]Among the most interesting of the rather large body of work on liberty can be found Robert Webking, *The American Revolution and the Politics of Liberty* (Baton Rouge, 1988); Joyce Appleby, *Capitalism and a New Social Order* (New York, 1984); H. T. Dickinson, *Liberty and Property: Political Ideology in Eighteenth-Century Britain* (New York, 1978); Lawrence Leder, *Liberty and Authority: Early American Political Ideology 1689–1783* (Chicago, 1968); and Isaiah Berlin, *Four Essays on Liberty* (Oxford, 1969).

nies convened a Continental Congress at Philadelphia; delegates left only after they had signed the Declaration of Independence. This document, which enumerated colonial grievances against the British regime, formally dissolved the bonds between the local and imperial governments. It marked the official start of a bloody war and, eventually, served the United States as a clear statement of the philosophical principles upon which the nation rested. And behind this important text lay a definition of independence. Because the Declaration's thrust was principally political and intellectual, scholars of American history and government generally use the term "independence" in only these contexts.[3]

Throughout the second half of the eighteenth century transient Scots in Jamaica as well as in the Chesapeake remarked that they wanted to become "independent." What did they mean? Certainly, as their behavior indicated, they did not desire the dissolution of the bonds between Britain and its American colonies. For them, as for most other eighteenth-century Europeans, "independence" was an economic condition.[4] The idea probably extended no further than the notion of personal freedom to exist without having to work for a living.

Indeed, Harold Perkin maintained that the "leisured gentleman was the ideal at which the whole society [England] aimed, and by which it measured its happiness and ambitions." But, he continued,

> leisure . . . did not necessarily mean idleness, although the right to be idle if one so wished was an integral part of the concept. It meant strictly the freedom to pursue any interest, taste or pleasure . . . without the further need to demean oneself by earning a living.[5]

Though Perkin's observation is based upon English sources, it applies in equal measure north of the border. For sojourners, being independent meant having the financial ability to live comfortably at home in Scotland.

The West Indian proprietors in London (and later Glasgow) and the tobacco lords demonstrated a whole range of leisured activities from phi-

---

[3]Indeed, while there has been no formal history of the word independence, the *Oxford English Dictionary* uses the Declaration as an example of the term's early usage (2d ed., prepared by J. A. Simpson and E. S. C. Weiner [Oxford, 1989]).

[4]The terms "sufficiency" and "competency" had similar implications. The *Oxford English Dictionary*'s definition (4b) of "independent" reads as follows: (a) not dependent on any one else for one's living; (b) not needing to earn one's livelihood; possessing a competency. (Vol. 7, p. 847.) The dictionary gives example of this usage in 1732, 1786, 1790, and 1802. As Charles Dickens remarked in the Pickwick papers, "She possessed that most desirable of all requisites, 'a small independence.'" Also see "competency", *OED*, v. 3, p. 604, definitions 2 and 3a; and "sufficiency," v. 17, p. 127, for similar related definitions.

[5]Harold Perkin, *The Origins of Modern English Society, 1780–1880* (London, 1969), p. 55.

lanthropy and public service to self-indulgence. Those who achieved this state did not worry about either the source of their revenue or its amount from one year to the next. Nor were they plagued by having to pay back accumulated debts. Any financial obligation to others remained small. With assets that greatly outstripped their liabilities, such people could do as they pleased.

Economic independence, meaning fiscal autonomy, brought increased political and social status. Those who acquired their "independence" generally had easier access to the government (and its benefits) both at home and abroad. Many could easily procure sinecures for friends and family members who needed them. Others sought political influence, if not office, in order to protect their interests. Still others had no intention of doing anything but drinking tea and visiting their friends. In short, becoming independent represented the pinnacle in the process of upward social mobility to which great numbers of the British population subscribed. There was nothing remotely revolutionary about this idea of independence. Indeed, it was directly tied to the traditional socioeconomic class structure. As Perkin suggests, "clergymen, lawyers, physicians, bankers, and overseas merchants knew, and showed by their ambitions that they knew, that the only worthwhile thing to be in the old society was a completely leisured—which . . . meant landed—gentleman."[6]

Many people who lived permanently in the American colonies also understood "independence" in the same way as their sojourning neighbors. This understanding almost certainly derives from the colonists' self-identification as British subjects. Living in America surely brought most of them higher standards of living than they could have expected in Europe. Prosperity encouraged them to work for even greater financial benefits. Once they had secured these, they believed, they could stop working and live without fear of either debt or downward social mobility.

But the permanent colonists' definitions and conceptualizations of independence evolved in the years before and during the American Revolution. Many American residents became convinced—rightly or wrongly—that the only way for them to achieve individual economic independence required the colonies collectively to separate from Britain and establish political independence. This realization, and the resulting actions, put them into conflict with the Scottish sojourners.

The era of rapid change after 1763, which Thomas Paine characterized as an "age of Revolutions," generated new ideas about the mechanism for

[6]Perkin, *Modern English Society*, p. 56; also p. 61, for a description of the upflow of new men into the "aristocracy" and the downflow of younger sons to the middle ranks. Also see R. H. Campbell, "The Landed Classes," in *People and Society*, p. 96.

achieving "independence" among a growing number of Americans.[7] No longer were promises of upward mobility enough to satisfy the population. Those on the patriot vanguard successfully managed to convince their apathetic or less fervent neighbors that the British authorities and their imperialist, mercantilist policies were holding them back.

> As John Murrin has pointed out, the colonial resistance movement that ended in Revolution began as a typical old-regime quarrel between the corporate bodies over the boundaries of their respective privileges and authority. It turned into a rebellion when the American elite failed to control the ordinary colonists who had leapt into the fray with grievances of their own.[8]

The problem was simply that everyone in the colonies, sojourners and immigrants, elites and yeomen, skilled and unskilled, was striving for the same thing, that is, increased social status and economic power. Upper-class colonists jockeyed for position with their British counterparts. Middling and lower sorts in the colonies hoped to achieve greater socioeconomic mobility within the colonies than they already had. Rather than creating a solidarity among aspiring people, this situation led to substantial conflict. Those who battled the British for political independence believed that imperial policy hurt their chances for upward mobility. Many of those who remained loyal, like the Scots, did so because they believed that their positions and advancement depended upon the continuation of the very British authority against which their neighbors fought.

Certainly, the positions that the Scots held within the colonial economic structures lend credibility to this notion. In Jamaica, they capitalized upon the island's need for skilled white workers. Had the colony not been producing sugar, which was protected by British mercantile policy, there may not have been jobs for them, or not the jobs they had. The Scottish presence as tobacco factors placed them in a similar position within the Chesapeake. If imperial policy had not made their trade profitable, the way in which the Scots went about achieving their economic independence might have been more tolerable to their neighbors. But the fact is that the Scots sojourners had become expert at manipulating the British colonial system to their own advantage. In order for the Scots to achieve *independence*, the colonies had to remain *dependent* upon the British empire for their political and economic policies. It is not a little ironic that these very policies were at least partly

---

[7]See Paine, "The Rights of Man, Part I," in *The Thomas Paine Reader*, ed. Michael Foot and Isaac Kramnick, (London, 1987), p. 262.

[8]Appleby, *Capitalism*, p. 12. Also see Murrin, "The Myths of Colonial Democracy and Royal Decline in Eighteenth-Century America," *Cithara* 5 (1965).

responsible for the Scots' belief that they could procure more outside of their native country than within it.

A relatively new concept in the eighteenth-century Atlantic world, political independence suggested that imperial policy did not uniformly benefit all those in the empire. Holding great appeal for the colonial elite because it generated new opportunities for them to control their own destinies, the definition of independence based on natural rights also attracted the middling and lower classes.[9] Many had become persuaded that imperial policies and those who implemented them, like the Scots, kept them in subordinate positions. By eliminating undesirable rules and completely breaking with a far-removed country, they believed that their opportunities for advancement would increase. For if nothing else happened, they did not believe that they would be any worse off.

In Jamaica, as in most of the colonial Caribbean, political independence did not come until the middle of the twentieth century. Why was this so? The answer is fairly simple. I believe that the economic elite in the Caribbean recognized that the individual economic independence for which they strove could amply be achieved within imperial economic boundaries. The infusion of credit from the metropole allowed whites living in Jamaica to retain the appearance of wealth and economic independence. They recognized that they could become independent as long as Jamaica continued to depend on Britain to support sugar prices, direct trade, and provide requisite provisions and manufactures. Rather than hindering, imperial authority over the sugar islands aided the colonial elite. Without economic and political support from Britain, the islands would have collapsed under pressure from huge black majority populations with completely different notions of independence.

In both places, the Scots did not change. They held steadfastly to their ideas and notions of independence. Their colonial sojourns had allowed them the liberty to pursue property. For this they were grateful. They, therefore, understood that in order for them to become independent, they and the colonies needed to remain in a state of dependency.

[9] I do not want to give readers the sense that the ideological origins of the revolution were insignificant. Indeed, I find them to be one of the period's principal legacies. But I also do not believe that these theories of natural rights developed outside of the context of more tangible imperial policies. The best work on the subject remains Bernard Bailyn's *The Ideological Origins of the American Revolution* (Cambridge, Mass., 1967). An alternative position can be found in Jack P. Greene, "Political Mimesis: A Consideration of the Historical and Cultural Roots of Legislative Behavior in the British Colonies in the Eighteenth Century," *American Historical Review* 85 (1969): 337–60.

Bibliography

PRIMARY SOURCES

MANUSCRIPTS

Archives, Scotland
  National Library of Scotland, Edinburgh
    John Cunningham Letters Acc. 7285
    Graham of Airth Papers MS 10924–26
    David Herd Letters MS 1924
    Alexander Houston Records MS 8796
    McLeod of Geanies Papers MS 19297
    MacMurdo Family Papers Acc. 7199
    Nisbet Papers MS 5464–5484
    Robertson-McDonald Papers MS 3945
    Charles Steuart Papers MS 5025–5041
  Scottish Record Office, Edinburgh

AC	Admiralty Court Records
GD 247	Cunninghame and Company Records
E	Exchequer Records
GD 345	Grant of Monymusk Papers
GD 142	Hamilton of Pinmore
CS 96	Extracted Processes, Court of Session (Lawson and Semple Records)
GD 1	Miscellaneous Letters
GD 121	Murthly Castle Muniments
GD 47	Ross Estate Muniments
RH 2/4/12	"Scotch Importation of Foreign Goods and Merchandize"
GD 248	Seafield Muniments

GD 136   Sinclair of Freswick Papers
GD 241   Thomson, Dickson, and Shaw Collection.
Aberdeen University Library, Manuscripts Department
                                  Duff House Papers
MS 1160   Gordon of Cairness Manuscripts
MS 2226   Tayler Manuscripts
Edinburgh University Library, Manuscripts Department
M. 1430   Campbell of Inverneil Papers (Microfilm)
M. 23   Alexander Hamilton's Letterbook (Microfilm)
MS La.   Laing Manuscripts
                                  Matriculation Rolls, Edinburgh University
Glasgow University Archives
                                  Hamilton of Rozelle Papers
Mitchell Library, Manuscripts Department, Glasgow
                                  Bogle Papers
                                  Minute Books of the West India Association of
                                  Glasgow, 1807–1853.
Strathclyde Regional Archives, Glasgow
A-TD 1   Dunlop of Doonside
TD 168   Alexander Henderson Letterbook (photocopied)
T-MJ   Mitchels, Johnston, and Company
TD 167   John Robinson's Letterbooks (photocopied)
TD 1   Smiths of Jordanhill
T-SK   Stirling of Keir Papers
Privately Owned, accessible through NRA(S), Edinburgh
                                  Campbell of Kilberry Papers
                                  Hunter of Hunterston Papers
                                  Moncreiff of Tullibole Papers
                                  Scrymgeour-Wedderburn Papers
                                  Stirling of Garden Papers
                                  Tweedie-Stodart of Oliver Papers
                                  Wardlaw-Ramsay Papers
Archives, England
Liverpool Record Office, Liverpool
920 Cur   Currie Manuscripts
920 Par I–IV   Parker Family Papers
British Library, London
Add. Mss 12,435   Long Manuscripts
Public Record Office, London
CO 142/31   Jamaica Landowners, 1754
CO 137   Jamaica Papers, Colonial Office
T 79, AO/12–13   Loyalist Claim Materials
CO 700   Manuscript Maps of Jamaica
T 71   Slave Registration Returns
CO 5/1444–1450   Virginia Shipping Returns

Archives, United States
  Henry E. Huntington Library, San Marino, California
                            Brock Collection
                            Loudoun (Scottish) Papers
                            Stowe Manuscripts
  Maryland Historical Society, Baltimore
    MS 854   Tuesday Club Records
  New York Public Library, New York
                            American Loyalist Transcripts
  Historical Society of Pennsylvania, Philadelphia
                            Alexander Johnston Section, Powel Papers
  Virginia Historical Society, Richmond
    Mss 1   Lee Family Papers
    P 4686   Peyton Family Papers
  Virginia State Library, Manuscript Division, Richmond
    Acc 13   William Allason Papers
    Ms 19894–19921, 22174 John Hook Papers
                            County Personal Tax Lists
                            County Property Tax Lists
  Library of Congress, Washington
                            Dunlop Family Papers
                            Glassford and Henderson Papers
                            Neil Jamieson Papers
                            James and Henry Ritchie Papers
Archives, Jamaica
  Jamaica Archives, Spanish Town
    1B/11/4   Accounts Produce
    1B/11/3   Probated Estate Inventories
    1B/11/17   Letters Administrative
    1B/11/18   Letters Testamentary
                            Jamaica Powers (of Attorney) Series
  Institute of Jamaica, Kingston
                            Plats and Parish Maps
  Island Record Office, Spanish Town
                            Deeds

PUBLISHED

Anonymous. *The British Antidote to Caledonian Poison: Consisting of the most Humourous Satirical Political Prints, for the Year 1762*. London, 1762.
——. *The Medical Register for the Year 1780*. London, 1780.
Breslaw, Elaine, ed. *Records of the Tuesday Club of Annapolis, 1745–56*. Champaign-Urbana, Ill., 1988.
Bridenbaugh, Carl, ed. *Gentleman's Progress: The Itinerarium of Dr. Alexander Hamilton*. Chapel Hill, N.C., 1948.

Burt, Edward. *Burt's Letters from the North of Scotland.* Reprinted. Edinburgh, 1974.
Currie, William Wallace. *Memoirs of the Life, Writings and Correspondence of James Currie, M.D., F.R.S.* London, 1931.
Defoe, Daniel. *The Advantages of Scotland by an Incorporate Union with England.* Edinburgh, 1706.
Devine, T. M., ed. *A Scottish Firm in Virginia, 1767–1777: W. Cunninghame and Co.* Edinburgh, 1984.
Edwards, Bryan. *A History, Civil and Commercial, of the British West Indies.* 5th edition. London, 1819.
Falconer, William. *Falconer's Marine Dictionary.* London, 1769.
Falls, Ralph Emmett, ed. *The Diary of Robert Rose: A View of Virginia by a Scottish Colonial Parson, 1746–51.* Verona, Va., 1977.
Farish, H. D., ed. *The Journal and Letters of Philip Vickers Fithian, 1773–1774.* Williamsburg, Va., 1957.
Greene, Jack P., ed. *The Diary of Colonel Landon Carter of Sabine Hall, 1752–1775.* Charlottesville, N.C., 1965.
———. *The Laws of Jamaica* (St. Jago de la Vega, 1792).
Leslie, Charles. *A New History of Jamaica.* London, 1940.
Long, Edward. *History of Jamaica.* London, 1774.
Micklus, Robert, ed. *The History of the Ancient and Honorable Tuesday Club.* Chapel Hill, N.C., 1990.
Riley, Edward Miles. *The Journal of John Harrower: An Indentured Servant in the Colony of Virginia, 1773–1776.* Williamsburg, Va., 1963.
Schaw, Janet. *Journal of a Lady of Quality.* Ed. Evangeline Andrews. New Haven, 1921.
Sinclair, Sir John. *A Statistical Account of Scotland.* Edinburgh, 1793.
Smith, Adam. *The Theory of Moral Sentiments.* Ed. D. D. Raphael and A. L. Macfie. Oxford, 1976.
Williamson, John. *Medical and Miscellaneous Observations Relative to the West Indian Islands.* 2 vols. Edinburgh, 1817.
Wright, P., ed. *Lady Nugent's Journal of Residence in Jamaica from 1801 to 1805.* Kingston, 1966.

SECONDARY SOURCES

BOOKS

Addison, W. Innes. *The Matriculation Albums of the University of Glasgow from 1728 to 1858.* Glasgow, 1913.
Appleby, Joyce. *Capitalism and a New Social Order.* New York, 1984.
Bailyn, Bernard. *Ideological Origins of the American Revolution.* Cambridge, Mass., 1967.
———. *Voyagers to the West.* New York, 1986.
Becker, Carl. *The Declaration of Independence.* New York, 1942.

Beeman, Richard. *The Evolution of the Southern Backcountry.* Philadelphia, 1984.

Berlin, Isaiah. *Four Essays on Liberty.* Oxford, 1969.

Berthoff, Rowland Tappan. *British Immigrants in Industrial America.* Cambridge, Mass., 1953.

Blalock, Herbert. *Towards a Theory of Minority Group Relations.* New York, 1956.

Bodnar, John. *The Transplanted: A History of Immigrants in Urban America.* Bloomington, Ind., 1985.

Bonacich, Edna. *The Economic Basis of Ethnic Solidarity.* Berkeley, Calif., 1980.

Brathwaite, Edward. *The Development of Creole Society in Jamaica.* Oxford, 1971.

British Association for the Advancement of Science. *The North East of Scotland.* Aberdeen, 1963.

Brock, William. *Scotus Americanus.* Edinburgh, 1982.

Brown, Callum G. *The Social History of Religion in Scotland since 1730.* London, 1987.

Brown, Wallace. *The Good Americans: The Loyalists in the American Revolution.* New York, 1969.

———. *The King's Friends: The Composition and Motives of the American Loyalist Claimants.* Providence, R.I., 1965.

Bumsted, J. M. *The People's Clearance: Highland Emigration to British North America, 1770–1815.* Edinburgh, 1982.

Butler, Jon. *The Huguenots in America.* Cambridge, Mass., 1983.

Cage, R. A., ed. *The Scots Abroad: Labour, Capital, Enterprise, 1750–1914.* London, 1985.

Calhoon, Robert. *The Loyalists in Revolutionary America.* New York, 1965.

———. *The Loyalist Perception and Other Essays.* Columbia, S.C., 1989.

Camic, Charles. *Experience and Enlightenment: Socialization for Cultural Change in Eighteenth Century Scotland.* Edinburgh, 1983.

Campbell, R. H. *Scotland since 1707.* Oxford, 1965.

Clemens, Paul. *The Atlantic Economy and Colonial Maryland's Eastern Shore: From Tobacco to Grain.* Ithaca, N.Y., 1980.

Craig, Mary Elizabeth. *The Scottish Periodical Press 1750–1789.* Edinburgh, 1931.

Craton, Michael, and James Walvin. *A Jamaican Plantation.* New York, 1970.

Cressy, David. *Coming Over: Migration and Communication between England and New England in the Seventeenth Century.* New York, 1987.

Cundall, Frank. *Historic Jamaica.* London, 1919.

Daiches, David. *The Paradox of Scottish Culture.* London, 1964.

Davis, Ralph. *The Rise of English Shipping.* London, 1962.

Deerr, Noel. *The History of Sugar.* London, 1949–50.

Devine, T. M. *The Tobacco Lords.* Edinburgh, 1975.

———, ed. *Conflict and Stability in Scottish Society, 1700–1850.* Edinburgh, 1990.

———, ed. *Improvement and Enlightenment.* Edinburgh, 1989.

Devine, T. M., and Rosalind Mitchison, eds. *People and Society in Scotland I: 1760–1830.* Edinburgh, 1988.

Dickinson, H. T. *Liberty and Property: Political Ideology in Eighteenth-Century Britain.* New York, 1978.

Dodgshon, R. A. *Land and Society in Early Scotland.* Oxford, 1981.

Donaldson, Gordon. *The Scots Overseas*. London, 1966.

Drescher, Seymour. *Econocide*. Pittsburgh, 1977.

Dwyer, John. *Virtuous Discourse: Sensibility and Community in Late Eighteenth-Century Scotland*. Edinburgh, 1987.

Dwyer, John, Roger A. Mason, and Alexander Murdoch, eds. *New Perspectives on the Politics and Culture of Early Modern Scotland*. Edinburgh, n.d.

Ekirch, A. Roger. *Bound for America: The Transportation of British Convicts to the Colonies, 1718–75*. New York, 1987.

Faragher, John Mack. *Sugar Creek*. New Haven, Conn., 1986.

Ferguson, William. *Scotland: 1689 to the Present*. Edinburgh, 1968.

Flinn, Michael, ed. *Scottish Population History from the Seventeenth Century to the 1930s*. Cambridge, 1977.

Fraser, Sir William. *The Chiefs of Grant*. Edinburgh, 1883.

———. *Stirlings of Keir*. Edinburgh, 1858.

French, C. J. "The Trade and Shipping of the Port of London, 1700–1776." Ph.D. dissertation, University of Exeter, 1980.

Goveia, Elsa. *Slave Society in the British Leeward Islands at the End of the Eighteenth Century*. New Haven, Conn., 1965.

Graham, Henry Gray. *The Social Life of Scotland in the Eighteenth Century*. London, 1937.

Graham, Ian. *Colonists from Scotland*. Ithaca, N.Y., 1956.

Greene, Jack P. *Pursuits of Happiness*. Chapel Hill, N.C., 1989.

Greene, Jack P. and J. R. Pole, eds. *Colonial British America*. Baltimore, 1984.

Hall, Douglas. *In Miserable Slavery: Thomas Thistlewood in Jamaica, 1750–1786*. London, 1989.

Hamilton, Henry. *An Economic History of Scotland in the Eighteenth Century*. Oxford, 1963.

Hancock, David. "Citizen of the World: Commercial Success, Social Development, and the Experience of Eighteenth-Century British Merchants who Traded with America." Ph.D. dissertation, Harvard University, 1990.

Handlin, Oscar. *Boston's Immigrants: A Study in Acculturation*. Cambridge, Mass., 1941.

———. *Immigration as a Factor in American History*. Englewood Cliffs, N.J., 1959.

Hast, Adele. *Loyalism in Revolutionary Virginia*. Ann Arbor, Mich., 1982.

Haws, Charles. *Scots in the Old Dominion, 1685–1800*. Edinburgh, 1980.

Higman, Barry. *Slave Population and Economy in Jamaica, 1807–1834*. Cambridge, 1976.

Holmes, G. K., ed. *Britain after the Glorious Revolution 1689–1714*. London, 1969.

Hont, Istvan, and Michael Ignatieff, eds. *Wealth and Virtue: The Shaping of Political Economy in the Scottish Enlightenment*. Cambridge, 1983.

Hook, Andrew. *Scotland and America: A Study of Cultural Relations*. Glasgow, 1975.

Houston, R. A. *Scottish Literacy and the Scottish Identity: Illiteracy and Society in Scotland and Northern England, 1600–1800*. Cambridge, 1985.

Houston, R. A. and I. D. Whyte, eds. *Scottish Society, 1500–1800*. Cambridge, 1989.

Insh, George Pratt. *The Company of Scotland*. London, 1932.

Isaac, Rhys. *The Transformation of Virginia*. Chapel Hill, N.C., 1983.

Jones, Alice Hanson. *Wealth of a Nation to Be*. New York, 1980.

Kammen, Michael. *Spheres of Liberty: Changing Perceptions of American Liberty*. Madison, Wis., 1986.

Kulikoff, Allan. *Tobacco and Slaves*. Chapel Hill, N.C., 1986.

Kyd, J. G., ed. *Scottish Population Statistics*. Edinburgh, 1952.

Land, Aubrey. *Colonial Maryland*. Millwood, N.Y., 1981.

Landsman, Ned. *Scotland and Its First American Colony*. Princeton, N.J., 1985.

Lecky, W. H. *A History of England in the Eighteenth Century*. London, 1887.

Leder, Lawrence. *Liberty and Authority: Early American Political Ideology, 1689–1783*. New York, 1978.

Lenman, Bruce. *An Economic History of Modern Scotland, 1600–1976*. London, 1977.

Leyburn, James G. *The Scotch-Irish: A Social History*. Chapel Hill, N.C., 1962.

Light, Ivan, and Edna Bonacich. *Immigrant Entrepreneurs: Koreans in Los Angeles*. Berkeley, Calif., 1988.

McCusker, John. *Money and Exchange in Europe and America, 1660–1775*. Chapel Hill, N.C., 1878.

McCusker, John, and Russell Menard. *The Economy of British North America, 1607–1789*. Chapel Hill, N.C., 1986.

Macfarlane, Allan. *The Family Life of Ralph Josselin*. Cambridge, 1970.

Main, Jackson Turner. *The Social Structure of Revolutionary America*. Princeton, N.J., 1985.

Marshall, Dorothy. *English People in the Eighteenth Century*. London, 1956.

Mason, Roger, ed. *Scotland and England, 1286–1815*. Edinburgh, 1987.

Meinig, D. W. *The Shaping of America: Atlantic America, 1492–1800*. New Haven, Conn., 1987.

Mintz, Sidney. *Sweetness and Power*. New York, 1985.

Mitchell, B. R. *British Historical Statistics*. Cambridge, 1988.

Mitchison, Rosalind. *A History of Scotland*. New York, 1982.

Mitchison, Rosalind, and Peter Roebuck, eds. *Economy and Society in Scotland and Ireland, 1500–1939*. Edinburgh, 1988.

Moore, John Bassett. *International Adjudications, Ancient and Modern*, 3d series, v. 3. New York, 1931.

Morgan, Edmund. *American Slavery, American Freedom*. New York, 1975.

——. *The Stamp Act Crisis*. New York, 1962.

Munford, George Wyllie. *The Two Parsons*. Richmond, Va., 1884.

Nelson, William. *The American Tory*. Oxford, 1961.

Norton, Mary Beth. *The British Americans: The Loyalist Exiles in England, 1774–1789*. Boston, 1972.

Pares, Richard. *Merchants and Planters*. Cambridge, 1970.

——. *A West India Fortune*. London, 1950.

Parry, M. L., and T. R. Slater, eds. *The Making of the Scottish Countryside*. London, 1980.

Patterson, Orlando. *Slavery and Social Death*. Cambridge, Mass., 1982.

——. *The Sociology of Slavery*. London, 1967.

Perkin, Harold. *The Origins of Modern English Society, 1780–1880.* London, 1969.

Phillipson, N. T., and R. Mitchison. *Scotland in the Age of Improvement: Essays in Scottish History in the Eighteenth Century.* Edinburgh, 1970.

Pocock, J. G. A. *The Machiavellian Moment.* Princeton, N.J., 1975.

Prebble, John. *Culloden.* London, 1961.

——. *The Darien Disaster.* London, 1961.

Preisser, Thomas. "Eighteenth-Century Alexandria, Virginia, before the Revolution, 1749–1776." Ph.D. dissertation, William and Mary, 1977.

Price, Jacob. *Capital and Credit in British Overseas Trade: The View from the Chesapeake.* Cambridge, Mass., 1980.

——. *France and the Chesapeake.* Ann Arbor, Mich., 1973.

Ragatz, L. J. *The Fall of the Planter Class in the British Caribbean.* New York, 1963.

Sanchez-Saavedra, E., ed. *A Description of the Country.* Richmond, Va., 1975.

Sewell, William. *Work and Revolution in France: The Language of Labor from the Old Regime to 1848.* New York, 1980.

Shaw, John Stuart. *The Management of Scottish Society.* Edinburgh, 1983.

Sher, Richard. *Church and University in the Scottish Enlightenment: The Moderate Literati of Edinburgh.* Princeton, N.J., 1985.

Sheridan, Richard. *Doctors and Slaves.* Cambridge, 1985.

——. *Sugar and Slavery.* Baltimore, 1974.

Sinclair, Sir John. *Analysis of the Statistical Account of Scotland.* Edinburgh, 1829.

Siu, Paul C. P. *The Chinese Laundryman.* New York, 1987.

Smout, T. C. *A History of the Scottish People.* London, 1969.

Sowell, Thomas. *The Economics and Politics of Race.* New York, 1983.

Spadafora, David. *The Idea of Progress in Eighteenth-Century Britain.* New Haven, Conn., 1990.

Steele, Ian. *The English Atlantic, 1675–1740.* Oxford, 1986.

Sunter, Ronald M. *Patronage and Politics in Scotland, 1707–1832.* Edinburgh, 1986.

Thomas, Brinley. *Migration and Economic Growth: A Study of Great Britain and the Atlantic Economy.* Cambridge, 1964.

Timperley, Loretta R., ed. *A Directory of Landownership in Scotland c. 1770.* Edinburgh, 1976.

U.S. Census Bureau. *Historical Statistics of the United States, Colonial Times to 1957.* Washington, D.C., 1960.

Ward, Robin, and Richard Jenkins, ed. *Ethnic Communities in Business: Strategies for Economic Survival.* New York, 1984.

Weber, Max. *The Protestant Ethic and the Spirit of Capitalism.* Trans. Talcott Parsons. New York, 1958.

Webking, Robert. *The American Revolution and the Politics of Liberty.* Baton Rouge, La., 1988.

Whittington, G., and I. D. Whyte, eds. *An Historical Geography of Scotland.* London, 1983.

Wolf, Stephanie. *Urban Village.* Princeton, N.J., 1976.

Wood, Peter. *Black Majority.* New York, 1974.

Yans-McLaughlin, Virginia, ed. *Immigration Reconsidered.* New York, 1990.

ARTICLES

Berthoff, Rowland. "Independence and Attachment, Virtue, and Interest: From Republican Citizen to Free Enterpriser." In *Uprooted Americans: Essays to Honor Oscar Handlin,* 99–123. Boston, 1979.

Bonacich, Edna. "A Theory of Middleman Minorities." *American Sociological Review* 38 (1973): 583–94.

Bushman, Richard. "This New Man: Dependence and Independence, 1776." In *Uprooted Americans: Essays to Honor Oscar Handlin,* 79–96. Boston, 1979.

Canny, Nicholas. "Identity Formation in Ireland: The Emergence of the Anglo-Irish." In *Colonial Identity in the Atlantic World, 1500–1800,* ed. N. Canny and A. Pagden. Princeton, N.J., 1987.

Eisenstadt, S., and L. Roniger. "Patron-Client Relations and a Model of Structuring Social Exchange." *Comparative Studies in Society and History* 22 (January 1980): 42–77.

Fagerstrom, Dalphy. "Scottish Opinion and the American Revolution." *WMQ* 11 (1954): 252–75.

Higham, John. "Immigration." In *The Comparative Approach to American History,* ed. C. Vann Woodward, 91–105. New York, 1968.

Karras, Alan. "The World of Alexander Johnston: The Creolization of Ambition, 1762–1787." *Historical Journal* 30 (1986): 53–76.

Kenney, Alice P. "Dutch Patricians in Colonial Albany." *New York History* 44 (July, 1969): 249–83.

Klingaman, David. "The Significance of Grain in the Development of the Tobacco Colonies." *JEH* 29 (1968): 286–78.

McDonald, Forrest, and Ellen S. McDonald. "The Ethnic Origins of the American People, 1790." *WMQ* 37 (1980): 179–99.

Mayer, Adrian C. "The Significance of Quasi-Groups in the Study of Complex Societies." In *The Social Anthropology of Complex Societies,* pp. 97–121, ed. Michael Banton. London, 1966.

Price, Jacob. "Buchanan and Simson, 1759–1763: A Different Kind of Glasgow Firm Trading to the Chesapeake." *WMQ* 40 (1983): 3–41.

——. "New Time Series for Scotland's and Britain's Trade with the Thirteen Colonies and States, 1740–1791." *WMQ* 32 (1975): 307–25.

——. "The Rise of Glasgow in the Chesapeake Tobacco Trade, 1707–1775." *WMQ* 11 (1954): 179–99.

Sheridan, Richard. "The British Credit Crisis of 1772 and the American Colonies." *JEH* 20 (1960): 161–86.

——. "The Crisis of Slave Subsistence in the British West Indies during and after the American Revolution." *WMQ* 33 (1976): 615–41.

——. "The Role of the Scots in the Economy and Society of the West Indies." In *Comparative Perspectives on New World Plantation Societies,* pp. 94–106, ed. V. Rubin and A. Tuden. New York, 1977.

Siu, Paul C. P. "The Sojourner." *American Journal of Sociology* 58 (1952–53): 34–44.

Soltow, J. H. "Scottish Traders in Virginia." *EHR* 12 (1959): 83–98.

Thistlewaite, Frank. "Migration from Europe Overseas in the Nineteenth and Twentieth Centuries." In *Population Movements in Modern European History,* ed. Herbert Moller, 73–92. New York, 1964.

Thomson, Edith E. B. "A Scottish Merchant in Falmouth." *Virginia History Magazine* 39 (1931): 108–17, 230–8.

Thomson, R. "The Tobacco Export of the Upper James Naval District, 1773–1775." *WMQ* 13 (1961): 393–407.

Tully, Allan. "Englishmen and Germans: National-Group Contact in Colonial Pennsylvania, 1700–1755." *Pennsylvania History* 45 (1978): 237–56.

Turner, Jonathan H., and Edna Bonacich. "Towards a Composite Theory of Middlemen Minorities." *Ethnicity* 7 (1980): 144–58.

Walsh, Lorena. "Community Networks in the Early Chesapeake." Unpublished. Presented April 1, 1984, at "Maryland: A Product of Two Worlds," St. Mary's City.

Wilkie, Mary. "Colonials, Marginals, and Immigrants: Contributions to a Theory of Ethnic Stratification." *Comparative Studies in Society and History* 15 (April, 1977): 67–95.

Wokeck, Marianne. "The Flow and Composition of German Immigration to Philadelphia, 1727–1775." *PMHB* 105 (1981): 249–78.

Wolf, Eric. "Kinship, Friendship, and Patron-Client Relations in Complex Societies." In *The Social Anthropology of Complex Societies,* pp. 1–22, ed. Michael Banton. London, 1966.

Zuckerman, Michael. "Fate, Flux, and Good Fellowship: An Early Virginia Design for the Dilemma of American Business." In *Business and Its Environment: Essays for Thomas C. Cochran,* ed. Harold Sharlin, 161–84. Westport, Conn., 1983.

Index

Library of Congress Cataloging-in-Publication Data

Karras, Alan L.
    Sojourners in the sun : Scottish migrants in Jamaica and the Chesapeake, 1740–1800 /
    Alan L. Karras.
        p.   cm.
    Includes bibliographical references and index.
    ISBN 0-8014-2691-X
    1. Scottish Americans—Chesapeake Bay Region (Md. and Va.)–History–18th century.   2.
    Chesapeake Bay Region (Md. and Va.)—History.   3. Scots—Jamaica—History—18th
    century.   4. Jamaica—History—To 1962.   I. Title.
F187.C5K37   1992
975.5'18'0049163—dc20   92-52763